The Naval Brigades in Belgium, France & The Dardanelles, 1914-15

The Naval Brigades in Belgium, France & The Dardanelles, 1914-15

With the Armoured Train Guns and the Anson Battalion at Gallipoli during the First World War

Naval Guns in Flanders 1914-1915
L. F. R.

At Antwerp and the Dardanelles
H. C. Foster

The Naval Brigades in Belgium, France & The Dardanelles, 1914-15
With the Armoured Train Guns and the Anson Battalion at Gallipoli
during the First World War
Naval Guns in Flanders 1914-1915
by L. F. R.
and
At Antwerp and the Dardanelles
by H. C. Foster

FIRST EDITION IN THIS FORM

First published under the titles
Naval Guns in Flanders 1914-1915
and
At Antwerp and the Dardanelles

Leonaur is an imprint of Oakpast Ltd
Copyright in this form © 2025 Oakpast Ltd

ISBN: 978-1-917666-32-9 (hardcover)
ISBN: 978-1-917666-33-6 (softcover)

http://www.leonaur.com

Publisher's Notes
The views expressed in this book are not necessarily those of the publisher.

Contents

Naval Guns in Flanders 1914-1915   7
At Antwerp and the Dardanelles   129

Naval Guns in Flanders 1914-1915

HIS MAJESTY'S ARMOURED TRAIN "JELLICOE"

Contents

Fortune's Favour	11
The Evacuation of Antwerp	19
The First Battle of Ypres	35
Winter Before La Bassée	72
Neuve Chapelle	100
The Yser, 1915	107
Appendix 1	116
Appendix 2	122
Appendix 3	125

Chapter 1

Fortune's Favour

Shortly after 8 p.m. on the evening of Thursday, October 1st, 1914, the two long tables of the Officers' Mess in a naval establishment in a southeastern county were both full. The assembly represented every branch and calling of His Majesty's Service, combatant and engineer, doctor and paymaster, permanent and temporary, reserve and volunteer. Two of the variety referred to afloat as "Guns," seated together, were engrossed in a heart-to-heart exchange of moans. Each expressed his particular opinion of Dame Fortune and criticized the persistence with which she forgot his existence. They compared their own dull life, sticking it out on the drill-ground and in the classrooms, endeavouring to train some of those many thousands of recruits, and to prepare them in some fashion for being drafted to sea, upon which domain the envied and fortunate brethren were already playing their part.

Opposite these two sat a younger officer, who was holding forth upon the merits and the endless possibilities of his own new arm of warfare—the Air Service. To a bewildered audience of equally inexperienced messmates around him, he was explaining how he was about to take an ex-cross-Channel packet-boat into the Heligoland Bight, and from her send out aeroplanes to bomb the Germans out of the Kiel Canal, or at any rate destroy their gates.

I hope by now he has learnt the full meaning of the Silent Service.

And so on throughout this assembly of officers almost everyone discussed "shop" in one form or another, for when peace was no more, so likewise went the taboo on that subject.

Of a sudden a resounding crash brought everyone back to a general alertness as the table vibrated under the blow of the "presidential" hammer, and in response to a voice toasting "Gentlemen, the King!" all stood as one and drank. War had brought no change to this old custom, but where previously the repetition of the toast and a prayer, "God bless him!" would have completed the ceremony, now in almost every mind ran the addition "and damn the Hun."

After the assembly was again seated anyone could rise and leave at will, and with a few remarks on the work each had to do during the evening, both the "Guns" left the mess.

As they passed out through the heavy doors and across the tiled hall, their commanding officer approached, and addressing one of them, said: "R——, I want you for a moment"—moving to the right and so down a passage. When out of earshot of the hall this officer stopped, and laying his hand on his junior's arm said: "The C.-in-C. has just called for an officer for active service. I have submitted your name. You had better rush off and pack up some gear, as you will probably leave in an hour's time."

"Where am I going to?" asked the junior.

"I do not know exactly, but it is to Belgium," was the reply.

"Thank you, sir."

And so did Dame Fortune smile my way at last.

A few minutes ago, I had been moaning and bewailing my fate at having to fag out the boring existence of a training school; now I was suddenly pitched into a fever of excitement at the prospect of immediate active service—"off to the front."

Rushing off, I fled to my room. An hour's grace and so much to be done! However, within that space of time I was again in the hall, with sword and revolver, wearing my C.O.'s Sam Browne gear, and kit-bag in hand.

The commanding officer was awaiting me, and said "it was approved"; simultaneously another officer approached and said: "Here are your orders."

Copy of Admiralty Telegram.

(Secret.)

From Admiralty to Commander-in-Chief, The Nore, dated October 1st, 1914.

(Priority. Urgent.) Following ratings are to proceed to Antwerp *viâ* Ostend tonight, sailing in *Engadine* as soon as she can be ready.

(Then followed the details of the draft of seventy active service ratings and the orders to report to the Belgian Government on arrival.)

>   To Lieutenant (G.)
>   For information and guidance.
>   Richard Poore.
>   Admiral.

A thrill of excitement passed through me, and I had bewildered visions of some unexplainable nature.

"The men are assembling now in drill-shed," said my C.O. "I'll see you there later."

Hurriedly I requested the hall porter to forward my mail.

"Where to, sir?" said he.

"I don't know," I replied, "but Commander Halahan will tell you later."

"Aye, aye, sir." And with that same old expression of understanding and acknowledgment ringing in my ears, I passed out of the quarters and away to the drill-sheds, where a sense of hustle and subdued excitement filled the air. On one side stood the commodore, viewing the scene with critical eye. A long queue of bluejackets stretched away through the doors into the square and darkness beyond. At the head of this queue was a collection of officials: Word had quickly and as quietly been passed round that some stunt was on, and that all seamen gunners were to muster at the drill shed in No. 4's, with a clean shift and personal gear in hand.

Rumours passed from mouth to mouth, and eagerness to get into the show, whatever it was, soon caused this endless queue of volunteers. Of the many who came forward, a large number had to pass away, for only those who were ready in every detail were selected and marched to one side to be medically examined, then on to be fitted out in field gear, reinspected, and finally passed on to give in name, rating, etc., to the clerk who recorded the full details of each man.

A white cap, no knife, no soap, a faulty bootlace, no collar—even the smallest detail did not escape the quick eye of the police. There was no second chance, for hundreds waited in the rear ready and equally eager.

Within half an hour seventy ratings had been selected, and were fallen in ready for final inspection.

Meanwhile I had visited the paymaster and secured seventeen sovereigns, which would probably come in handy before long, and had made arrangements about my affairs.

Two days' iron rations were then served out all round.

"What's the game, Bill?" "Where are we off to?" "What's up?" and similar expressions were to be heard murmured in the excited ranks. At last, I was informed that everything was ready, was given the nominal list, and took charge, forming the draft into marching order, and reporting all ready to the commander.

He in turn reported to the commodore, who wished us good-luck and Godspeed. I then learnt that we were being despatched to form the crews of six 6-inch guns which had been sent to Antwerp to reinforce the forts.

Rejoining my men, I marched them out of the drill-shed and out into the night. I noticed several forms joining up, and before we had proceeded many yards on the way to the dockyard gate the party had increased considerably in numbers.

Halting before the gate, I called the roll and passed each of my own men through; the extras disappeared into the darkness; their last effort foiled. Once again, we moved off, and the gates behind us closed with a bang. It seemed as if this sudden clanging of the gates resounding in the still night air had startled the senses of most of us into realising that we were alone and on some venture into the unknown, certainly for the men, who as yet were not aware of their errand. The moment seemed to require relief, so I called for a song, and at once the dockyard walls resounded with the refrain of "*Tipperary*."

We did not have far to go, and shortly before 11 p.m. boarded the launch, which bore us downstream on the way to our transport. Collecting the men together, I informed them of our destination and our errand—a surprising piece of news, at first received with much excitement, but soon followed by silence, for each had his own thoughts to occupy him, either of his own future or of those who were left behind.

An hour's silent journey brought us alongside the *Engadine*, which till lately had been a cross-Channel packet-boat. She was completing with coal and busily preparing for her journey. I got the men comfortably settled for the night, and then tried to sleep myself, but with little success, for excitement was too intense.

By 1 a.m. the *Engadine* slipped from her buoy and out of the black harbour. On our way we were to pick up Lieutenant Ridler of the *Severn*, who was to join the party, and had been so informed by wireless. A mist lay over the sea, but we eventually found and picked him up at the Girdler; unfortunately, however, the ship herself was allowed to drift on to a sand-bank and delayed us.

At daylight the mist was quite thick, but we continued on our journey as fast as the turbines could drive us. Hot coffee and biscuits was served out and the draft detailed into seven sections. As we were approaching Ostend the following signal was received by wireless, adding greatly to our excitement and making everyone even more determined to do his best.

Admiralty to Engadine.

First Lord wishes representatives of the Royal Navy now going into action at Antwerp good-fortune and Godspeed. The cause which they are to serve is the preservation of the National Life of the Belgian people, who are in the extreme distress of a cruel, terrible, and unprovoked attack. A million men in the British Isles now getting ready to take part in the struggle will watch the feat of arms expected from the small number of naval ratings employed.

To this we made reply:

"Engadine" to Admiralty.

To First Lord.

Officers and men now in *Engadine, en route* for Antwerp, wish to send their heartiest thanks for, and to express their cordial appreciation of, your message conveying such encouraging attention.

Later in the forenoon we made out the marks of Ostend, and proceeded up the harbour about 11 a.m., berthing alongside the Railway Quay, (Oct. 2nd). A train was waiting for us, so we disembarked at once, exchanging cheers with the crew of the transport and also with the populace, a great crowd of which were gathered round the precincts of the station.

"Third return Chatham, please, miss!" shouted the wag.

"Berlin and b—— the *Kaiser!*" replied the rest.

And so on, with compartments labelled "Berlin" and hoglike caricatures of the war lord, we steamed out midst cheers, and so forward to the unknown. Our first stop was at Bruges at 12.30 pm. Immediately the train had pulled up a crowd of civilians and guards, men and women, rushed along to greet us, bringing food, fruits, and drink. This wholesale display of kindness and hospitality was at first most embarrassing, but not so much so as the one great question which was on everyone's lips:

"Thank God, the English have come! But how many are coming, and where are all the others?"

Their anxiety was terribly apparent, and yet there was only one thing to say:

"Many thousands more are following behind us."

We could but give some encouragement, though in reality we knew not whether thousands or none were to follow; in fact, we knew less of what was behind than what was in front of us, and that was very little.

One thing, however, was quite apparent —that if this sort of drinking and feasting continued all the way to Antwerp the men would soon be all intoxicated, so a stop had to be put to the former part of the menu. That afternoon we continued a very slow journey eastwards along the Dutch frontier loop *viâ* Lokeren, and so on to St. Nicholas, stopping at most stations, where we always met with the same everlasting questions and with the same gifts.

At St. Nicholas we had a prolonged wait; everywhere things were busy, and many trains were going westward. A troop train full of Belgian soldiers passed us, and as soon as they saw who we were, they gave a terrific cheer and yell of "*Les Anglais!*"

Off again, we slowly moved east, passing crowds of soldiers and a great quantity of military material, earthworks and barbed-wire entanglements, and so on, till about 6 p.m. we passed the forts and stopped at the station of St. Anne. Here we were told to disembark and to board a ferry at the quay. I noticed a large pile of boxes and luggage under a guard on the quay, and was informed that it was the baggage of the queen, who was to leave that night.

It was by now quite dark, but the city (Antwerp) was brilliantly lit, though, in spite of this, the reflections of the flashes away to the south showed the sources of the constant rumble, as the guns continued their work.

And so, at last, was heard the sound of battle at hand and we were thrilled with excitement. We crossed the Scheldt and disembarked, but had to wait for a Belgian staff officer to join us, who was to show the way to our quarters. When in half an hour's time he arrived, we set out on our march through the city, till in its eastern quarter we came to the so-called barracks wherein our men were to be lodged for the night. Then things began to happen. No one ever knows how a crowd will spring up in a city street, apparently by magic, and here suddenly we were being surrounded by a crowd of women, men, and children.

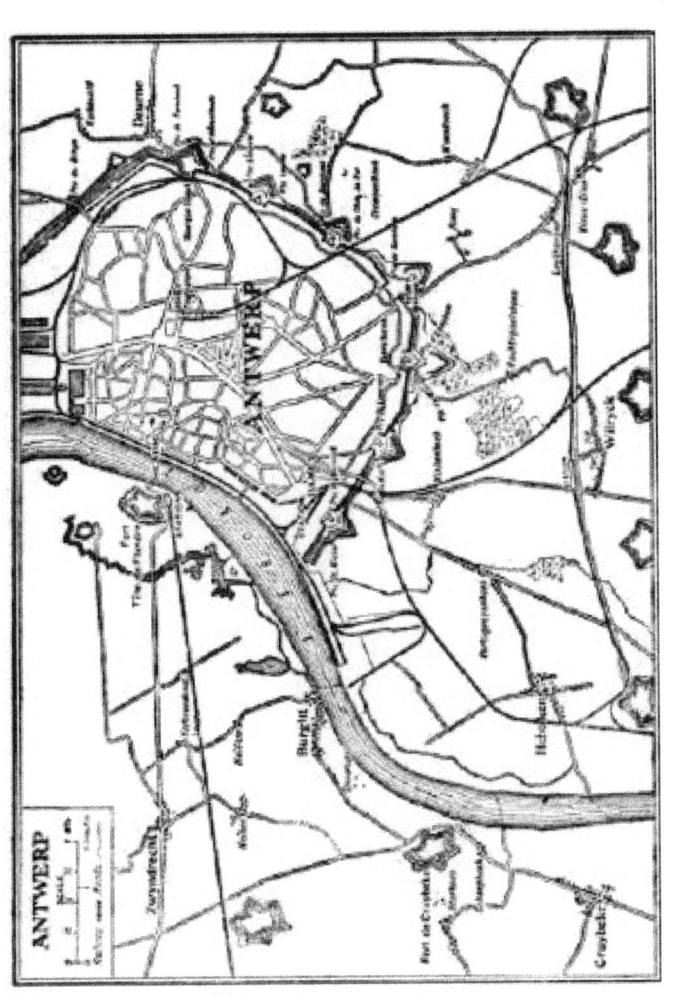

"*Vivent les Anglais!*" they shouted. "*Vive l'Angleterre! A-ah, ça va bien! Ils arrivent.*" The men called in answer: "*Cheer-o, monsoo! Vive Belgique!*"

Before very long we were a surging mass instead of only seventy sailors, the crowd disguising our small number. Again, and even more eagerly, the same questions were asked: "How many are coming, and where are they?"

But to our small band the welcome was so whole-hearted from these people who had met us at their gates, that we all felt very proud of being Britishers. It was good to feel that Britain had not failed her friends, though the obligation were only a moral one. Yes, one felt proud as never before.

Our quarters consisted of two bare rooms on the first floor of an equally bare large building. We were able to arrange for hot coffee and some biscuits, and then, tired by the day's journey, most stretched out on the floor and tried to get some sleep. Ridler and myself then rejoined the Staff Officer in his car and went off to the Headquarters. Here things seemed to be somewhat busy, and we could not get any immediate instructions, so decided to go out and get some dinner first, for it was now 9 p.m.

The *Hôtel St. Antoine* was recommended, so thither we went, and were very thankful for a decent warm dinner after such a tiring journey.

Chapter 2

The Evacuation of Antwerp

My instructions were to get in touch with a certain naval officer who was already in Antwerp with other naval guns and men; so, it seemed advisable to see what our Embassy could do, as they were quartered at the time in the *Hôtel St. Antoine*. We eventually got in touch with one of the Secretaries, and after a further short wait were requested to go in, as His Excellency wished to speak to us. On entering, we were very cordially greeted by an elderly gentleman, who then said:

"Well, gentlemen, I am sorry to tell you that you have come too late. The authorities have just decided that the city is to be evacuated. The Belgian Field Army is leaving now for the west with His Majesty the King, and only the garrison are remaining to guard the city and cover the retreat."

He told us that the majority of the forts in the southern sector of the outer ring of forts had already been blown to bits by heavy guns and had fallen, and that it was certain that the city could not be saved from capture.

This was very sad news for us indeed; there seemed to be no time to waste thinking about it, but to attempt to find the senior British naval officer present in the city and report.

After parting with His Excellency, we returned to the hotel lounge, and then I caught sight of a British naval officer. An exchange of greetings and names showed that this was the very person whom we sought. He had crossed from England during the preceding month with six 4.7-inch guns for the same purpose as ourselves, but they proved much too feeble; however, he obtained the necessary permission and had mounted them on railway bogies, forming a couple of armoured trains.

The idea was first tried with one gun which was mounted on

the bogie of a large wagon, and upon completion about the middle of September proved quite a success. All six guns were subsequently so mounted, and by this time were out in action daily, forming two complete trains of three guns, two engines, and two magazines each, all protected by steel plating five eights of an inch thick, sufficient to stop splinters and rifle bullets. We learnt that our six 6-inch guns were in a certain engineering yard, but that their use in the matter of reinforcing the forts was considered negligible.

He had heard rumours of the anticipated evacuation, but ours was the first definite news which reached him, and he had as yet received no orders on the subject. At this moment Rear-Admiral Oliver appeared upon the scene and inquired at what hour the armoured trains would be ready to leave Antwerp for the west, for we were all to clear out as soon as possible; it was thereupon decided that all could and would be ready at 4 a.m. next morning. It was now midnight, so I borrowed a car and went to the men's quarters to warn them to be ready.

The whole city seemed to be full of cars, and every officer owned one. One hardly saw an officer on foot at all. Our men were all dead to the world, tired out. But I told them to be ready to fall in at 3 a.m. Returning to the hotel, I asked for a room, and was soon asleep on top of the bed. After a couple of hours' rest the night porter called us and brought a welcome cup of coffee. Arriving at the barracks, I found the men ready, so we fell-in at once and started our march across the city.

Once more in pitch darkness, but guided by our car, three-quarters of an hour's marching brought us to the *Gare des Dames*, where we found the armoured trains. The engines were still shunting about, filling with coal and water, and a certain amount of confusion prevailed. I divided the men into six parties putting one in each gun wagon.

By 4.30 the trains were ready, and we were about to start on our return journey to Ostend, when the order came to "stop." From somewhere a message had arrived, and the rear-admiral said the trains and men were to remain where they were in readiness for the time being.

Ridler went off to try and collect the 6-inch guns, and to see what was possible with them, whilst I accompanied the rear-admiral back to the hotel, where we got the news from the Embassy that the First Lord of the Admiralty and Staff had left London for Antwerp, and were expected about midday; meanwhile we were to wait.

In the interval it was decided to get on with the work with the 6-inch guns. They were to be placed in positions chosen between the forts of the inner ring as part of the defences being built there, mounted on crossed double 10-inch girders sunk in the soil. The Antwerp Emergency Company started the work at once, and Ridler took over the task of superintending.

The First Lord (Churchill), arrived at the hotel about 1 p.m. Seeing me, he asked whether I belonged to the Royal Naval Division, and, learning the nature of my errand, wanted to know how long it would take. He appeared satisfied with the estimate I gave, and remarked that "we were going to hold out."

This was the first news I had heard that the newly formed Naval Brigades were to arrive in this neighbourhood.

However, with the Staff came more details, (Oct. 4th), and also rumours of the despatch of troops of the British Army.

Our own particular job was clear: we could continue the work begun on the 6-inch guns and the 4.7 trains could carry on with their normal programme. These latter had done nothing during this day but remain in readiness to leave, a diversion from their usual activities which caused their local Headquarters to ask "Why?" That was smoothed over when all was explained and orders for the following day's work were issued to them.

Commandant Lefevre, a Belgian Engineer Officer who had been largely instrumental in the building of the trains, joined us at dinner in the evening, as also Captain Servais, a retired Belgian Artilleryman who commanded one of the sections of the armoured trains. That night we slept at the latter's house. Next morning Ridler took some of the men and continued with the 6-inch, whilst I split the remainder up amongst the 4˙7 guns.

Till now Lieutenant-Commander Littlejohns was actually in charge of both trains, and generally went out in one section, whilst Captain Servais took charge of the other. From the beginning the guns had been manned by British naval gunlayers assisted by volunteer Belgians. It was now decided that my bluejackets should assist, whilst I went out with Littlejohns to help him, and eventually take over the train to give him more freedom to go to Headquarters, and so on.

Leaving at 5 a.m., we took his section out *viâ* Wilryck and prepared for firing at Waerloos.

The methods of laying and training the guns were most primitive, for up till lately all firings out to the southward of the Nethe had been direct. Now that the Germans had advanced and were actually assaulting the city's defences, cover was necessary, and in such flat country firing had to be indirect, or blind.

A position was chosen where the map showed a straight piece of line, the line of the rails being taken as the zero for training. Bearing and ranges were taken off the map. The guns were laid to the elevation corresponding to the range required, and a bearing arc was painted round the pedestal, the zero pointer being a plumb-line slung from beneath the mounting.

With such means success in indirect laying was a matter of luck, and it was obvious that calibration and greatly improved ideas were necessary.

As soon as the train stopped, telephone communication was always established with the Headquarters under which the train was working at the time, and so kept in touch ready to fire whenever required.

The target was a battery position to the southeast of Duffel at a range of 5,000 yards, and over this area a steady fire was placed. A hostile captive balloon was observed to ascend, so I asked Littlejohns if I could try and down it. We opened fire on it with long-range shrapnel, and after four rounds it was hurriedly hauled down. However, it had time to see us, so we retreated a few hundred yards; and sure enough, after a lapse of some minutes, our previous position was subjected to a searching but weak fire from some battery.

About midday we advanced beyond Waerloos, stopped just short of the bridge over the line, and opened fire on another battery at 6,500 yards. The First Lord and his Staff arrived during this performance. He remarked: "We cannot have too many of these trains." Two members of the Staff inquired whether the firing-line was visible; we informed them that if they went on top of the bridge in front of us, they would be able to get a good view. They went out, and hardly reached their destination when shell began falling in the neighbourhood of the train and shrapnel crackled overhead. I do not suppose those officers had run so fast for many a day, for their time for the distance separating them from the shelter of the train was remarkably fast.

As for myself, it was the first time I had been under fire. I heard an awful shriek overhead, so dived into a ditch alongside. It did not take very long to learn that a shrieking shell had already passed overhead and out of danger. A shell which will be unfortunately near one gives little or no time to get clear after one catches the first sound of its shrieking passage through the air.

A Taube appeared high up and coming towards us, the first hostile aircraft I had seen. Determined to have a shot at a Hun myself, I laid the 6-pounder anti-aircraft gun with which we were fitted, and opened fire on him.

Perhaps he did not expect that sort of reception, for he immediately banked steeply to the right and went off home; however, he no doubt saw us and would report our position, so we again withdrew the train a few hundred yards.

Most of the houses around us had already been deserted, but some of the inhabitants still lingered.

That evening Littlejohns and myself met Temporary Colonel Sir P. Girouard at the Antoine and dined with him. The sad state of the white shirt and collar I had worn when leaving England was too apparent, so he offered me a khaki substitute in lieu from his kit.

Early next morning, (Oct. 5th), the train went out again, and this time I took charge of one section in place of Littlejohns, who remained in Antwerp for a conference on the question of the 6-inch guns. It was decided to abandon the idea of placing the guns in the positions chosen, but to place the girders on a railway bogie and mount the guns similarly to the 4.7s. This was rather an experiment, for we could not estimate whether the recoil would be so severe as to prevent the gun being fired much out of the fore and aft line of the truck, for fear of upsetting it.

I took my section out *via* Vieu Dieu and stopped at Kleine Meil, on the Brussels line, in a position which was screened by a dense wood over which we could fire. Headquarters telephoned the position of two targets which were to be engaged—the bridge over the River Nethe east of Lierre, which village had been evacuated by the Belgians and was being occupied by the advancing German troops; and the Ander-Stad-Farm on the southern bank of the Nethe, more to the westward. I was informed that the Belgians had all crossed this river and were taking up positions along its western bank as far west as Willebroeck. The above farm was a little shelter from which the Germans would launch an attack to cross the river.

I opened fire on these two objectives and continued a slow bombardment at irregular intervals. In the early part of the forenoon a battery commenced searching for us, but, beyond an occasional uncomfortably close one, most of the shell did not fall close enough to look dangerous, so I held on to our screened position.

In the late afternoon an order came to return and go out on the Lierre line, and from there open fire on the Duffel Bridge over the Nethe and on the "S" bend of the river immediately west of Lierre, as Germans were massing to attack at these two places. Arriving at a point on the line marked K. 7 on the map, which denotes the position of the seventh kilometre signpost, I opened fire and continued till dusk, when we returned to Antwerp for the night. Thus, my first days of independent work came to a close.

It was the general principle that the train should not work at night, when the flashes would draw hostile fire on their surroundings and so interfere with the passage of reliefs and food, etc., moving up to the front, and also stray shells were liable to cut the rails in rear and cause a derailment in the dark.

During this afternoon a French armoured train joined us, and opened fire on Walheim. It was a very good unit, mounting two short 7.5-inch guns of considerable ranging power, but before firing the mountings had to be secured to the rails and supports rigged out from the truck so as to hold it all in place; so that it was not mobile as we were, for we could fire when in motion at any point of the compass.

The methods and customs of our Ally amused the men, but this amusement caused that light-hearted gaiety which is quite irresistible in the endeavour to surmount trifling difficulties in a foreign land. In like circumstances the British bluejacket is at his best, and volumes could be filled with the anecdotes of their adventures in Belgian and French villages. "Knowalls" who for ever are trying to introduce the universal language could certainly draw some useful hints from the "blue" in a strange land. He is soon equally at home in China, Pacific Islands, Amazon, or in the wilds of Africa.

The only thing which seemed to stump their ideas was the alarming manner in which the children so soon picked up the language. Grown-ups, yes; they of course would learn it in time; but the fluency and speed of the children's jabber was beyond them.

Somehow, they got on much quicker with the womenfolk—a subject for the student; but the whole-hearted welcome admiration and wonderment of the womenfolk for the men, and their own patient sufferings and hardships, seemed to produce a sort of favourable medium.

At daylight next day, (Oct 6th), I took the section out again and stopped at Kleine Meil. Our first target was again the bridge east of Lierre, upon which we opened fire. I learnt that during the preceding night the enemy had built pontoon bridges across the river and had attacked just west of Lierre, succeeding in forcing the Belgians out of their trenches. This advance was checked and the trenches cleared by

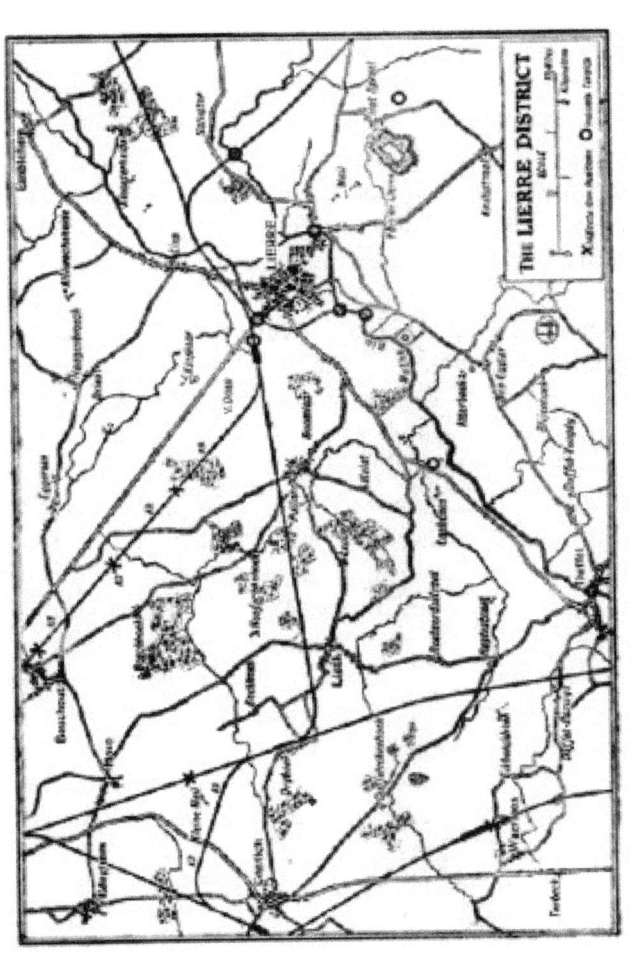

the arrival of the Royal Naval Brigade under General Paris, belonging to the Royal Naval Division. These fine soldiers from the sea had attacked as soon as they arrived on the field, and though they retook the lost positions, had not been able to force the Germans off the north-western bank of the river.

Our line now ran along the main road between Lierre and Duffel Bridge.

Early in the forenoon I got orders to return to Waesdoirck and go out on the Lierre line. At the first place I picked up Girouard and Littlejohns and whilst passing through Bouchout Station one of the gun bogies was derailed, causing a delay. All round this area were many London buses drawn up by the roadside. They had come straight from the London streets and had been used to rush up the Naval Division from Dunkerque. We were reminded of home by the brilliant advertisements of the theatres, etc., such as the one I photographed with Girouard at the controls and Littlejohns as the conductor.

We left the derailed bogie behind with a salvage party and went on with the other two guns to a position behind the Donk Wood beyond K. 8. In this position we were in front of most of the field artillery, which were barking away on both quarters and only a mile from our own marines holding the line in front of us west of Lierre.

Our first target was a double battery of field guns which a Belgian balloon observed to be in action in a position at Blijenhoek, 2,000 yards to the south-west of Lierre. We opened fire with lyddite and shrapnel, and after half an hour we were informed that the enemy had ceased fire and were moving away. We were told to open fire on the pontoon bridges used in last night's attack, so a slow bombardment was directed on this area. After about twenty minutes we must have been spotted by the balloons, for a battery opened on us with shell of a medium calibre. Their first salvo straddled us—one shell landed and exploded 100 yards on one side, and another as much on the other, whilst one landed—a "dud"—in the ditch alongside the train.

We did not wait for more, but went back to K. 7, and from there watched the continued shelling of our previous position, which made several breaks in the rails. At this time further orders arrived to fire at once on Lierre Station and the north-western portion of the village itself, as the Germans were debouching from this part and massing in the station area ready for an attack. Lyddite was fired on these areas slowly for the remainder of the forenoon, during which time the derailed bogie arrived and joined in.

GARE ST. NICHOLAS.

THE GEARLESS BUS AT BOUCHOUT.

At noon we had to return to Antwerp for water, and on the way passed Ridler, who had succeeded in getting the first 6-inch mounted, and was on his way to test it with a few trial shots at the Hun. A second 6-inch was completing and expected out to join him. This was a good piece of work, for only forty-eight hours' continuous working sufficed to mount the two.

Passing through the inner line of forts, we met the other brigades of the Naval Division, who were busy digging themselves in, on the trench system between the forts. In front of this system was about 75 yards of solid barbed-wired entanglements, and a further 50 yards' width of "too-de-loos" in front—a nest of pointed wooden pegs, points up.

All the area in front for hundreds of yards was being systematically cleared of woods, houses, and villages to leave a clear open space over which the enemy would have to advance if he got so far in.

Whilst the engines were preparing to go out again Littlejohns and I visited the General Headquarters, and there I met the Commander-in-Chief, General De Guise. He congratulated us upon the apparent success of the shoot that morning against the double battery.

We were soon out again on the Lierre line, and from K. 7 I opened fire on that part of the northern bank west of Lierre where the pontoons landed. This continued for a short while until a further order to concentrate on the Duffel Bridge arrived. It was said that the attack on Lierre had been checked, but that another was being pressed on our right flank at Duffel.

All the afternoon we kept up a steady fire upon this area until dusk arrived, when we had to return and try to obtain a replenishment of the greatly depleted shell supply, for the heavy day's firing had caused a big expenditure. Whilst searching round trying to find where the reserve trucks had been shunted to, I got a message that I was to report at once at the Antoine.

There I met Girouard, who said that the Germans had succeeded in forcing back the Belgians on our right, and that we were to clear out with what guns we could save, and destroy the remainder. We were to leave at 11 p.m., so there was plenty to do to get the trains all connected up ready to depart.

There was only one way out, which we hoped might be still clear—*i.e.,* over the Boom Bridge—but the Germans had been in sight of it for two days, and by now might be holding the southern bank. However, it was our only chance, and once across the bridge only derailment could stop us. It was not till 11.30 that we eventually got away with both the 4.7 trains, for the 6-inch were held up still at Hoboken, but were to follow.

All went well till we reached Wilryck Station. The night had become as red as day, as the glare of the burning houses and buildings everywhere mounted to the sky in huge streaks of light, showing where everything was being blown up, burnt, and destroyed in the endeavour to open up the area in front of the inner defences. The roads were packed with a seething mass of men, women, and children of all ages, household effects, and hundreds of soldiers, all streaming towards the city in headlong retreat before the threatened advance of the Huns.

It was such a picture as only an artist could give us on a canvas. No man is more tender to the helpless than the British "blue," no one more cheerful; and not one of us but felt his heart wrung by the infinite pathos of this terror-stricken mob.

As we drew up at Wilryck the station-master started waving his arms in frantic gesticulations, and told us that we could not go on *viâ* Contich, as that village was already occupied by the enemy. There was still one way left by which we could reach the Boom Bridge—the single line round by the bank of the Scheldt *viâ* Hoboken.

It was now just past midnight, (Oct 7th), and our chances of getting away in the darkness seemed to be getting thinner and thinner. However, we started off on our new line, but had hardly got a mile before we were brought up all standing with a grinding of brakes. Jumping out to see what was in the way, we found about a hundred trucks and wagons barring our path, all in the various stages of unloading but quite deserted by the owners, the Naval Divisions, and not another engine in sight. Such a load was beyond the power of our own two engines, and even then, we could not push all this lot out in front of us, so after a few moments' consideration we decided to abandon the train and walk to Hoboken, where if we could not get out by rail, we could cross the river and get away to the west on foot.

The railway-side was strewn with all manner of articles and foodstuffs. Littlejohns borrowed a bicycle, and as soon as we met a road made off for the city. Girouard took charge and led the way along the line, all stumbling over the rails and sleepers in the darkness, but trying to keep as quiet as possible, with a very much open eye to the left for the enemy, who might pop up at any moment on our flank. Behind us the villages were burning, whilst to the south the roar and flashes of the guns showed where the battle was raging.

Half an hour's tramp in this fashion brought us to the Hoboken yards where the 6-inch were still held up. After a certain amount of signalling and arguing, we persuaded a tug to come alongside and take us all across to the western bank.

When once landed, everyone, I fancy, gave vent to a sigh of relief. There we found a small estaminet and were able to stir the inmates into activity, getting them to serve out a tot of schnapps to each man, Girouard signing a chit on behalf of the British Government for the cost. The innkeeper seemed quite content, saying, "Oh, the English will pay." It was bitterly cold, but the liquor put fresh life into us all. Once again, we set out, and eventually brought up in a village named Cruybeke. The place was full of Belgian soldiers, from whom we learnt the whereabouts of their local Headquarters.

There we learnt the latest news from Antwerp, and as there did not seem to be any urgent need to hurry on, we sought out a friendly barn, and all lay down for an hour's rest. From the smell of the place, it must have been sacks of fertilizer upon which we lay.

At 4 a.m. we again visited the Headquarters and got into telephone touch with the city. They said that Contich was clear of Germans, and that the Boom Bridge was still in our hands, so there still seemed a chance of retrieving our trains if we retraced our steps and tried once more. This course was decided on, so I shook up the men and returned to Hoboken. There we got the 6-inch under way, whilst Girouard left us and went into the city to find Littlejohns, who was to follow in the 4.7 trains.

By the time all was ready it was almost midday, and once again we got to Wilryck Station, which was now deserted. Farther on Contich hove in sight, but not a rail had been touched, and we began to doubt whether the Huns had ever been there at all. What was more likely was that the personnel had deserted the station, and when Wilryck could get no reply had assumed the worst. We steamed slowly on, keeping a good lookout for a broken rail, and a better one for a surprise from the enemy from the east, till at last the bridge itself came in sight.

Continuing slowly, we saw Belgians working there, so that seemed hopeful; but the man in the signal-box had had no orders about us, and would not give us the signal, so we jumped out, put it to "clear" and passed on.

As soon as we arrived at the bridge, we could see it clear and intact, so the throttles were opened wide, and we were soon racing as fast as possible, over the river, across the canal, and on into the trees, all eyes

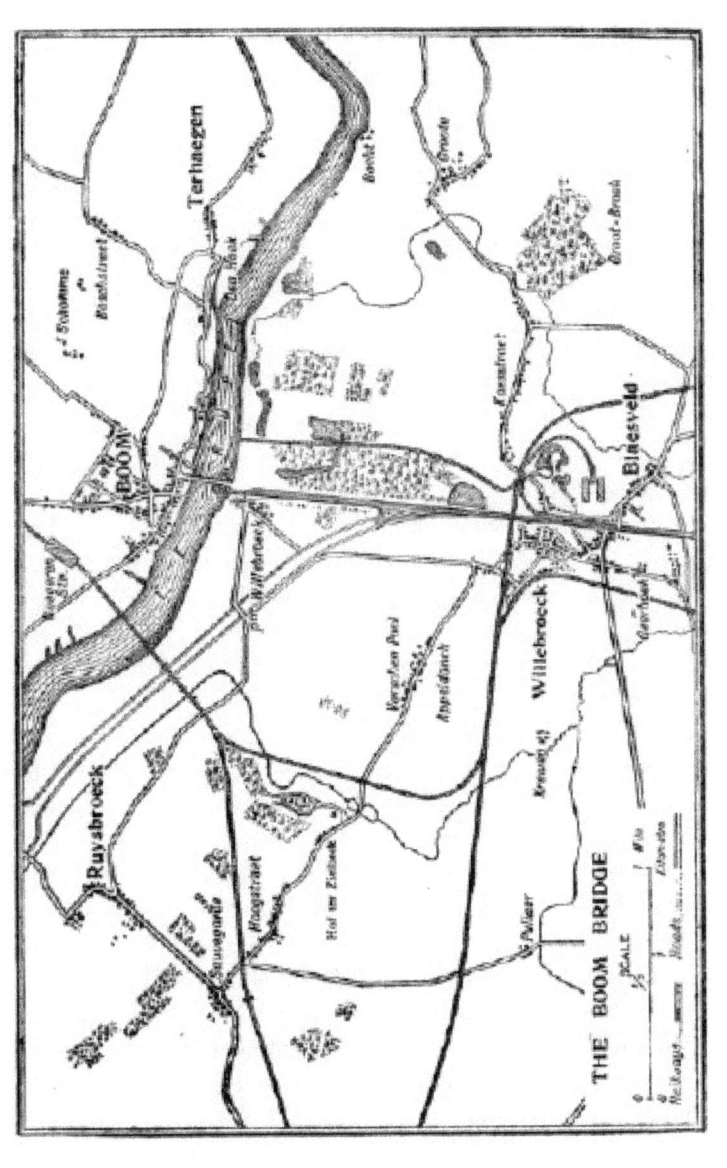

on the watch for a sign of the Huns or a broken line, but not a sign did we see. At last, we turned round to the west and on to Puers, when everyone let out a yell of delight, for we reckoned we were clear at last, this time with our own guns.

As we passed over the canal at Tamese we saw the Belgians entrenching on its northern banks, waiting for an attack from the south; our appearance from that direction was a surprise. Once we passed again through the awful spectacle of the retreating masses, all moving west, till at last we stopped in the station of St. Nicholas. Here we were to wait and see if Girouard and Littlejohns got through with the 4.7's. After some trying hours they arrived, and at last we were complete. They had been through even more exciting experiences, for after the other guns left behind had been destroyed, they got to the Boom Bridge only just in time to get over and away before it was destroyed by the retreating Belgian Engineers.

During the night we joined up together and left for Ostend, arriving there the following evening, after a very slow and jerky journey.

We learnt that Antwerp had capitulated during that day, for the bombardment of the city which had begun the night we left had continued, and the destruction of the city seemed certain. The Germans were attacking the inner defences, and the forts there were being demolished one by one. The Belgian Field Army and Naval Division got across the river, though part of the latter stayed till the Germans were actually fighting on the wire entanglements, and then the garrison alone remained behind to cover the retreat and destroy all they could. Awful tales of these last few hours were told in Ostend on their arrival As soon as possible we got some food for the men, for we had all been without supplies for two days, and then got a meal ourselves at the *Hôtel des Thermes*.

Ostend itself was in an awful state of chaos: the Belgian Field Artillery were moving through and to the west; the remnants of the Naval Division were arriving at intervals and embarking for England; the 4th Army Corps under General Rawlinson was disembarking and moving to the south-east to cover the retreat; whilst hundreds of thousands of refugees were seeking shelter and any possible means of putting the biggest distance between themselves and the Huns, fleeing into France or embarking in any old "ditcher" whose exorbitant price they could pay for a trip to England.

On Saturday, October 10th, orders were received from England to send the guns to Dover, so I had to prepare them for dismounting and

6-INCH GUNS AT OSTEND.

ready to be hoisted out into a transport. By 2 p.m. all were ready, and then orders came to delay, so I had to replace them and get ready for service again.

CHAPTER 3

The First Battle of Ypres

1.—YPRES.

It transpired that the 4th Army wanted all the guns it could get, and here were some ready, so a telegram or two soon arranged matters. Towards evening General Rawlinson sent for Littlejohns, and told him to send a train to co-operate with the 7th Division—General Capper.

Littlejohns sent for me and explained the affair, and offering me the job, said I could take a 4.7 section. During the evening, I arranged the train, selected my own full three crews of bluejackets, and two engines with their own mechanics. We also filled up with what few tinned provisions I could find and plenty of ammunition. By 3 a.m. all was ready; I had my charts, and had orders to report to the Headquarters, which would be found at a place called Eeringhem. *Ordre de marche* and red-tape held me up, so that it was 4.30 before I could get clear of Ostend Station, but once again we were off to action somewhere— this time with all hearts full of pride, for we were to be with the grand old B.E.F.

An hour's journeying brought us to the destination, which we found deserted except for a few civilians, who said the English had moved on. We followed, but they were not at Istexghem, so I telephoned to Thourout and found that British Cavalry were there. Meanwhile I was able to persuade the kind lady at the hotel to give us all a cup of hot coffee. We moved on to Thourout, and from there got into touch with the Headquarters of the 3rd Cavalry—Brigadier-General Byng being at Coolscamp.

Whilst I was explaining the situation a despatch-rider arrived with an order. It appeared that there had been some mistake made in the original orders I got before leaving Ostend.

This order read:

> *To Officer Commanding Armoured Train.*
> Please despatch the armoured train immediately to Ghent. On arrival there report to Major-General Capper, commanding the 7th Division.
>   (Signed) M. F. G——,
>   Lieut.-Colonel, 3rd Cavalry Division.

At the same time General Byng himself arrived and explained the mistake in the original orders, so I at once set off to Bruges and on to Bellem, where I picked up an officer of the grenadiers. Arriving at St. Pierre Station, Ghent, about 4.30 p.m., I found the Divisional Headquarters installed in the *Hôtel de Ville*, and arrived in time to join in the afternoon tea. Everyone was busy working on maps and writing out orders, but in the end, I met the general and reported, explaining what sort of engine of warfare I commanded. He gave me the details and explained the withdrawal of his division that evening from the precincts of Ghent towards Bruges, and told me to go to Melle and report there to Brigadier-General Lawford, commanding the 22nd Brigade, who would give me orders as to how to co-operate with him. Lying on his table was a German helmet, which I was in the act of admiring when General Capper remarked:

"That is the division's first trophy. Would you like it?"

Flabbergasted, I replied: "Yes."

"Then it is yours," said he; "take it, with the good wishes of the 7th Division."

That helmet is now one of my proudest possessions.

Accompanied by a staff officer, we left Ghent after dark and went as far as a point from whence we had to strike across country on foot to find the Brigade Headquarters, falling into ditches and climbing fences, eventually bringing up at a most insignificant cottage, where we found the general. He explained his plan of withdrawal and his wishes that from 8.15 p.m. I should open fire for an hour, one gun searching each of the three roads from Oordegen, Oosterzel, and Muelte, whilst at 8.30 he was to commence retiring from his position.

We returned to the train and carried out the programme, afterwards returning to Ghent. There I found the French evacuating their hospital, and they asked me to carry away a load of the effects of their wounded, which I loaded into a truck and eventually left with the railway authorities at Bruges. I bought a quantity of loaves for the

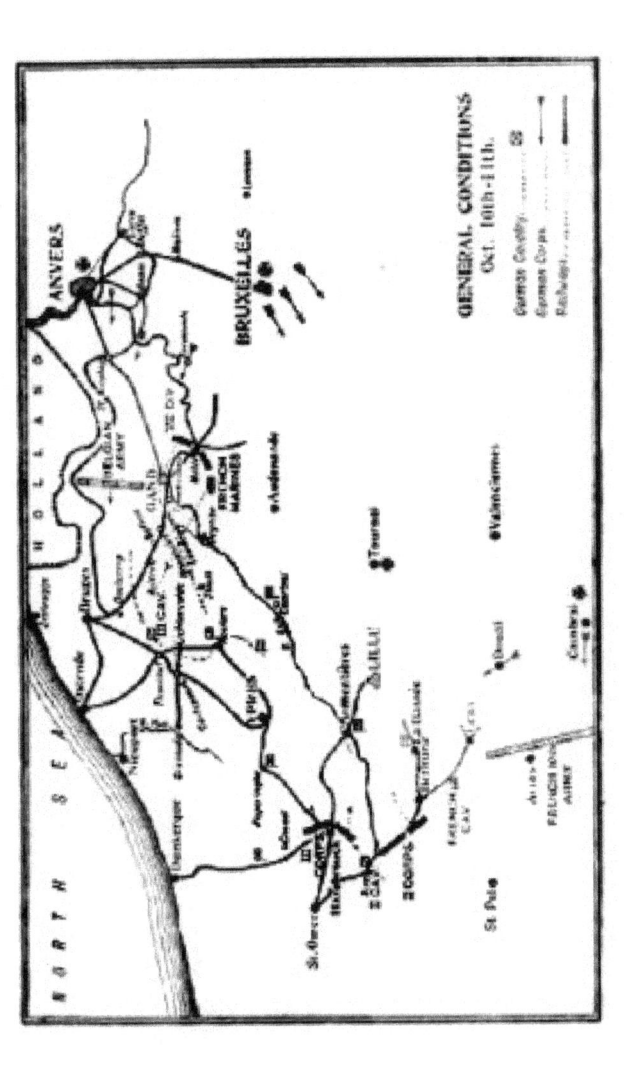

men, and at 11.30 p.m. proceeded to Aeltre for the night.

I was to report to Divisional Headquarters at Hansbeke next morning, Oct. 12th, but on arriving there at 6 a.m. found that they had left, and were then on their way to Bellem, so I returned there to wait for them. At 10 a.m. they arrived, and on reporting, the general said: "Well done! You may probably have held up an attack at the moment of our retirement." He directed me to advance to the canal bridge at Landegem to communicate with the outposts and patrols there, and co-operate with them as I thought fit.

Arriving there, I got into touch with them, and at 1.15 p.m. advanced out with one gun to Helsendrieck to look for a sign of any enemy patrols. Nothing turned up by 2 p.m., so I returned with that report. An hour later I advanced again as far as Tronchiennes, and here they said that the Germans were passing round to the north of Ghent in large numbers, and that a *Uhlan* patrol had been sighted north-east of this village itself. I saw the Belgian Engineers blow up the Assel Bridge over the canal in front of me, so returned and reported again at Hansbeke.

The train now required water, so we returned to Bruges, where I ran into an awful chaos of traffic, and that small evolution took six hours before I got clear again. Shortly before midnight we got into position just west of the Landegem Canal Bridge to support our cavalry, who were detailed together with the Belgian Guides, to hold it that night. It was a pitch-black night and very quiet, and one could almost imagine phantom Huns watching from the other side of the canal as I walked along the bank in my search for the Cavalry Headquarters.

As it was, I almost fell into a trench which was dug into the railway embankment, wherein were installed a section of the Northumberland Yeomanry. I eventually found the farm which was their Headquarters, but learnt that they had all moved off some time before, the section on the railway not having retired with the main body.

Returning to the bridge, I found the Belgian Guides and spent some time with them, but as they were about to retire, I told the Yeomanry to get aboard, and we retired also. We passed Bellem, picking up a horsebox with a fine charger in it and a wagon full of regimental impedimenta, then retired to Aeltre, and, (Oct. 13th), reported by telephone to the Divisional Headquarters, which were now at Thielt. Things must have been very busy there, for it was not till the noon that orders arrived to send the troops across country to Roulers, and

THE CREW OF THE FENIX.

to proceed myself to Bruges and there await orders.

During the forenoon a Taube flew over us very low, so we opened fire with the 6-pounder and all our rifles; he seemed to get very annoyed, dived and dodged about, and flew away to the southeast, still very low. At Bruges orders came to report to the Corps Headquarters at Roulers. I learnt that all our forces had reached Roulers, and that the Germans had entered Thielt, though our cavalry were still working about Thourout; *Uhlan* patrols were reported as having been seen all over the neighbouring country, so that the cut across country between the two forces looked as if it might be an exciting one, though as long as the lines were not actually cut I saw no reason why we should not get through. All along our route we never saw a sign of soldiers, either our own or the enemy's, and eventually arrived at Roulers at 4.15 p.m., where I sought out the Corps Headquarters and reported myself.

I was ordered to proceed to Dunkerque, fill up with ammunition, and go back that night. At Cortemarch we were held up for one and a half hours, and only got as far as Dixmude by 11.30 p.m. Here I was again held up, but was told that another armoured train was coming from the west. Guessing that this would be Littlejohns with the 4.7-inch Belgian section, I decided to await his arrival before returning to Roulers; an hour later he arrived, and we equalized our supplies of ammunition. However, it took almost as long to return, and it was 8 a.m. before we were all back at Roulers. There we found the corps gone, but General Capper had our orders. Our troops were evacuating Roulers, retiring to the high ground east of Ypres, and we were detailed to protect their rear.

We left Roulers at 9.30 a.m. and shortly afterwards the Germans' patrol entered that town in our rear. By 3.30 p.m. the job was finished, so we moved on to Ypres Station and reported. Whilst I was away on this errand, one of my machinists sighted a stray *Uhlan* patrol, opened fire with his rifle, and emptied two saddles. We saw a Taube shot down; the pilot was wearing the Iron Cross, which decoration he had received for being the first aviator to drop a bomb on Antwerp.

Scattered firing could be heard from the direction of Mt. Kemmel, and we learnt that the cavalry of our main army had just taken the position—one of great importance in the days to come. It was said that our 2nd Corps were advancing south of us and had already occupied Armentières, whilst our cavalry filled the gap between them and ourselves, so that now we were back with Sir John French's troops at

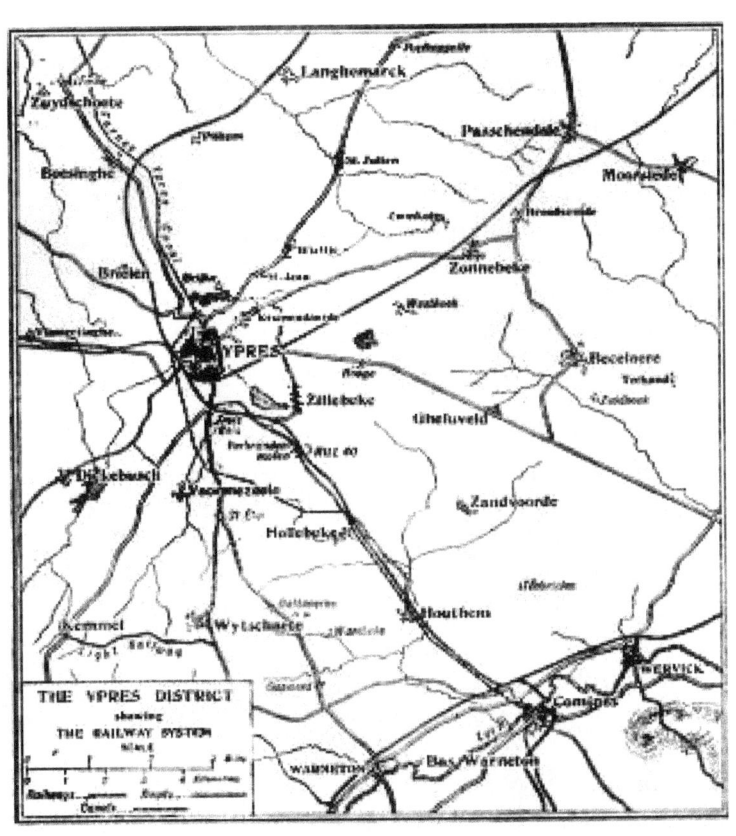

last and held his left flank.

That evening, I had an excellent dinner in the splendid little *Hôtel de Châtelaine*, a famous place which fed us all for many days, the plucky proprietor keeping it going til he was eventually shelled out when the Germans gave vent to their disappointed feelings at being unable to take the town some two weeks later, and commenced their systematic destruction of the main square, the hotel itself being nearby the famous Cloth Hall and Cathedral. A great many of us have good reason to bless this hotel-keeper's brave family.

Early in the following morning, Oct. 15th, I was sent out to the Menin road-crossing to report to General Capper, whose Headquarters had been installed in the famous Houge Château. There was nothing doing during the day, for the enemy had not come up with us, and we were busily engaged in selecting our positions on the ridges.

During the afternoon my train was inspected by Prince Arthur of Connaught. In the evening, I got a message from Littlejohns saying he was returning to Dunkerque, Boulogne, or Havre to form a base for the trains. Captain Servais left with his train for another area, and Ridler had gone to Boulogne to complete the armouring of his two 6-inch gun bogies.

The next morning, I was sent to the Frezemberg Halte on the Roulers line, and from there on to Zonnebeke to report to the Headquarters of the 22nd Brigade, where I had breakfast with General Lawford and got a plan of our positions. On our extreme left our 3rd Cavalry Division was still reconnoitring to the eastward of Passchendaele; the 22nd Infantry Brigade were astride the Roulers railway; the 21st to the Menin road; and the 20th on our right when we were in touch with the 2nd Cavalry Division at Kortewilde. Everywhere things were very quiet, but all on our side were extremely busy on their positions.

Returning to the Menin crossing, I met General Capper, who told me to go out on the Commes line and operate. The Gordons were resting at this crossing and were greatly amused at our quaint piece of artillery. Arriving at Houthem, I found the Scots Greys there, and from them obtained the details of the hostile positions along the bank of the Lys from Warneton to Bousbecque.

Moving on to a position at K. 23, I opened fire with lyddite and shrapnel from all three guns on various selected areas along these lines. The country round here was absolutely flat and covered with trees, ditches, and isolated farms. The firing was quite blind, as no such thing as an observation post was possible; whilst aircraft spotting was still only being tried and no machines were available for us. Our advanced cavalry posts were in this position, but no enemy were seen, and at dusk we returned to Ypres.

Up till now the crews had been sleeping and living round their guns. Nights were getting cold, and the winter was at hand, so I obtained a guard's van and a couple of covered wagons from the railway authorities. In the former I made a cabin and office for myself in the "dicky" position used by the guard of a train, and built quarters for the petty officers in the body of the van. In a small timber-yard near the station we found a quantity of boarding and timber, from which each man was able to build billets for himself.

Their bunks were arranged three high all round, so that one wagon took eighteen men. Till now the train had been painted the Service grey, which was now the worse for wear, so I got a good supply of paint and brushes from the excellent *chef-de-gare*, and began painting the whole train in a camouflage design of yellow, green, and red, and before long we toned well with the autumnal colouring of the country around us.

By means of some telephones and wire I fitted up telephonic communication between all three guns and a centre position in the foremost magazine wagon, which had an armoured ventilation hood forming a most efficient conning tower in case of close fighting. Thus, I was able to control all the guns on all round firing, except right astern. For the normal shoots and bombardments I made out all the orders from my cabin, where I had a suitable table for maps, etc.

For any particular shoot the gunlayer was given the details for his rounds on a chit of paper, but when I could obtain the assistance of an observer, I used the control position at the guns, for generally the fighting sections—*i.e.*, the guns—were kept some distance in front of the unprotected living section, each section with its own engine. But even now the arrangements at the guns themselves were very primitive, and I badly required the bearing arcs and a clinometer.

In the morning, (Oct. 17th), I was sent out again to Houthem to repeat the firing of the previous day, but on arrival there the commander of the Greys objected, for he said he had located hostile batteries at Comines, and if I opened fire, I should draw a return fire upon his neighbourhood. This put me in a quandary, for mine were corps orders, but I obeyed the man on the spot and returned to Ypres to tell them so. They agreed to this and sent me out to Zonnebeke instead, to be at the disposal of the brigade there, but throughout the day things continued to be very quiet.

That evening, I had a hot bath, the first decent scrub since leaving England. Whilst at Houthem that morning Lieutenant ff.-Blake came on board; we had been shipmates in the old *Britannia* days, but he left us and joined the cavalry. He produced a German lance, which we erected on the top of my van and flew our ensign from it. I had bought the silk at Ypres and one of the men sewed it together.

That night the orders were issued for the advance, which was to take place next day, when we were to move towards Menin—that town famous for its leaf tobacco manufacture, of which the quantity put forth was out of all proportion to its quality of doubtful fragrancy. (See Appendix 1.) Though little did we realise that we should be moving forward in the face of numerous hostile formations the presence of which had not yet been felt. (120,000 against 20,00.) We were soon to discover, however, that descending upon us was the full weight of three German Army Corps, the 23rd, 26th, and 27th. Our noble 7th Division were about to bump up against a force hopelessly outnumbering it by six to one.

Throughout that night various additional orders arrived, and by 3 a.m. I had orders to be in two different places in the morning; however, I got this settled by the division, and by 5 a.m. got definite orders to act as General Capper himself wished.

At 6 a.m., (Oct. 18), I took up a position near Houthem, and opened fire on Gheluwe. The cavalry asked me to knock out a farm about 1,500 yards down the line, where they declared the Germans had posted a machine-gun which had already caused us some casualties. Leaving two guns in action on Gheluwe, I tried the other one, but the telephone wires were in the way, and a trial shot only missed over and hit the village of Comines beyond. However, I tried with the 6-pounder, and after exploding a few shell on the wires and posts, eventually blew a clear range through the wires and got on to the farm.

After a few rounds we steamed out towards it, but everything was very quiet, and if the Germans had been there before they certainly were not there now. From a hundred yards we put a few more shells into the neighbouring outhouses to make it certain, and then returned to the main train and rejoined in the work there. For some time this continued, also firing on Wervicq and Menin areas, and shortly after 9 a.m. I was informed that so far, our advance had progressed and that our men were just east of Trehand—an advance of quite two miles. Meanwhile I had shifted position 200 yards back, for it was not wise to remain firing in one spot for too long; and, sure enough, at 9.40 a.m. a hostile battery opened fire, four high-explosive shells bursting on the metals in the position vacated.

This caused some misgivings to the local cavalry commander, who asked me to move farther away still, so as to leave his area as clear as possible. I went back as far as K. 25, near Hollebeke, and continued firing on the Wervicq sector, and then back still farther to K. 27 and opened fire on Comines, which lay clearly in view before us. If it was any consolation to the cavalry in front of me, this succeeded in drawing the shell-fire back from them upon ourselves, for again we got shelled, but quite harmlessly.

The noise of battle gradually quietened and eventually ceased, so I returned and reported, being sent on to Poperinghe to report to the corps. There General Rawlinson wanted to know where Littlejohns was with his other train, but I could only show him the vague information I possessed on that point. I had to wait there till the orders for the continuance of the advance were issued for the morrow.

During the day our 3rd Cavalry had been able to wheel round on our left and were at St. Pieter, and our line ran south-east from there to Houthem. My orders arrived at 10 p.m. and also the plans for the next day. So far, we had not run up against any exceptionally hard obstacles, so were to take Klephoek and Gheluwe, and then follow up by occupying Menin, and thus the whole northern bank of the Lys, supported by the 2nd Cavalry on our right.

By dawn, (Oct. 19th), I was already in position at Houthem, where I had been directed to fire from, but this again disturbed the cavalry, whose horses were all sheltering in the village, so I moved back again to K. 26. Orders to commence the attack reached me at 9.10 a.m., when I began the bombardment of the hostile positions at Wervicq. During the forenoon Littlejohns arrived with the Belgian section and joined in the firing after I had explained what was wanted to him for the attack on Menin.

Further orders were expected, for I had already received a warning to be ready to rush round *via* Roulers and join up with our left flank; however, none arrived, though very heavy firing continued up in that direction.

Early in the afternoon orders arrived for us to go to Zonnebeke, but when we reached there things did not seem very disturbed, and

no further orders arrived till dusk, when we returned to Ypres, where we learnt that our attack had been stopped, and that we had begun to feel the pressure of the huge forces against us. During the forenoon our 3rd Cavalry on our left had been pressed in from the north, and in the end the whole dvision had to slowly retrace its steps, fighting all the way, till they reached their original positions of the previous morning.

The pressure on the north was increasing and things began to look dark, though our hopes were raised by the news that General Haig with his 1st Corps was coming up from the Aisne to our assistance. Next morning, (Oct 20th), we were out again, and went to Zonnebeke to assist our cavalry on the left, who were already as far back as Passchendaele-Keiberg. Our first objectives were the approaches to Moorslede, upon which all guns were turned. Later a message arrived that the French cavalry had been forced out of Passchendaele, and that we were to fire upon that village.

About noon orders came to open fire upon hostile infantry which were seen advancing from Keiberg, so we opened fire on that area, and from then on throughout the whole afternoon various orders continued to arrive, so that we had a busy time of it.

First Broodseinde—right in front of us—then Passchendaele, Goldberg, Passchendaele again, Nieuwemolen, and once again Passchendaele. All these places in turn were our targets—a call for help here, assistance ordered there, and so on— all hard to miss; the last we could see burning furiously. Though at first a novelty, it is easy to quickly tire of burning villages and of destroying the homes of our Ally, and even of firing away into the blue at the enemy and his positions, yet it was little bits of consideration such as the following, which arrived after a bombardment of Passchendaele, that go far to relieve the monotony and to invigorate the spirit:

From G.O.C. 5th French Cavalry.
The effect of your fire appears to have produced a most excellent result against the attack of the enemy, and we thank you for your able support.

That night after we all had returned to Ypres Littlejohns left for the Yser front to join up with the Belgians there. Out again at dawn I went to Zonnebeke under the orders of the 22nd Brigade, who gave me a battery east of Broodseinde as the first target; and upon this we began a searching fire. All round shells of various calibres were flying and exploding in any place, aimed at nothing in particular apparently, and certainly the very great majority did no more than plough into the earth harmlessly; but in front, all along the ridge, shelling and rifle-fire showed where the two forces met and where the heavy fighting was taking place.

My firing at the battery was quite indirect, for the ridge and woods hid everything to the east except a few prominent villages and spires, etc.

Later in the morning a message arrived saying that our left had been pressed back, so I retreated behind the Ypres road to K. 8, and from there opened fire on Passchendaele once more. This continued to be my target up till noon, when I was sent back to Ypres and out to Boesinghe, there to report to the 1st Division—General Lomax. This was the first I had heard of the actual arrival of the 1st Corps, and their arrival must have cheered up everyone, for the menace on our flank looked very black.

By 2 p.m. I had found the Headquarters, and was directed to go out and shell Poelcapelle, from which direction our troops were being hard pressed. It seemed that during the forenoon the Divisions had started their advance as soon as they had arrived on the field with the idea of forcing the enemy back towards Bruges, but after an initial success they were very soon brought to a stop by masses of the enemy and intense artillery fire. At 4 a.m. my objective was changed to the station itself, which would be visible if I advanced a few hundred yards. This I did and opened a direct fire on it at 2,000 yards, so that it was soon in flames. Wallemollem also was given me as a target, so I opened on this as well.

Half an hour after this was begun, I noticed a mounted officer dashing up to us, who when he arrived said that the French cavalry on our left had been driven in, and that the Germans were 500 yards on my left flank. A quick retreat seemed advisable, so I ran back to K. 46 and continued firing from there, for I did not relish the idea of finding the Huns too close behind me. However, the French were soon rallied and able to hold back the threat. At dusk I returned to the Headquarters and then on to Ypres for the night.

The following morning, (Oct. 22nd), I was again sent to join the 22nd Brigade and ran out to Zonnebeke, but at the Ypres road crossing I found the Warwicks busily engaged in digging reserve trenches, so that after a few hasty words I retreated to a less prominent position at Frezemberg Halte. The Warwicks told us of the awful shelling

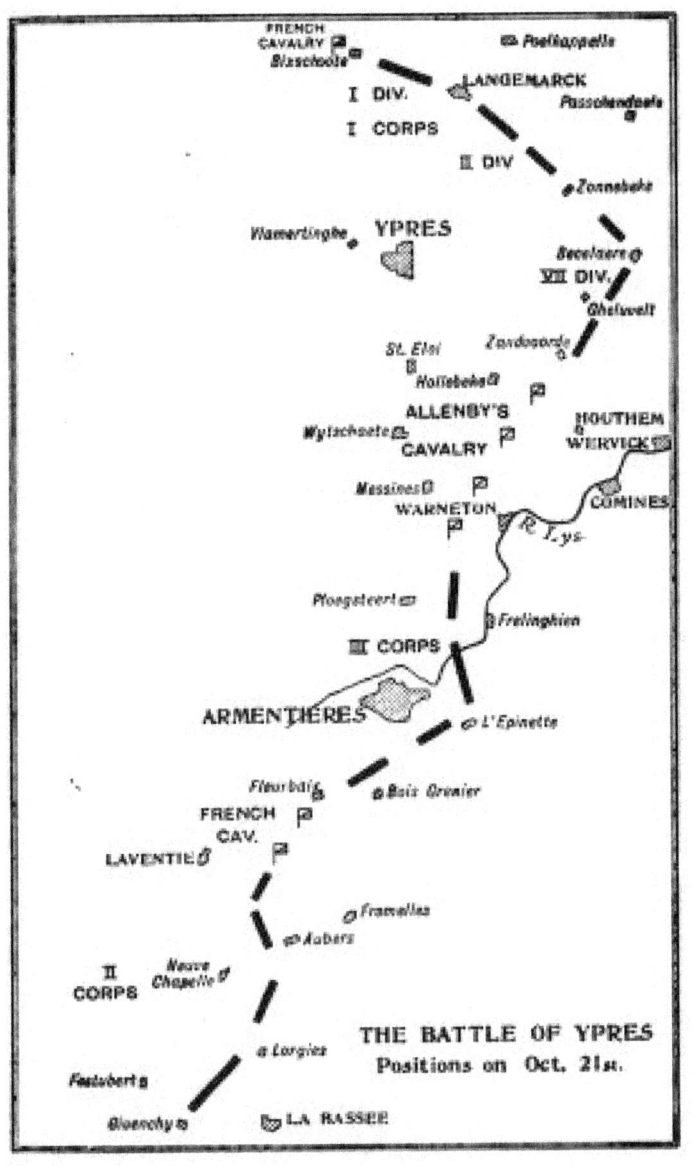

they had experienced during the night, and indeed, poor fellows! they looked as if they had been through everything.

I learnt the whereabouts of the new Brigade Headquarters, for their old quarters in Zonnebeke was now a pile of bricks and dust, and set out to find them. On the way I met the remnants of the 1st Welsh Fusiliers—6 officers and 300 men; the others had fallen during the last few days in the awful fighting, but most of them during yesterday's and last night's shelling. Early in the afternoon we opened fire on Becelaere and Gheluvelt, but had not been long on this job when orders arrived for me to report to the 3rd Cavalry, who had now moved round to the right flank of the 7th Division and were in the line at Zandvoorde.

I found General Byng at his temporary headquarters at Klein-Zillebeke and then got more precise details of the positions in the sector. My first target was Houthem, which was in full view after moving out as far as Hollebeke. The range was 3,000 yards, so that the effect of the T.N.T. upon the unfortunate houses and roads was most brilliant for our forty-five minutes' bombardment. Various members of the cavalry force came on board and were very loud in their praise of the effect of our shell, which firing they had watched during the shelling on Passchendaele in front of them when they held that sector; it was something to know that we were doing good, for if it was so then, why not generally?

That evening, I had to report to the 4th Corps at Ypres. For the last two days I had sent various telegrams off to the base for more ammunition, because our supply was direct from England to ourselves *via* Dunkerque instead of through the army channels, which would have been much more convenient; now I had only sufficient left for one day's heavy shoot. Each evening, we had to return to Ypres to clean fires, and fill up with fuel and water, for the engines had now been under constant steam for three weeks, and only careful nursing would keep them in perfect order.

Early in the morning, (23rd), I was out again under the 3rd Cavalry, and went forward to continue the bombardment of Houthem. Firing was going on all along the line, and it was obvious that hard fighting was in progress. This cavalry division was on the right of the 20th Brigade, who were being heavily shelled, and occupied the line between Zandvoorde and round Kortewilde. Various types of shell were flying around, and the roads were a certain target of shrapnel. So, I opened a direct fire on the roofs, etc., of Houthem, and soon got back a reply from some battery concealed on the left of the line, but it got no nearer than bursting high shrapnel overhead. It seemed as if its concealment stopped it bringing a direct fire upon us; however, it was eventually located an hour later, when I turned on to them.

About 1.30 p.m. more precise details of the hostile trenches and gun positions were sent to me, so I sent a messenger to ask if I could run out along the line and get a direct fire at them, but the general said he thought it too risky in view of the prevailing uncertainty ahead. All this time shrapnel was bursting on our left in the trees and shells were falling around in all directions, but from the hundreds which fell, extremely few did any harm, due to this form of unobserved firing. Throughout the whole afternoon we were engaged continuously on any of six different targets to the south-eastward, and at last towards dusk came to the limit of my supplies—a sad state, which I reported to the Headquarters, and then returned to Ypres to see if a replenishment had arrived.

Telegrams brought no reply, and by the following forenoon I was exasperated and in perplexity as to what to do. At last, at 11 a.m. I got news that a 6-inch gun with trucks of ammunition and stores had left Boulogne, and was told to go to Hazebrouck to meet them. I reported this to the corps, and by 11.25 got away, arriving there at 1 p.m. From there we were sent to St. Omer, but nothing was known there of my quarry.

At this time General Headquarters were in this town, so I sought out the Director of Transport, through whom I got the news that such a gun and wagons had been seen shunting about Boulogne during the forenoon, and again, later, further news that they had left attached to a train at 11 a.m.

It was not till 8 p.m. that the train arrived, bringing me 300 rounds for my 4.7 guns and a 6-inch gun which was now armoured and provided with a quantity of its own ammunition. But just as we were about to go east again, orders arrived that I was to remain at St. Omer. Meanwhile I had sent the engines into the sheds for their much-needed cleaning.

That evening the following communication was received, as it was to be communicated to all troops from the Field-Marshal Commander-in-Chief:

23rd October, 1914.

The Field-Marshal Commanding-in-Chief wishes once more

to make known to his troops how deeply he appreciates the bravery and endurance which they have displayed since their arrival in the northern theatre. In circulating the official information which records the splendid victories of our Russian Allies, he would remind the troops that the enemy must before long withdraw troops to the East and relieve the tension on our front, and he feels it quite unnecessary to urge officers and men to make a determined effort and drive the enemy over the frontier.

Towards noon next day we got orders to proceed again to Ypres, at which place we arrived by 4 p.m., when I reported to the 4th Corps. However, General Rawlinson told me that now the armoured trains had been taken over by the General Headquarters, and that he must get instructions from them before he could give me orders to work under him; meanwhile I was to wait in Ypres. At 3 a.m. (Oct. 26th), I was rung up by the Corps Chief-of-Staff, General Montgomery, who asked me to go out in the early morning on his responsibility and engage the guns at "America," for they were causing great trouble to the 20th Brigade holding Kruiseecke. By dawn I was in position at K. 27 on the Comines line and opened fire on the area indicated.

About 8 a.m. the Germans began a violent shelling of Hollebeke on my left, and started making a dead set at the church, which, from our point of view on the flank, made a most picturesque bit of shooting. They first ranged on the church with high explosive, and then burst into salvos of shrapnel. After first straddling the roof with a line of high bursts, they next hit, then never missing, the roof and building, so that within a few minutes it was in flames.

In time our turn came, and someone directed his attention on to our position, for we were straddled three times in succession, after which I withdrew round the bend and into the shelter of the woods for a while, where at 10.30 a.m. I got orders to return to Ypres. The station was occupied by hospital trains and a train of trucks filled with German prisoners, who were being despatched in large numbers. The Red Cross Sisters came on board and told us that they had first heard of us from the wounded German prisoners, who had told them that our presence was well known to them and that we were very much disliked; also, that a hot time was in store for us if we were caught, for their Emperor had offered £1,000 for our capture. (See Appendix 3). Naturally we felt something proud, but as equally determined that he was to be disappointed and perhaps inclined to raise the price.

GERMAN PRISONERS AT YPRES.

Whilst at the Corps Headquarters, I had a look at a large crowd of Germans who were assembled in the famous Cloth Hall. Such a motley crowd in that fine building looked very out of place, for they were going through a process of search and interrogation. Everything except their clothes and personal belongings was collected in.

During the preceding day the Germans had found the exact range of our lines around Kruiseecke, and their defenders had been going through the same awful experience as their comrades of the 22nd Brigade some days before. They—the 20th Brigade—had been attacked, all day long and during the night, and after their trenches had been blown to bits, they had to abandon the position and take up another line between Zandevoorde and Gheluvelt, the brigadier being wounded and the remnants of the brigade itself relieved and withdrawn.

At 2 p.m. orders came to go out and fire again on the "America" positions and on Kolenberg; twenty minutes later we were in action again.

Fighting could be seen to be in progress in front of us at Kortewilde, and on our right at Hollebeke. Some of our troops were passing under the bridge beneath us and forming up in open order in front of us abreast the Hollebeke Château, and were advancing towards Kortewilde as if they were at drill. Meanwhile shells and shrapnel were flying all round. During the firing on our targets a note arrived signed by "Scottie"; whoever he was I never found out, but he wanted a certain trench shelled, the position of which was 1,000 yards just in front of us. Keeping everyone behind the armour, I took one of the guns out and at 600 yards range opened fire with the 6-pounder. The railway was so highly banked that the 4.7-inch guns could not depress enough, so we had to stand up in the open and use the 6-pounder anti-aircraft gun.

Our own line of trenches was quite noticeable, for at every round fired khaki heads kept popping up to see either if we were still there aiming at them or at the Boche, but probably they were as anxious about their own heads as I was, for owing to the very short distance separating the two lines and the flat trajectory of the shell at such short range the projectile could only have been missing them by a few feet overhead.

A quarter of an hour was long enough as we were in full view of the enemy and might at any moment become a point-blank target for some gun if I stopped, so I retreated to the remainder of the train. I hoped that if we did not do all that the troops hoped for or-expected, at any rate we put up a small show for their amusement which varied the monotony of their day. (See Appendix 2.)

That evening when I returned to report I got orders to proceed to Bethune with the 4.7 guns and join the 2nd Corps, and that Ridler was coming up with his other 6-inch gun and so form his train. Naturally I was very loth to leave this field of operations, but was consoled with the knowledge that things were just as lively at the right as on this the left flank of the battle.

That evening we left at 10.25 p.m. and arrived at Bethune at 4 a.m.

The following are extracts from the *Corps Bulletin*:

"In the diaries of captured German officers the most unreserved compliments are paid to the shooting both of our infantry and our artillery. Our guns, they say, drop their shells with such marvellous accuracy on the target that there is only a yard or two between one shot and the next. One officer wonders whether we locate our targets mainly by means of our aircraft, which, he says, are always flying over their troops, or whether we are in telephonic communication with observers behind their own lines.

"As for our infantry, he remarked that our fellows 'shoot extraordinarily well'; as soon as a head shows above the trenches bullets begin to whistle past. On one occasion the Germans found themselves under a deadly fire, when they were near the village of Koelborg, but at a considerable distance from our trenches. So sure were they that the bullets could not come from us that they set fire to the village as a punishment for supposed *franc-tireurs,* who, in fact, did not exist. A compliment to us, but rather rough on the villagers.

"An officer captured the other day by the 7th Division has a sufficiently extraordinary tale to tell. In the course of our advance he found himself left with about twenty men in a house within our lines. He stayed there for three days before he was discovered and made prisoner. The moral is that the fact of a building being within our lines does not prove that it harbours none of the enemy.

"Amongst the enormous and varied booty captured by the Russians in the brilliant victory is the German Crown Prince's car containing his own most personal belongings. There is a rumour, so far lacking confirmation, that in order to facilitate their rapid retirement before the Russians when the roads are blocked with their own fleeing troops, the German commanders and princes are in future to be provided with Zeppelins.

2.—Givenchy.

On arriving at Bethune, I received a message to return to Hazebrouck and intercept Ridler, who had more ammunition and some stores for us. I had not seen him since I left them all at Ostend on the 10th, and all this time he had been forced to remain at the base completing his train, and naturally was very eager to go out and begin work with his two 6-inch. I was back again in Bethune, by 11 a.m. and sent on to Beuvry Station to report to the 5th Division there— General Morland.

By the time I found the Headquarters and got the maps and details of the positions it was already dark, so I got the orders for the next day and returned to Bethune, where there was at last a decent engine workshop which my engines could use. A hot fight was in progress at Neuve Chapelle, the remains of which village eventually were left in the fringe of the German lines a few days later. The Lahore Division under General Willcocks was in the neighbourhood in support, so that all around us we met these big Indian soldiers. Most of the batteries were using telephonic communication. with their observers in front, but that was as yet beyond me; however, I was to have the assistance of an aeroplane to spot for me. Verey coloured lights were used for a code to indicate the fall of shot.

On arrival at Beuvry next morning at dawn I found that all the points were locked to foul, and as there were no authorities at the deserted station, I had to smash the padlocks to pass through. I ran out to a position about 1,000 yards west of Cuinchy Station and proceeded to clear the poles and telephone wires out of the way, for they ran along the northern side of the lines and thus were foul of my guns. This took much time, for the wires had to be kept clear, some of them being used to form part of the signal system between the posts in front and the positions in rear. My orders were to engage two particular batteries at Voilaines until the airman arrived, and then to use him for spotting. By 9a.m., Oct. 28th, I was ready and commenced. firing. A French battery of 75's just on my left were somewhat surprised at my curious form of artillery.

In this locality again direct firing was out of the question, for the ridge in front and the village of Givenchy and Cuinchy filled the horizon, though the steeples of La Bassée and Douvrin Churches were outstanding on the skyline. But we were a bit better off here than at Ypres, for the maps showed every house, and it was possible to lay for a particular spot on the skyline on a bearing in line with the actual target beyond.

At midday the airman arrived overhead to co-operate with us. He signalled the first salvo as falling to the right and next as line correct. For some reason he now sailed home again, so I continued firing on this line for an hour. Meanwhile he had landed and sent me a message saying that we were just too far over the target, but all the shell were landing into the village itself, which we had put in flames—a fact which Headquarters were not displeased with, for they said that damage to persons and material must have resulted.

We were to try again, but the airman broke his propeller on leaving the ground and did not arrive again till 3.30 p.m. At first, he had some difficulty in spotting the lyddite in the broken country, but eventually we got line and range correct, continuing on this target till dusk. When he landed, the airman sent a report that when he left, we were straddling the right-hand gun of the hostile battery, so that there was little doubt that we were warming them up, to say the least of it.

During this afternoon the French General Commandant of the 116th Brigade had sent me details of his positions in front of Givenchy, and requested that I should tell him what he could do to give me his most complete co-operation.

This brigade was on the right flank of our 2nd Corps, and was thus the connecting-link between the two national armies. That evening, I returned to Bethune.

My orders for the next day, Oct. 29th, were to wait out in position ready to continue with the airman when he arrived. However, the morning was very foggy and there seemed no early chance of making a start.

Meanwhile heavy shelling and much rifle-fire was going on in front at Givenchy and to the north, shells were flying round in various odd fields and spent bullets continued to buzz about, some of them flattening out on our armour. I learnt that an attack was being made by the enemy, and that they had entered our trenches held by the Manchesters.

The airman must have reported on the impossibility of his co-operation, for at 8.10 a.m. I was told to carry on independently as yesterday; so that we again opened fire on the Voilaines batteries; this firing and the buzzing ricochets from the fighting going on in front kept us busy during the forenoon.

About midday the following message arrived from Headquarters:

To 108th, 114th, 2nd Siege, and Armoured Train.
Airman reports that at least three batteries have evacuated their positions since yesterday. He is not sure about two others. The G.O.C. congratulates you on your excellent shooting.

This was a very encouraging beginning. By 4 p.m. the fog had reduced so little in density that the day's original programme seemed doomed to be a wash-out, so I opened fire on an area at "*les 3 maisons*," where a large crowd of wagons and horses were congregated, and at dusk returned to report.

We were out again early, Oct. 30th, and waiting for fresh orders. Reports stated that our bivouac target of last night had disappeared, so we must have moved that lot, and soon directions to search the Voilaines positions arrived. Whilst engaged on this firing the French Brigade asked me to destroy a house 200 yards in front of their own troops at Givenchy, but I could not do this, for what with the uncertainty of indirect laying and having no observation, it seemed almost as likely that I should hit the French as the house; moreover, I had my own work to do.

That evening, I was told that an airman had reported our shell were falling round the position of the battery—our target, also that the 2nd Corps were being relieved by the Meerut Division, General Willcocks; the former was practically in a state of complete physical exhaustion owing to the want of sleep and incessant labours during the past weeks, and the dreadful thinning of their ranks. This sort of warfare with unseen enemies and big explosions would be new to these Indian warriors, but it was hoped they would get used to it, as, indeed, they soon did after the first few experiences, which resulted in unnecessary loss due to their imprudent gallantry.

All the next forenoon, Oct. 31st, we were busy on the Voilaines positions, whilst more fighting was going on at Givenchy. The French informed me that they had attacked and had succeeded in advancing as far as the western apex of the triangular system of railway-lines, a small part of France which was going to play an important part in our winter campaign in the near future. That night I was ordered to return to Boulogne to refit the train.

Accordingly, we left Bethune, arriving at Boulogne at 4 a.m., where I had my second hot bath since leaving England and at last slept in a bed. I found Littlejohns and reported. He had an office in the *Métropole*, from which he controlled the three trains. Some weeks before it

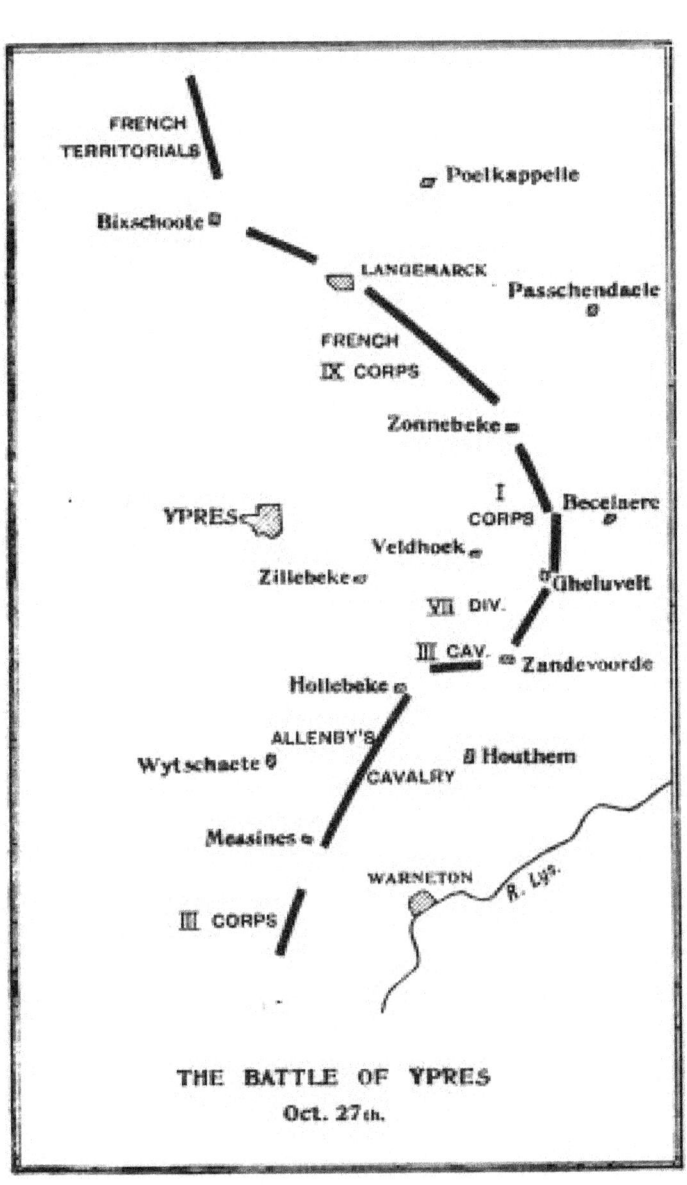

THE BATTLE OF YPRES
Oct. 27th.

had been decided to give each train a distinguishing name, and I had chosen the name of the C.-in-C. of our Grand Fleet for mine; now our cap ribbons had arrived, and every man wore "*H.M.A.T. Jellicoe*" on his cap.

I took the train into the repair yard and had the guns lifted out so as to get at the mountings for complete overhaul. Proper large bearing arcs were engraved and fitted to each mounting, and after a certain amount of argument I got a clinometer from England. Our living quarters were decently and more comfortably fitted out, and a small cooking-stove was purchased for each wagon, whilst an additional truck was secured and fitted up as a storeroom. The camouflaging was done up and each gun wagon given a name, those of our famous admirals—*Drake, Howe,* and *Nelson*—being selected.

By November 7th we were ready again for service, but Littlejohns went to London and I remained in Boulogne to take charge of the base in his place. During this period Boulogne was a very sad spectacle, for it was filled with our wounded who continually streamed in from the terrible battle raging all along our front and especially at Ypres. Everywhere hospitals had been started and were full; as fast as they were cleared into hospital ships, they were filled again from more trains from the east.

On November 11th Ridler sent a message to say that his train had met with an accident, a derailment having caused a certain amount of damage which put his unit out of action. Littlejohns returned from England and said that our shell supply ought to be at Dunkerque. The next day I received orders to go to Ypres, so arranged to go to Dunkerque first to see if our ammunition was there, and if so to fill up. This course was approved and we got away the same night, but an accident forced us to go *viâ* Calais, St. Omer, and Hazebrouck. However, we arrived at 9.30 a.m. and found the shell. At the same time, we were able to fill our provision wagon with various food-stuffs from the Naval Division stores, which were still there; this supply of luxuries, such as tinned salmon, marmalade, sugar, milk, cheese, and rum, was a great blessing during the winter months to come.

3.—Ypres again.

We eventually got a clear route again that evening and arrived the same night at Poperinghe, where I found the Headquarters of the 1st Corps, whose Artillery Chief, General Horne, now was my commander. I found there one of Ridler's 6-inch guns which had not

THE TRAIN BEHIND GIVENCHY.

been damaged in the accident, and this was attached to my train with a third engine. Ridler himself took the remainder of his unit off to Boulogne for repairs. In rearranging the train, I put the 6-inch behind the 4:7 section, so that when going out to action I could keep the two calibres separated, and where possible on opposite pairs of rails. All joined together we made a big and heavy train, and much too big a target in an advanced position; the living-wagons with their engine were always kept well in the rear.

From the Headquarters I got the details of the positions and a short summary of recent events. When I left the front a fortnight before, the battle was spread out all along the line; lately it had very much bunched up in this particular sector.

The French 9th Corps were on the right. Our 1st Corps were holding the line from Reutel round the edge of Polygon Wood to Veldhoek, and a large salient round Hill 60, as far as the Comines Canal, where we joined the French 16th Corps.

On the 11th the 1st Corps had held up a terrific attack, and yesterday it had been the French turn; the two armies still held their ground. Sometime before, the Germans had commenced destroying Ypres with guns of all calibres, in brutal vengeance at being defeated in their efforts to break through.

I was told that the station at Ypres had especially suffered and would need some reconnoitring before I could use it, which I did on the following day, finding that there still remained one complete line through the station, though the other six had been destroyed. As luck would have it, the complete line was a siding running on the southern side and nearest to the Germans, whose shells going over it just missed.

My targets consisted of six different battery positions to choose from for daylight firing, and certain areas which were probable places of assembly of supply and relief columns to be bombarded each evening at dusk. At dark I was to return and report at Headquarters. During the afternoon we passed through Ypres and took up a position at K. 2 on the Roulers line, opening fire at 3.45 on three different batteries with both calibres for forty-five minutes, repeating the firing at 4.30 p.m. At dusk we carried out the evening's programme of bombardments and then returned to Poperinghe. All day long snow and sleet had been falling.

I found that there was only one and a half miles of clear run on the Roulers line and of two on the Comines line, which I could use so long as the way through Ypres remained unbroken. If that was smashed beyond repair, I would have to resort to the Boesinghe line and fire over Ypres itself, for the main line to Poperinghe was too close to our own main roads of communication, upon which it would not be wise to draw fire.

We were well provided for in the matter of "food," for in addition to our own stock on board we drew rations and bread from the A.S.C. Moreover, to the east of Ypres were a number of deserted plots where some vegetables continued to grow, from which we were able to draw an occasional supply. I have also recollections of an occasional chicken getting run over, and being subsequently cooked. The following menu for a day is a standard of our living:

Daylight	Cup of tabloid tea.
Breakfast, 8.30 a.m.	Army rasher and fried bread; tinned butter; marmalade; tabloid tea.
Dinner, noon	Tinned rabbit; cheese and bread; rum.
Tea, 4pm.	Tea; bread and jam.
Supper, 8 p.m.	Bovril tabloid; beef and a vegetable; bread and jam; tea.

The beef and rabbits were sometimes varied according to circumstances by tinned salmon or the proceeds of a farmyard accident.

That night, (Nov. 16th), we received the sad news of the death of Earl Roberts.

Early next morning the congested traffic between Vlamertinghe and Poperinghe held us up, so that we did not get clear before noon. The shelling of Ypres was in progress, and in view of the chance of having the lines cut behind me, I decided to remain west of Ypres except when actually going to carry out a shoot.

Firing orders arrived in the early afternoon, so we went to the same spot as yesterday and opened fire, the 6-inch engaging a battery at Zandevoorde and the 4.7's a battery near Hollebeke. This firing continued at intervals during the afternoon until it was time to repeat the evening's programme. Zillebeke and the area in front of us was getting a good shelling from both big and small guns, whilst the shells fired at Ypres passed shrieking over our heads. At one time a few salvos of large stuff, about 8.2-inch, fell too close to us, one 75 yards short of the metals, making a huge hole measuring 6 yards in diameter and 15 feet deep.

It had been a miserable day, for rain had fallen on and off all the

IN ACTION AT YPRES.

time. That night I got permission to use Vlamertinghe as a base and so be clear of the traffic. I could obtain water from there for the engines, and used one of them alternately to run me to Poperinghe each night, and whilst I was away reporting, the engine filled up with fuel. Surprising to say, the water service at Ypres Station was still intact, so that on peaceful occasions we could fill up there when passing through.

Next morning, (Nov 17th), was even worse, for it was blowing as well as raining, but we went east and opened fire at 9.30 a.m. on three different targets. However, we had hardly warmed up to the work, when we were beautifully straddled by a salvo of four medium-calibre shells from some unkind fellow away in the south. This reception was repeated four times, hitting my office and my servant, who was in the act of dressing a chicken for dinner, so we cleared out to the west for a spell. At this time a hostile airman came up and manoeuvred about overhead whilst we were shunting. When he had gone, we went on again to the Comines line and opened fire again from K. 33.

Ypres and Zillebeke were being shelled again, and we could see stuff falling around our other position which we had just left. Three hostile balloons were seen going up away to the south, and some time afterwards a battery started shelling the station behind us. Not liking the trap, we retreated and fled through the station to wait on the other side of it till they had finished, informing the Headquarters of this; in reply I was told that the Hollebeke battery had not fired since our last firing at it, and was thought to have been forced to move at last. The Hun eventually tired of it, so after seeing all clear through the station, we ran out again on the Roulers line in time to carry out the dusk bombarding programme, and then return for the night.

That evening we received a copy of the following telegram, sent on to us from Littlejohns at Boulogne:

> *From First Lord of the Admiralty.*
> Am very glad to hear of good work of the armoured trains. Tell your men.

The Germans had attacked during the day, but we had apparently expected it, for an officer made prisoner the day before had stated that they were going to make a last effort to break through, and that if they failed, they were going to give it up and take up defensive positions. The 2nd Corps had borne the major part of the attack between the Menin road and the canal. At first, we lost a few trenches, but our troops returned to the counter-attack and retook them. Later in the afternoon the enemy tried again on a small sector held by the 3rd Cavalry Division, but the, latter stood their ground and drove them back.

Our own casualties had been grave enough, but it was said that those of the enemy's were frightful. In one small section alone a thousand German dead bore witness to our men's fine courage. A lot more French troops were arriving in the area and were to be met everywhere. I learnt that they were going to take over the whole front here from us during the next few days.

In the morning, (Nov. 18th), we went off to the Comines line, and the 6-inch opened fire from K. 321 on to a battery south-west of Zandevoorde, whilst I took the 4.7 section up farther to see if a nearer position was possible; however, the lines were too badly wrecked abreast the Zillebeke Lake, where there was no cover or straight line, so I had to return to the 6-inch position, and join in from there. Towards midday a battery commenced dropping shells in our area, and some fell too uncomfortably close, so we shifted position on the Roulers line: To get there I found we had to run the gauntlet of some shelling of the south-east corner of Ypres, and in fact had a narrow escape of being knocked off the line by a salvo which passed between the two sections and landed in a pond on the far side of the railway embankment.

At 2.30 we were in action again with the 6-inch on the Gheluvelt targets and the 4.7 on Zandevoorde. Within a quarter of an hour, we got the same reception as yesterday, being straddled again, splinters from the second salvo hitting the 6-inch bogie and its engine, and wounding the driver. Farther in rear a shell landed alongside a wagon loaded with 4.7 cartridges and riddled it, but luckily did no other damage, though I removed a splinter from the base of one cartridge where it was embedded alongside the adapter, having passed through the box and metal case containing four of the cartridges.

At the same time the station was being shelled, so in getting clear we had to pass through that, which we did as fast as possible, regardless of the steam-cloud we sent up. The Germans then let the station have it properly, turning on a battery of "Jack Johnsons" for over an hour. I had to report that both lines east of the station were untenable and the station impassable at present.

At 4.30 the shelling ceased and I went forward to look at our line. It was still intact, but there was an awful mess all round; I counted forty huge craters within a space of 100 yards square, but it was now too late for us to go out again. A record to the effect that we had been

6-INCH GUN IN ACTION.

heavily shelled but were undamaged appeared that evening in the *Corps Bulletin*.

As we approached the station on our way east next day a greeting of heavy shells landed in the station and stopped our progress in that direction; but not to be balked, I took the 6-inch into the station between two salvos and shunted on to the Boesinghe line, where we found a position at K. 55 and opened fire on one of the Zandevoorde targets, Sleet was falling, turning later to a steady snowfall.; Early in the afternoon the shelling ceased, for the Germans had perhaps stopped for dinner as usual, so I ran out on the Roulers line with the 4.7 section and opened fire for half an hour to relieve the 6-inch and then returned. We had timed the Huns' meal hour nicely, for the shelling of the station soon began, continuing till dusk.

Things were very much quieter as we passed eastward in the morning, (Nov. 20th), though the main square was still receiving the usual marked attention; we went straight into action with all guns on the new positions of two batteries in front of Klein-Zillebeke, returning after half an hour's firing. Whilst coming back through the station a battery opened fire on it, one shell of the first salvo landing under the tail of the last 4.7 bogie, smothering it with mud. From the apparent direction it seemed to be the same fellow as had chased me off the Comines line previously, but this time there was no doubt as to his line, for when the shelling ceased, I went forward and found seven holes in my line; six had burst and blown up the rails, but the seventh was a dud, and the base of the shell was clearly visible down the hole in the hard clay. It was a 4.1-inch, and the direction of the hole gave the line of the battery quite easily.

Unable to go east any more, we put the 6-inch into action again from the Boesinghe line, and then went back to Poperinghe after dark.

When I reported my line of direction at Headquarters the general said I was quite right, and that airmen had today located a battery hidden in the front edge of the wood, and there sure enough was the line of direction I had laid off. He also told me that now all our troops had been relieved by the French, and that he himself was off in the morning, so that our co-operation here was at an end. He made some kind remarks on our work when I said *au revoir*, and later sent the following report to the base:

The Armoured Train 'Jellicoe,' under the command of Lieutenant R——, joined the 1st Corps on November 15th. The train has been employed daily in connection with the operations east of Ypres in firing upon the batteries, roads, communications, and places of assembly of the enemy. Owing to the enclosed nature of the country, all firing has been conducted by map and compass, and no direct observation has been practicable. It is therefore not possible to state with any certainty what the effect of this fire may have been, but prisoners have admitted that our guns have been a source of loss to them. Lieutenant R—— has displayed great energy and keenness, and he and his crew of the armoured train have done excellent work. They have been under fire daily, and it is due to the skill with which Lieutenant R has manoeuvred his train that he has escaped without casualty.

(Signed)   H.T. Horne,
              Major-General, R.A., 1st Army Corps.

The following extract from one of the local dailies is of amusing interest:

To fill the times of silence there is the armoured train which rages under the very ramparts of the city and whose largest piece sends its projectiles 20 kilometers. This diabolical machine is operated by an English sailor who smokes his pipe with frightening composure. The detonation is such that the ramparts themselves are shaken, and the air pierced by the shell vibrates to the end of the horizon. 'Little Willy' is the name of the canon, is a very inconvenient neighbour, but he must do a good job.

During the afternoon I was able to telephone to Littlejohns at the base, and arranged to go to Dunkerque to get rid of a large number of empties and to fill up with ammunition. Our guns also were considerably coppered and required cleaning or replacing by others. During the afternoon we arrived there and went on the quays; there I joined the hospital yacht *Liberty* alongside, and aboard her enjoyed a hot bath and a most excellent dinner. Later the Belgian train of 4.7s arrived with Captain Servais; it was now known as the "*Deguise*," so named after our recent commander-in-chief at Antwerp. They had been engaged with the Belgian Army before Dixmude on and off for the last month.

Six more 4.7 guns arrived from England, so I had the job of shifting all our guns and sending the old ones home.

When this was completed, I left for Boulogne and laid up the

MY OFFICE.

train for a rest at the station of Wimereux. Some of the men were sent home on four days' leave, (see Appendix 3), and for the first time since leaving two months ago, the crew were paid; they thoroughly enjoyed the chance of spending a few coins, for the only money on the train had been the few pounds I had brought out with me.

On December 1st I got leave myself and went home to England for seven days.

CHAPTER 4

Winter Before La Bassée

Upon return from leave I found that things were very quiet at the front, and that only one train was being used at a time, Ridler being at Ypres with his repaired 6-inch guns. All our own repairs had been completed, and with the exception of a few men who got leave to go home in turn, we were ready for service when required. Meanwhile to keep fit we started a routine of route marches each forenoon, whilst each afternoon we arranged a football match, followed by a couple of hours' leave in the village.

However, plenty of rain and gales interrupted our work and made times rather boring, so that the joy was unanimous when we received orders on December 21st to get ready at once and leave for Bethune that night.

Arriving there the same night, a message greeted us saying that at the moment the 1st Corps were taking over the sector from the Indians, and orders would be issued to us from the former later on. We learnt that the enemy had attacked Givenchy on the 20th and forced our troops back almost to our guns

Our first counter-attack, (Dec. 22nd), had only succeeded in regaining Givenchy itself, but the 1st Corps had arrived and today were going straight into the fight. That something extra lively was in progress at the front was obvious from the din we could hear as far back as Bethune, and it was quite irritating having to wait to join in. By the end of the day our men had driven all the enemy back to his original lines.

During the afternoon of the following day General Horne, who still commanded the corps artillery, came on board and told me to meet him next morning at Beuvry. On arriving as arranged, he took me to the Headquarters of the 1st Division, where I met Brigadier-General Fanshawe, C.R.A., under whom I was directed to work.

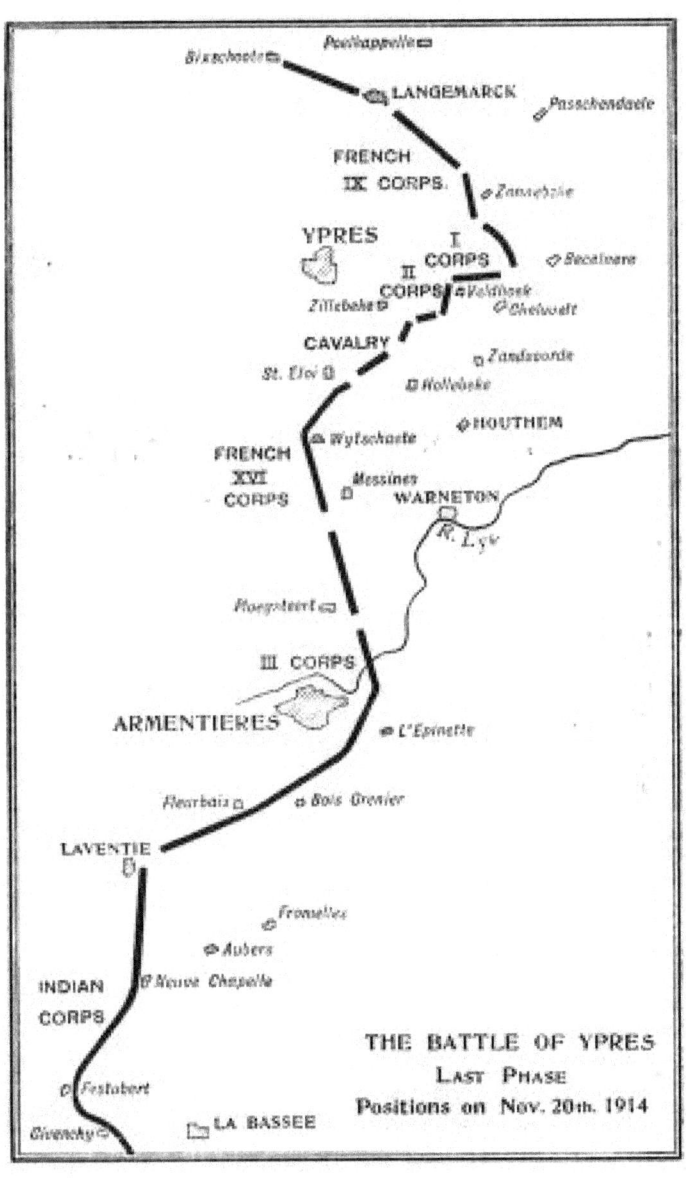

It was decided that I should begin by co-operating with aircraft, the means of communicating now being by Smith's Morse lamps and a code, and so get a decent calibration of my new guns. That afternoon we went forward and selected a position ready to open fire, but no airman arrived. The nights were very cold now and the dawn showed a heavy frost on the ground—a proper white Christmas morning.

I had a large selection of targets to choose from, and found a very convenient position to the east of the canal junctions. A dense wood lay close by us on the left, behind which we could go for shelter in case of the necessity of a screen, but in front of this it was possible for anyone on the La Bassée church to spot our gun-flashes. A field battery was posted in emplacement on each of our quarters, the 113th and 118th.

No particular firing orders were given me for the day, perhaps because it was Christmas, but my first list of targets included a wood and *château* at Coisne, which was said to be the cover of a bivouac and supply columns, and this seemed to be a nice spot upon which to leave our Christmas card. At a quarter past noon, I ran the train out and fired five salvos of high-explosive into the area and then returned to our dinner.

We had our Christmas mail of parcels, but by some unfortunate accident the Royal presents which were served out to every man in France missed us. This was the fault at the base, but we got them some three months later.

On returning to Beuvry, I found that the Headquarters had moved to a more permanent billet in Bethune, where I enjoyed an excellent dinner with the Divisional Commander, General Hashing, and his staff. My midday present to the enemy had amused them, and indeed it seemed curious compared with the rumours we heard of peace, picnics, and a football match with the Saxons just north of us. Opinion on this item varied.

Beuvry Station became our Headquarters each night, but I had to run back to Bethune on an engine to report as usual.

After a hard frost during the night the day, (Dec. 26th), was brilliantly clear; we waited behind the cover of the woods for our observer to arrive. The method of co-operating employed was that the aeroplane would fly towards the target, and when he could see it clearly, the round would be fired as he turned to one side to watch for the burst. When he had seen it, he returned and signalled the result by lamp. The aeroplane was generally kept to one side of the line of

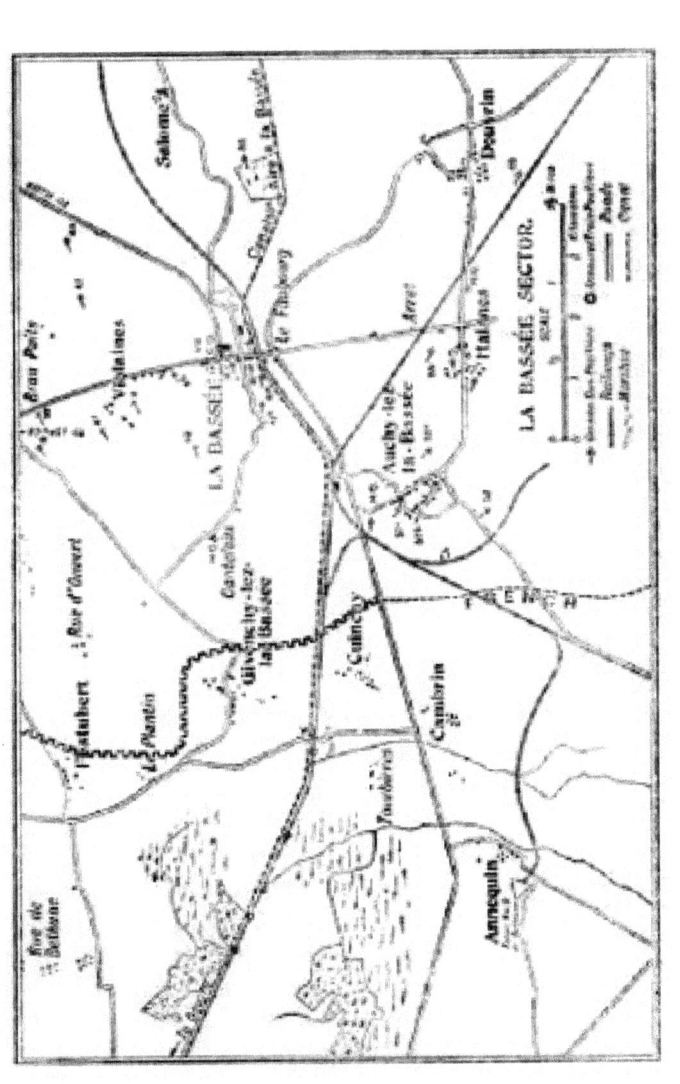

fire and in no particular constant position relatively to the guns, so as not to become too obvious an indication of their position and range.

In these early days of the war wireless had not reached the state of perfection required for spotting and signalling which it did later on. Our airman appeared overhead about 11 a.m. and we opened fire, but after several trial shots I had to give it up, for he could not see the bursts, which were hidden in the woods. Later when he tried again on another target, he said it had come over too misty to spot, so we had to give it up for the day.

We tried again next day, the airman saying he could see No. 41 clearly enough for spotting, but when we got going the mist was very hindering; however, we were eventually able to start, and were soon put on the mark. It is very difficult to judge what allowances to make for the cordite when it is open to all changes of temperature; a 10 *per cent.* drop in range was often experienced.

Each evening whilst at Bethune I was able to purchase a copy of *The Times* of the preceding day for the sum of thirty *centimes*; this was a great blessing.

For the next two days we had a strong gale, and the rain came down in torrents, so aeroplane work was quite impossible, and artillery at a standstill. The only shelling of any note was the evening's plastering of Annequin slag-heaps and a few stray shots into Givenchy.

Half along the line towards Pont Fixe and a couple of hundred yards in front of our firing position there were two high standards which in times of peace were used for carrying the cables of the canal electric system. On the top of one of these I rigged a block, so that I could be hauled up in a boatswain's chair. So long as I kept on the rear side of the trellis-work structure, it was possible that I should not be seen by the enemy's observers. From that height I could just make out the general lines of the trench system, except when the rise of Givenchy shut out the view; also, I got a particularly good view of most of the railway triangle in front of Cuinchy.

La Bassée was in full view, and with glasses I could descry figures moving about in the tower of La Bassée church; they were no doubt German observers, and I itched to have a shot at them, but so long as the Germans did not shell Bethune it was understood that we would not shell La Bassée, where there were still large numbers of civilians. Our airman did not arrive overhead till noon next day, (Dec. 30th), when we started ranging on No. 41, but he did not stay long, and went down home after several signals of "Unobserved." He ran out to see us and saw that some other battery was firing at the same time as ourselves, so that he could not pick out our bursts, which were short; the cordite must have still been frozen, though the weather was now milder. Whilst we had been firing a German sausage went up in the direction of Lorgies and as he must have seen us, we might expect something over us soon, so retired a bit to wait. However, nothing arrived in our area. Late in the afternoon we ran out to behind Cuinchy Station, bombarded the cross-roads at Illies for twenty minutes, and then returned home. That evening, I had a bath and dined at the Headquarters, a pleasure which became a weekly occurrence each Thursday.

By now arrangements were in operation so that the troops coming out of the trenches were taken to the baths at Bethune, their uniform thoroughly cleaned, and their underclothing changed; my own sailors went through this once a fortnight. This excellent service must have improved the general health of everyone considerably, besides checking the objectionable little friends that used to visit so many of the men.

After we had gone out next morning, (Dec. 31st), a chaplain visited us and held a Communion Service. I went forward to our reserve trenches to look into the possibility of making a forward observation post for us; but the brewery at Pont Fixe seemed the best, for though being some short distance in rear, it afforded an excellent view of the terrain. Towards 4 p.m. a violent shelling broke out in front of us and around Givenchy and Pont Fixe. No special orders arrived, so we opened fire on the Coisne area. The firing died down in front, so we went home, where I learnt that the Germans had attacked and occupied an advanced machine-gun post of ours.

Everyone had been very careful with their ammunition, as it was very scarce; we were better off than anyone, for our allowance averaged three times that of other batteries per gun. At midnight I struck "sixteen bells" on our ship's bell, for which a 6-inch cylinder served the purpose.

During the following forenoon, (Jan. 1st), orders arrived to bombard the eastern apex of the triangle, and a note to be prepared to increase the rate of fire if ordered. From my position up the standard the target was in full view, so we started in at once and continued slowly. Soon afterwards a battery of small calibre commenced shelling us, but everything passed over my head and fell into the canal in front of the train. Again, during the afternoon whilst we were firing it came back, but much closer this time. I began to think that my friends in the

H.Q. STAFF AND THE CREW.

church at La Bassée could see me moving up and down the standard.

After a couple of shrapnel bursts behind me and one almost alongside my ear, I thought it time to get down. Hardly had I set foot on the ground before they hit the top, knocking it clean off, and sending my block to bits at my feet. First thoughts were best that time, and I felt very glad that I had not stayed up there too long to think about it. We learnt that the German attack yesterday had eventually succeeded in taking a trench of ours. Later a general bombardment was ordered for five minutes, my particular target being the Lorgies cross-road.

The following day was very miserable; raining and blowing a gale. Movements of troops and the work of keeping up the supplies for those in the front line must have been nearly impossible, but though the A.S.C. people told awful yarns of their trials, they seemed to get there all right. The trenches were no more than drains cut through the country, where existence was an everlasting punishment—thoughts of which made us realise how deuced fortunate we were in our warm train.

Our own rations were left each night by the A.S.C. at the Beuvry Station as they passed through on their way to the front, and with some additions from our storeroom our menus continued to be quite exceptional. The word passed round, so that my office soon became a stopping-place for those officers who cared for a yarn and a cup of tea.

Littlejohns came up from Boulogne on a visit, so that we were able to discuss the need and possibility of getting another officer lent to me to assist and do the observation work from an advanced O.P.

The next day, (Jan. 3rd), was much finer, so I set out for the ruins of what was once a cottage situated near our trenches, to get a closer view of the interior of the triangle and the general run of the buildings there.

Approaching Givenchy, signs such as "To the Casualty Station," "To Batt. Headquarters," "To Cross Bone Alley," etc., showed the way to the several positions named. The whole village was a maze of trenches, for use when the shelling made the open road too hazardous. Paths wandered in all directions—behind buildings, across gardens, into a house by a door and out again by a hole in the wall, behind heaps of bricks and then under a sunken arch—all selected so as to provide protection from stray bullets and shut out the traffic from the enemy's observers and snipers.

The village was in ruins from end to end—a battered sepulchre. No building was whole; all roofless, hardly a wall without a hole or a huge crack. The shattered remains of the fittings and furniture lying on the floors indicated the class of the former occupants. China crocks and ornaments lay shattered on the shelf. A child's cradle overturned in a corner, vivid pictures in pieces and at all angles on the walls, plaster from the ceiling and bare floor, were the few remaining signs of previous humble occupants; whilst the home of someone more fortunate was evident by the burst upholstering showing springs and padding of a settee, a smashed polished table minus all legs, torn carpets, and smashed bedstead hanging from the shattered beams of the first floor, a tiled hearth and discoloured, splashed wallpaper. Mixed up in all this dirt lay hundreds of empty tins, bits of service kit, sandbags; heaps of straw and old bedding showed where the soldier had tried to find rest and shelter.

Moving on, one approached the reserve trenches, the track to be followed being plainly marked by signposts bearing instructions and directions to various trenches, etc. If these were not closely followed a whistle of a bullet would soon force one to realise that these instructions were put there for other reasons than directing, as German snipers were ever on the watch for a chance of drawing a bead upon the unwary.

Arriving at the ruins, I climbed up very cautiously and carefully looked through a hole in the wall. From here the objects of the visit were in full view, whilst in the foreground was a splendid view of the trenches, the few moving khaki forms of the sentries, the walls of the trenches, the piles of sandbags, the shadows of the dug-outs, and beyond the neutral strip of grass-covered ground, bordered on both edges by a jungle of barbed wire.

There on the German parapet lay a few dark objects—dead Huns shot down at night or tumbled out over the parapet by their own comrades after being killed in their trenches, and there left to rot. The extraordinary silence over the whole field was occasionally broken by the sharp crack of a rifle as a sniper tried his luck on some minute object seen to traverse his line of fire laid on the opposite trenches by his observer at the periscope.

On our way back I found a tortoise-shell cat wandering about Cuinchy which looked as if she wanted a home, so I brought her back with me. That afternoon we bombarded a factory in the triangle, spotting from the standard, from which I could locate each burst quite distinctly. A battery replied, but the shells flew wide. Hoping to deceive the other fellow that he had got our line and range, I ceased fire for a spell; he then started firing high-explosive shells for some minutes. When he stopped, I continued again. At any rate, if we went on like that it might induce him to expend shell in ploughing up the field on our left, thinking he was keeping us quiet, whereas it was the limit of the day's expenditure that kept us so.

A thick mist hung over the country all next day and no action was taken. Our general visited us and showed me some more targets and areas which required attention.

The Germans found amusement in bombarding a bit of waste land in front of the wood on the left of our position with 8.2-inch guns. The high-explosive they used made huge craters in the wet mud; those had detonated, but the majority only exploded with a loud squelch. I retrieved a fuse intact, which was the type used by the Belgians and made in a Belgian factory. That night our sentry fired on a light which was flickering along the telephone wires and did not reply to challenges. Later again in the early morning someone was seen hovering round our guns; the challenge got no reply, so the sentry opened fire, upon which some of the other men jumped out and joined in.

However, no trace could be found of any visitor, but rumours of spies were quite common; and orders had been made that no single person was to approach any battery at night, and fire was to be opened at once on any loitering figures.

We heard that Ridler had returned to England, and that another officer, M. Gould, had come out to take over his train.

The following morning, (Jan. 5th), was again misty, but clearing later in the day, we were able to carry out a bombardment for half an hour on the far corner of the triangle. During the day one of the 6-inch guns arrived to reinforce my train. I now kept the 6-inch on one set of metals and the 4.7 section on the other. Whilst shunting in Beuvry during the evening my wagon was derailed, but with the assistance of a wreckage gang from Bethune we got it replaced by midnight.

Light rain began falling during the following day, although we had had a frosty night. During the forenoon I calibrated the 6-inch on a target in the triangle, relieving it by the 4.7's later. In the afternoon I tried the effect of the 6-inch on some railway-trucks which were still on the railway forming the south-western face of the triangle. It was said that these trucks had been lately turned into machine-gun shelters, whilst the high embankment itself beneath, which had a concrete face on the far side, was a warren of dug-outs. We got a couple of

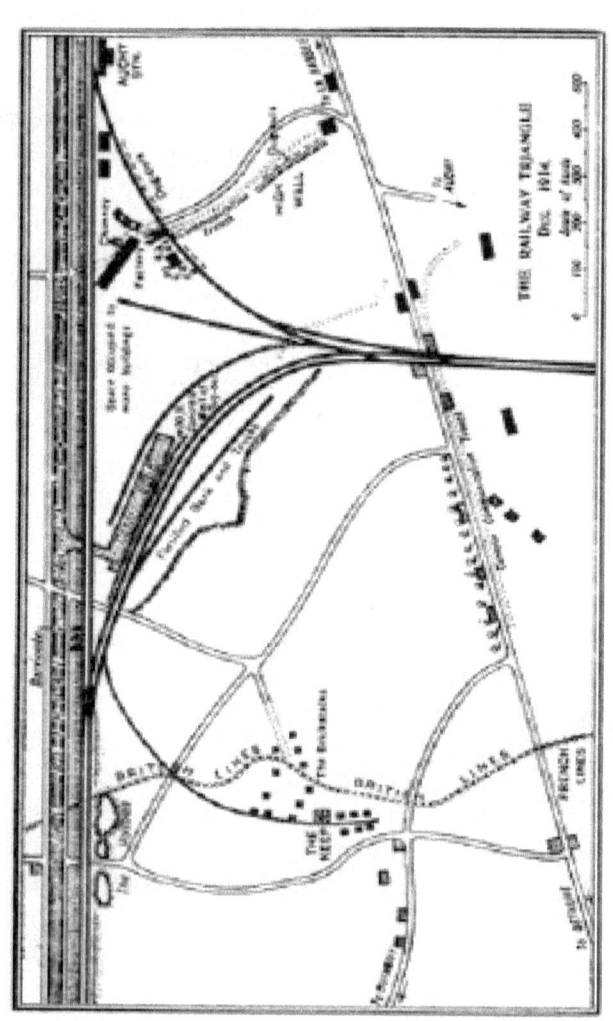

direct hits on the trucks, lifted one up on to another, and the bursting of the common shell against their sides was quite picturesque. The 4.7 section shelled some barges lying in the basin which were used also as shelters for troops.

At Beuvry that evening the chaplain boarded us. and held a service. During the night my cat wandered off, but was brought in at dawn by my Belgian railway guard.

Another period of gales and rain intervened, and then we commenced the programme of systematically ranging all the various batteries of the corps upon portions of the triangle; those of our own division (the 1st) were allotted the forenoon— each battery having a certain period of time in which to register—finishing up with all batteries doing a combined bombardment for a few minutes. This triangle was rapidly becoming a most important area; it afforded very good shelter for the assembly of troops, and compared with the surrounding country was a very excellent jumping-off ground for an attack. However, we were going to make it as untenable as possible for whichever battalion was there as a garrison.

Our period was from 10 a.m., when we commenced registering each gun upon the line of trucks, we had previously shelled. From my spotting position up the standard I could get a good view, and once again one of the 6-inch shell disarranged a truck; at 12.45 we all fired together, the result being a fury of shell-bursts and explosions which must have made things very uncomfortable for the Hun.

Later we learnt that our first round from the 6-inch which had ranged short had landed in a German trench, causing its garrison to bolt, and in turn became the target for our troops' rifles.

Naturally all this did not go on without drawing a reply, but in the area around us the shell continued to fall harmlessly into the neighbouring field. A few large shells were thrown around the Beuvry Station during the day, and one landed in the courtyard of the Gorre Château, where it burst, killing fifteen Indians and wounding forty-two others.

The bombarding continued next day, (Jan. 9th), our period commencing at 10.30 a.m., when the 6-inch continued as before, but we were ranged along the. northern embankment facing the canal and on the barge ferry there. Field guns started placing unpleasant shell round my standard, so I had to come down; one lesson had been enough. More to the rear I tried a railway signal-post, from which a good view of the triangle was possible.

Nearby was a small house used by some old women, who still lived there in spite of their close proximity to the shells. Now that I had to come back near them, they asked what I thought about their safety in future, as things were daily growing warmer; and though I did not expect them to follow the advice, they eventually did so in the course of a day or so. What wonderful women these were, up till now tilling their small patch of soil daily, paying little heed to the bursting of shells around them, and so hardened that the sight of aircraft flying overhead did not even inspire sufficient curiosity to cause them to look at them.

And yet the houses in the east and their church on the skyline, which for all their lives had been within their view, were no longer, as they lay in tumbled heaps of bricks, stones, and mortar. A couple of white crosses in their garden mark the graves of two Englishmen who had fallen in their defence, as they had for their own kin. They were ever dressed in black, and knew too well that those noises and explosions always in their ears plainly told of more graves and more women that would wear black.

It is little wonder if few smiles are to be seen on the faces of such women. They have seen and heard the red anger of war, not in illustrated papers nor cinema shows, but at first hand, with their own eyes and ears—in the white clouds of shrapnel and black volcanoes of high explosives, in the flames of burning houses, in the thunder of the guns and the shrieking of shells, in the groans of the wounded and the shattered forms of the dead.

All the country-side is full of such women, of whom one could say she has a husband, a son, or a lover out there in front, as every male relative and friend, old and young, wearing the blue uniform of France, is serving his country either in the battle or in the workshop.

During the whole remaining period of our stay on this sector and the many lively days to come, these women returned each day to carry on their work on the land, walking miles to and fro. Shells would plough huge holes in their field, but they were filled in during the day and the neatness of their plots restored.

At 1.23 p.m. the combined shoot took place with picturesque effect, bringing down a heavy shelling upon Givenchy, whilst large shells ploughed through the wood on our left, and a field gun got quite close to us. I was covered with mud from one burst, and another landed alongside my wagon, though far behind; still, we saw it out.

The German troops before us at this time consisted of battalions of the 7th and 14th Corps, of which the 56th, 57th, and 116th Regiments of the 14th Division were just north of the canal, and the 169th and 70th Regiments of the 29th Division were at the triangle.

On the next day, (Jan. 10th), we had our programme, promising much interest.

The guns of the whole corps were to check their registrations until 1.50 p.m., when a ten minutes' combined bombardment was to precede an attack by the 2nd Infantry Brigade upon the lost machine-gun post.

Our period began at 10 a.m., when the 6-inch opened upon the trucks till our aeroplane observer arrived overhead, then we shifted target to the bridge over the canal. The second round, which was too far to the right and thus into the triangle, hit some sort of magazine, putting up a large burst and flame. We at last got the line and straddled, scoring two hits. At 11 a.m. all guns of the Division opened fire for five minutes, after which the 2nd Division on our left carried on with their programme.

Shells from hostile batteries fell in various places, but the nearest to us were in the canal in front of us. Soon afterwards our observer came over to spot the 4.7's on to No. 41, but he went back after a few rounds, having met with some difficulty.

When the corps bombardment commenced, I put the 6-inch on to the trucks and the 4.7's on to the eastern apex and barge bridge, and for ten minutes there was an awful din; after which gun-fire was slower and less rowdy, for we all shifted on to hostile battery positions to keep their fire down whilst our men went forward. The rattle of rifle fire continued for some time, but slowly died away.

The Germans sent up three sausages, at which I fired, but was unable to reach. We continued the slow fire till 3 p.m., when the airman arrived over again, our fire shifting on to No. 41. I got "O.K." signals several times, which meant straddling and line correct, so continued on this target after he had left.

Before night we had achieved quite a good day's work with three successful shoots to our credit.

Good-fortune had followed our attack in the afternoon, for not only had we taken the post, but also an observation post in the Hollows, though it was thought that we would not be able to hold on to the latter position, which was too far advanced and so isolated.

A prisoner taken at the time said that the bombardment yesterday had killed 200 of the triangle's garrison.

That night we lost the advanced post, but firmly held our real objective.

The same artillery routine was carried out next day, (Jan. 11th), against the triangle, and as well as that firing, we again opened fire on the bridge, when the aeroplane arrived and got some more hits. At noon the combined bombardment continued for five minutes. That evening Headquarters told me that No. 41 had vacated his former emplacements and was now 500 yards more to the south-west, in position No. 41a.

Scattered hostile shelling had already commenced by the time we arrived out next morning, (Jan. 12th), and "whizz-bangs" were bursting over the field on our right. I was greeted by a few shrapnel which fortunately burst wide on one side, but I came back a bit. Before this small stuff stopped, they had hit the line, scattering a pile of loose metal and smashing one rail. After midday the shelling increased, and it looked as if something unusual was in progress, so we ran out and opened fire on the Coisne Château, target 41*a*, and the far apex of the triangle.

Shells continued to fall around us, but the only damage was from a few splinters striking the 6-inch bogie, and one man being slightly wounded with a cut in the neck from a piece which also carried away his cap in passing. By 3 p.m. the firing had died down, so we ceased also. We heard that the shelling had been the covering to a minenwerfer attack on the post taken by us on the 10th, forcing our garrison out and leaving it once more in the Germans' hands. Towards dusk we gave the *château* grounds another bombardment and then returned. That evening a suggestion to relieve us by another train was made from the base, but eventually dropped after Headquarters reported on the idea as undesirable.

Two days' heavy rains followed, making things impossible for most; even our troops in front of Festubert had to come out of their trenches to drier ground in the buildings behind them. However, towards the close of the second day we were able to run out and bombard the *château*, No. 41*a*, and Illies for an hour.

An 8.2-inch howitzer battery had now, (Jan. 15th), been located on the western edge of the *château* woods, so we were directed to shell it upon arrival out next forenoon, during which process we got it back fairly hot, though as usual the direction was wrong, and all we received was a bath of mud and water all over the 6-inch gun, one shell falling alongside it. Whilst the crew were going through the baths in Bethune that evening, Admiral Tufnell, who was working with the

Red Cross here, came on board to visit our curious ship.

A long spell of miserable weather followed, during which very little work was done by anyone. The 8.2 howitzer continued each day to try and smash up our lines, but nearly always missed—dropping into the wood on the left, the front edge of which was gradually moving to the west, as its trees were blown up or cut off short by the incessant shelling. It was seen that No. 41 had again moved his position, and was now in two sections in emplacements labelled 41*c* and 42*d*. We managed to get in an hour's firing one day, when we levelled a series of buildings inside the triangle. Snow fell very heavily one night, affording some amusement, including an unsuccessful attack with snowballs upon the train by the Headquarters units of the 3rd Infantry Brigade.

It was not till Wednesday the 20th that we were able to get to work again. For almost two hours that forenoon we fired slowly at several of the targets round La Bassée, and once again we were told that 41 had shifted; this time he was south of the canal by La Faubourg. During the afternoon we opened fire on this position, each calibre in turn, for a couple of hours. This continual shifting of position showed that he did not like it at all, but it was rough luck that the weather was so bad that we could not get some aeroplane spottings and perhaps give more effective punishment.

That evening, I had dinner with the 26th Artillery Brigade, and for the first time for many a long day played auction.

The following day brought us a variation, for we had two shoots at a battery at Auchy, No. 57a, the forward observer of the 113th Field Battery spotting for us and passing his observations back through his battery to which I had run a wire. We got well on to our target both times; the Corps *Bulletin* that night stated that the battery had been silenced. That evening, I had dinner with the Headquarters of the 3rd Infantry Brigade, General Butler.

The morning was misty after the night's frost, and our programme with the airman fell through owing to his having to go home at once with engine trouble. A newer 6-inch gun arrived during the day to replace the old one, out of which we had already sent 3,000 rounds.

For the first time for a long while we had a German aeroplane over us, and must have been seen, for shortly afterwards the 8.2-inch started again. Luckily, they were a bit short and only one shell got the line, but that was enough to make a crater 30 feet in diameter and quite destroyed the left set of metals.

During this a most unfortunate affair occurred, for a company of South Wales Borderers came along on their way to the front. Seeing the shelling in front, the officer asked me what I thought about it, and I told him that if he passed over to the south and went up to Tourbierres, he should be safe. Unfortunately, on his way there the shelling checked, and probably thinking it was finished, the soldiers returned to the lines, only to receive the next two shells, which blew three of them to bits and wounded several more; the latter I sent back to Bethune on an engine.

These large shells have merely a local effect, for they plough into the ground and their burst is confined to a thin cone, all the energy of the explosion passing vertically upwards. Lately an officer belonging to one of our howitzer batteries in front of us stood unharmed whilst two of these shells burst, each 5 yards on either side of him. On the other hand, another officer was hit direct by one of the shell; not a square millimetre of flesh or clothing could be discovered anywhere in the vicinity after a three days' search.

A few days ago, during the heavy fighting in progress just south of us, the French got an opportunity of wreaking their revenge for a punishment the Germans had dealt them in a similar manner at Messines in 1914. The French got wind of an attack to be made on them, and which had to cross an open space on the west slope of the ridge. They silently brought up 6 batteries of 75's, and waited until three battalions of the enemy had topped the ridge and then opened fire. It is declared that not one escaped the frightful carnage which followed.

During the following forenoon, (Jan. 23rd), the Germans sent up a sausage from somewhere beyond Salome, quite out of reach of any of our artillery. Determined to have a bang at him, this time I ran out with the 6-inch to Pont Fixe and opened fire with shrapnel; he was pulled down at once and taken away. However, our advance to almost within 1,000 yards of the Hun had not been unnoticed by them, and they tried to give us a warm reception for our audacity, but the shells hit the roofs and houses around us instead; we did not delay when we saw the balloon off, but opened out the throttles and bolted, getting away without a scratch. The incident appeared in the evening report, but by far the most amusing result was a yarn in one of our home papers some days later. It ran as follows:

> One incident of interest has occurred in this quarter. A diversion was created by sending one of our English armoured trains

from Bethune to La Bassée. It steamed at a great speed along the line, and for fully three hours the roar of guns indicated that a furious duel was in progress. It was feared that the train had been put out of action, but towards evening it returned, its armour absolutely undamaged. Its gunners and commander were walking by its side, driving nearly 200 prisoners before them. Among these were two hunchbacks and a dwarf. In passing, I must mention the almost incredible good-fortune of our armoured trains. They have inflicted appalling damage on the Germans, and all are unscathed, their only casualty being one man slightly wounded. The armoured trains, or our land cruisers as they are called in the ranks, have annihilated whole companies of the enemy. They have fired even their biggest guns during the week. This gives the gunners a weird sensation, for the wheels of the trains jump the rails, but are so made as to regain their position.

Of course, the man who wrote that had some brain; though in one point he is correct, for we had fired the 6-inch broadside on, causing the wheels to rise slightly from the rails, but the bogie soon fell back again, for with its armour and a large number of rails suspended over the axles it is a very heavy mass to lift.

Early in the afternoon we registered upon some works in the western apex of the triangle upon which the enemy were expending much energy, the 113th F.B. observer again assisting by spotting us on. After hitting a few times we checked fire, repeating the process at intervals for the rest of the day.

Black Marias started searching us out again, but only damaged the signal-house near the line and a farm on our right; however, in the latter case some of our troops were hit, for when the shelling started, they ran out of the farm to see what was happening, and got the next salvo in their midst.

Later during the day Lieutenant Luard of the R.G.A. joined me to act as my observer from a forward O.P., a form of assistance for which we had long been waiting. We went forward in the morning, (Jan. 24th), and selected a position among the twisted beams and rafters of the Pont Fixe Brewery from which he could get a clear view, and ran out the telephone cables. At this time the Germans had turned their 8.2's on to the Givenchy locks of the canal, so we opened fire upon the position No. 56. This shelling of the locks continued all day, 125 shells falling all around it—11 tons of metal—but luckily not damaging it enough to break it.

It was soon realised that their aim was to smash the locks and flood the country behind our lines, for the water-level on their side was higher; and we afterwards learnt that they had formed a big head of water with which to complete the job. Any future attempt was stalled off by filling the lock itself with thousands of bags of sand, and sinking a barge full of sand, in bags, across the width of the canal.

During the afternoon we opened fire once more on the bridge over the canal by the triangle, Luard spotting from the new O.P. The bridge had been hit by us often before, but in spite of all twisted beams, etc., the Germans were able to run wooden planks across it and make a good enough passage. The only way out of it was to try and destroy one of the brick supports on one bank; then it would all fall into the canal.

Soon after our arrival out the following morning, (Jan. 25th), the enemy opened up a violent shelling, especially the area all round and in front of Givenchy. Realising something was up, I was in the act of moving the train forward to retaliate, when down came a salvo on top of the train, killing one engine-driver and wounding several of the crew. One of them, a driver of the other gun engine, was hit in seven places about his body, and his clothes were torn off him in ribbons. With his aid we got the guns back 200 yards, but before we were ready to go again large numbers of troops were assembling near us, so that we could not fire, for it would only draw down a fire upon them. It was said that the Germans had attacked and taken some of our positions, and that a counter-attack was preparing.

It was not till 9.45 that our area was cleared of the majority of the troops and at this time our orders, of particular interest to us, arrived and read:

To Armoured Train.
1st Corps have ordered La Bassée to be shelled. Will you please carry this out.

It appeared that the Germans had fired some shells into Bethune from a long-range gun, and we were to take our revenge in this way. I ran out and put all guns on to this target, picking out the position of the Headquarters of the 7th Corps, which were just beyond the church. We also fired at other good targets, such as the main bridge over the canal and the station in La Bassée.

Black Marias started coming over again, so that we had to drop back a hundred yards and recommence. During this a battalion of the Gloucesters were passing on the left of the canal, and unhappily got a couple of shells, which cost them several casualties, including an officer and three men killed.

Towards noon the details of the position in front and the orders for the counter-attack reached us, the latter being timed for 1 p.m., my particular target being the canal embankment of the triangle to hold reinforcements from that direction.

The Germans had mined and blown up the trench occupied by the Scots Guards, had captured it and others to the south, so that our line had fallen back into a straight line in front of Givenchy. A secondary attack in front of Givenchy had caused a small set-back, and the French on the south side of the La Bassée road had been driven back to our alignment. However, we still held the "Keep"—a brick fortress in the midst of the brick-fields, wherein our men were surrounded but holding out.

When the bombardment started, we kept the 4.7 section in action against the reinforcement and the 6-inch upon the 7th Corps Headquarters, where already two fires were raging as a result of our previous firing. By 2.30 p.m. the firing subsided, so we reduced our rate, occasionally firing a few rounds along the embankment.

Our counter-attack had completely driven the enemy from our lines at Givenchy, having been repulsed five times with heavy loss; whilst before Cuinchy we had cleared most of the brick-stacks, and with a small exception had regained our own lines again. Altogether it was considered that the Hun had come off second-best, for his losses were considerably higher than ours, and though he still held a small bit of our ground, he had not been able to withstand our counter-attack in the main part. The prisoners which filed past our position were a motley crowd, very much shattered and extremely glad at being our side of the lines.

At 4 p.m. the battery at Auchy was reported as being in action, so I turned our 4.7's on to it, quickly silencing the enemy, as was also reported from the 113th F.B. observer.

The following is an extract from a letter written by a German killed today. He writes:

> In La Bassée something special will happen in a few days. You will read of it in the papers, then the dust will fly. I have had luck here, and have several times looked death in the face. But

bad weeds don't fade. Peace must not be thought of. This must surely go beyond March.

Always lacking, never slacking,
Never for a bullet asking,

And when I come back, I will tell you about *Anno* '14-'15, and bring you a fine souvenir. Otherwise, I am in good health.

I was now left with only the 6-inch gun and one 4.7, the other two having been recalled to Boulogne. We made a determined attempt against the bridge during the forenoon, and got four direct hits out of twenty rounds, but the enemy had piled a heap of earth against the buttress, which had to be blown away first, so that little real damage was done. A revised list of targets received that night gave us the positions of four regimental headquarters requiring attention, and also the news that 41 had once again moved south of La Bassée to 416.

Next morning was very cold and snow was falling. I was directed to try and bring down a tall chimney in the triangle which was supposed to be an enemy observation post. For a long time, the enemy had been endeavouring to do the same to the Brewery smoke-stack, but though it now resembled a cullender, it had withstood every bombardment, as also our O.P. in rear of it.

It was by no means an easy matter to hit such a thin unseen target at 5,000 yards, but I used a landmark for laying and put lateral corrections on the deflection scale. After twenty rounds, during which we obtained three direct hits, one of which had removed a large portion half-way up, it still withstood our attempts to destroy its base, for I wanted to bring it all down together. At the same time the 4.7's kept up a steady fire upon 41*e* to keep him quiet.

During the afternoon a Hun machine flew over us and dropped three white fire-balls. Knowing that this was a ranging signal to their guns, we moved back, but nothing arrived over. They said that the Germans take ranges of the fire-balls which are dropped vertically over a target and use this range as a basis. At dusk we ran out and shelled the Auchy Headquarters, and then went home.

During the afternoon, (Jan. 29th), the Germans began shelling Cuinchy again, and word arrived that an attack was preparing in front of the 2nd Brigade, so we opened fire with the 6-inch on the Auchy corner of the triangle and the 4.7 on the northern embankment till 10.30, when all was quiet again.

The sausage went up again in the direction of Coisne, so out we ran again to Pont Fixe, but he was descending and being hauled away before our first shell had burst. Of course, we had been seen coming and two batteries opened fire on the station. We got clear, however, and then they tried to hit the line behind us, so that our return was most exciting, for it was only possible to hear the crash of the explosion above the roar and rattle of the train travelling at a terrific speed, and to look around and say, "Where did that one go?" Luckily the rails were not hit, or we should have made a nice pile of wreckage.

At dusk we bombarded for half an hour with the 6-inch guns on Douvrin and the 4.7-inch on Haisnes, both villages being used as rest quarters and reserve billets by the enemy.

The attack during the forenoon had been made by 600 troops of the 116th Regiment, who had till lately been facing the French at Hullock. A hundred of them were killed by our bombardment, but the remainder, carrying axes and scaling-ladders, rushed on against the "Keep." The Sussex were there and drove them off, leaving fifty dead Germans around the position. The Northamptons lost a bit of their trench at the first rush, but, recovering, counter-attacked, and killed every Hun in it. A prisoner taken stated that large numbers of Germans had been killed and wounded during the recent shelling of La Bassée; this looked like a feather for us.

The 2nd Division's guns were registering on the triangle during the next forenoon, (Jan. 29th), so we were quiet. The sausage, however, went up at Illies, so we at once ran out before he could get too high. This time we were able to get five bursts near him before he was run to the rear and pulled down. The usual reception greeted us on arrival at Pont Fixe, but we got through again without a hit after another exciting dash home.

The afternoon arrived with no apparent disturbances from the enemy, so we had another trial against the chimney, getting two more hits out of fifteen rounds; but it still stood up. Meanwhile No. 57c—a new position containing two 5.9 guns which had been firing on us lately—was kept quiet by the 4.7's.

A quiet day followed, during which we watched one of our 9.2 howitzers registering on the triangle. One of its shell fell into a Hun trench and delivered a Boche into the Munsters' trenches. The 169th Regiment had by now been withdrawn from our front because of its heavy losses on the 25th, being relieved by the 112th Regiment. During the night a party of them rushed an advanced post held by the Coldstreamers, and still held it in the morning in spite of a counter-attack.

The howitzers put down a ten minutes' stream of high-explosives, and then a party of Irish and Coldstreamers rushed forward, retaking the post, and passing on gained the other one we had lost on January 25th, making prisoners of an officer and thirty-one men, and capturing two machine-guns, all that remained of a company which had set out the night before; so that, one way and another, this had been an expensive amusement for the Hun.

All that forenoon I had been unable to fire, as the London Scottish were waiting alongside us as a reserve in case of need during the attack. All was clear in the afternoon, when orders came to engage 41e and 59, as they were shelling our forenoon's gains. This went on till things quietened, at 3 p.m., when we turned on to the chimney again, this time bringing it crashing down with a third hit and thirteenth round, the brick-dust from its fall putting a red cloud over the triangle.

On my return that evening I heard that it was intended to relieve the 1st Corps by the 2nd Corps, and also that my train would probably go back, so that our activities were to stop for a while; it had been very interesting in spite of the cold and awful rains. General Fanshawe paid us some nice compliments, and said he was sending a report to Littlejohns.

This report reads:

1st Division,
February 1st, 1915.

The armoured train has been in action daily and has done much good work against the triangle and the German guns about La Bassée and Auchy. The shooting has been good, and several direct hits have been scored. Today a high chimney used by the Germans as an observation station was brought down. When a German captive balloon has gone up out of range of any of the guns of the division Lieutenant R—— has taken his train up to Pont Fixe and obliged the balloon to come down.

The train has received a great deal of attention from the German guns, but by judicious handling it has so far escaped injury.

    (Signed)   E. A. Fanshawe,
    Brigadier-General, 1st D.A.

A day's downpour intervened, and then I motored to Boulogne for a conference, returning in time to go out on the afternoon of the 4th and open fire on a factory and another chimney to the north-eastward

SNOWBALLING.

A "BLACK MARIA" HOLE.

of the triangle, scoring several hits, but no definite result.

The troops of the 2nd Corps, under General Haig, were gradually taking over the line from the 1st Corps, and many troops were in the area, so that little firing was done. However, I was able to continue against the same target with the 6-inch, keeping $57c$ quiet with the 4.7's until after the twenty-second round the chimney crashed down, on its way knocking down the whole western wall and roof of the factory, which had already been made very rickety by our misses. Now the interior was in full view, so that it was rendered useless for cover and shelter.

An operation by the Guards Brigade was planned for the afternoon of the 6th, commencing with the registration of "Mother"—our 9.2-inch howitzer—upon the triangle's embankment and some brick-stacks held by the enemy. For a quarter of an hour prior to the attack the whole corps artillery joined in, the result being a huge area of explosions, fire, and brick-dust, all forming an immense red cloud covering the entire front. Our own particular job was the holding up of reinforcements by a barrage on the canal bridge and the far apex.

At 2.15 p.m. the Coldstreamers rushed the brick-stacks, and the Irish the trenches on their right. Within three minutes General Lord Cavan had won a further addition to his increasing bunch of successes, for the whole of the objective had been secured by his men, as well as twenty survivors of the original defenders, also a machine-gun and a trench mortar. Indeed, some units had gone too far and had to be brought back. So helpless had the enemy become that our Sappers were able to go out and erect 300 odd yards of wire before dusk, so that our line was now securely held east of the brickfield.

Soon after the attack had been launched, we shifted our fire on to $41e$ to keep Fritz quiet, some of our shells causing fires to break out around the canal bridge at this corner of La Bassée.

Shortly before 3 p.m. we again shifted the 4.7's on to Haisnes, which, being the position of the reserve troops, might also be the point of assembly prior to a counter-attack, so we put the 6-inch on the triangle communication trench.

Through the whole period the hostile fire in our area had been confined to a few "woolly bears" scattered harmlessly all round, but before long everything was quiet again and all shelling ceased.

An hour later we got orders to shell the interior of the triangle, for prisoners had stated this area was full of troops, so we opened fire with this object, till forty minutes later all the artillery was put on to Auchy, where quite two battalions had been seen preparing to attack; our fire dispersed them and the attack never materialized. Our total casualties for the day's work was only twenty.

Upon return that evening to Bethune, I had a farewell dinner with the brigadier, and thereafter came under the orders of the C.R.A. of the 2nd Corps, General Onslow.

The commander-in-chief sent a telegram to all the artillery which had been working under the 1st Corps during the last six weeks, congratulating them on their good work.

During that night a party of the enemy were seen approaching the front of the Coldstream Guards, who allowed them to come within a few dozen yards of their wire and then opened fire; thirty dead were found at daylight.

Quietness was the order of the day following our success, and it looked as if we were in for a rest, till about 4 p.m., when the enemy put down a heavy fire upon the Cuinchy front. As this increased in intensity, I joined in the reply by opening fire with the 6-inch on Auchy and the 4.7's on the southern apex. In our area large shells were ploughing into the wood on the left and along the canal, a couple of bursts unfortunately getting into some troops who were passing at the time. Before an hour had passed all was quiet again, and we learnt that a hostile attack had been launched, but was dispersed by the artillery's quick action. That evening, I had an excellent and amusing dinner with the Divisional Cavalry—the XVth Hussars.

A successful attack by the French on our right, to improve their position and get up more into the lines with us, followed, and then several days of wind and rain prevented all operations.

During this time the Belgian 4.7-inch section arrived under Captain Servais to relieve us, and on the 12th, I took him and his observer to the O.P. to show them the points of note and explain the working of the O.P. and other details. At the same time, we continued our attempt to destroy the bridge, but soon after starting this the enemy shelled the O.P. so heavily that our observer had to retreat to the cellars. We got going again later, but beyond sending various girders flying and doing similar less vital damage, even ten direct hits did not eat away enough of the support to cause it to collapse; a few 9:2 howitzer hits were necessary. That night I introduced Servais to the Staff he was to work with, and then I waited over a day or two to assist him to settle down in his new surroundings, strange after his experiences when working with his own people on the Yser.

After another wild and wet day, (Feb. 14th), Servais took his section out, and I went on with his observer to the O.P. to assist during the usual bombardment prior to a successful but restricted attack by the infantry near the brickfield. From this position in the O.P. the advance and the fighting could be seen and followed much as a spectator in the grandstand watches a football match. Through flashes could be seen every detail and movement of the fighters, even to the expressions on the faces, all seeming like the dumb-show of a cinema film: a rifle pointed, and a spit of flame from the muzzle without hearing the report, and officers obviously giving orders and gesticulating.

Not that we were too far off to hear such sounds, but they were drowned in the continuous roar of the battle itself. The struggle was interesting and exciting, even from a spectator's point of view, and more so from my own, as I was playing a part in the great game going on in front of me. Beyond our line of trenches white puffs of smoke continually burst, the shells passing overhead in a succession of rushing shrieks. Larger black volcanoes of mud and flame showed the fall of high-explosives destroying the enemy's line, whilst occasionally a flash and a huge red dust-cloud would show where one had landed in a pile of bricks.

All along the front, on both sides, our own and the German batteries were pouring down their shells, each battery dependent for the accuracy of its fire on its observer situated similarly to myself. In a few moments a stir was apparent in the British line, a glimpse of a row of khaki figures clambering from their trench and the flicker of their bayonets, and in an instant the ground beyond was dotted with moving figures, making a fair target for the German rifles and machine-guns—such as had survived the bombardment. Figures sprawled, some never to move again, others to rise and stumble on after their comrades, as yet more fortunate in being untouched.

The advance having started, the fighting-line surged forward, checked and halted, moved again—now rushing, now staggering, and so on till the edge of the German trench became dotted with bobbing heads and moving figures, the next moment to be hidden by the swarm of our men as they leaped upon them. Then suddenly this area became the object of the enemy's artillery, endeavouring to shell out the survivors of the victorious attackers and prevent the consolidation of the position won. Now it was our turn to look round and engage the enemy's guns and try to check their design.

We saw target No. 11 in action and attempted to get the train on to this objective. A large error in direction at the start looked suspicious, and upon return to the train I found the new bearing racers were a matter of 2 degrees in error, a fault which I corrected before leaving.

Next day we returned to Boulogne, and were able once more to send some of the men, a few at a time, home on leave again. As for myself I got to London for four days on March 1st.

CHAPTER 5

Neuve Chapelle

Returning from leave, I had to take charge of the work of completing the mounting and equipment of the new 4-inch guns which had arrived from home. This completed, the guns were sent out to join Gould; and I then carried out the erection of the 6-pounder from my train on a cliff west of the harbour of Boulogne, to reinforce a couple of French small pieces there for the defence of the port against U-boat attacks—our own men manning one gun day and night.

From now on I was directed to act as Gunnery Officer of all the sections, a job which included inspection of each unit at intervals, and of the preparations prior to the coming offensive on our own centre before Lille. For use in getting about the country I was provided with an Austin four-seater, a new car which gave me much pleasure in my efforts to obtain an up-to-date knowledge of driving under varying and often difficult circumstances.

On March 7th I set out for the train under Gould, and after reporting on the way at a couple of the Headquarters under which we were to work, reached La Gorge that evening. During the following day we sought out a position for the train when in action, and an O.P. in Laventie from which we could get a good view of the country over which the attack was to take place and our particular targets. Laventie Church was an excellent position for the latter, but too likely to become the object of hostile attention; however, we found that a good view could be obtained from a turreted house nearby, so there fixed up our telephones, etc.

Close to the position of the train, which was composed of one 6-inch, one 4.7-inch, and two 4-inch guns, we found the new 15-inch howitzer in the process of being erected under the supervision of R. Bacon (Temporary Colonel, R.G.A.). His observer joined us in our O.P. and used this position during the next few days.

THE FAMOUS PONT FIXE BREWERY.

That night I reported to General Montgomery, my friend of the early days of Ypres, who was now in charge of the southern group of heavy guns; and on the morrow visited the train still working under Servais before La Bassée.

That night the orders for the attack were issued. Our positions lay just to the west of Neuve Chapelle, which village was the first objective, whilst the Aubers Ridge beyond was then to be attacked, from whence an advance on to the plain of Lille would threaten the city, and also outflank La Bassée in the south. Three hundred guns of calibres varying from "Grandmother," the 15-inch howitzer, down to the small 12-pounders, were arranged in a large circle so that their converging fire could be directed upon the centre at Neuve Chapelle. The attacking troops were the 4th Corps under General Rawlinson and the Indian Corps under General Willcocks, whilst simultaneously the 2nd Army at Ypres and the 1st at Givenchy were to carry out a holding offensive to prevent the enemy from drawing upon these neighbouring sectors for reinforcements with which to meet the main attack.

At 7.30 a.m. (Mar. 10th), the first gun opened fire, and soon all 300 guns were concentrated upon the trenches and defences round Neuve Chapelle. The earth vibrated as if struck by a huge hammer. The first shells that hit the enemy's position raised a cloud of smoke and dust, so that throughout the bombardment we could see nothing but a mass of greenish lyddite fumes and great tongues of red flame and flying earth. Defences and parapets crumbled like sand, and revolting fragments of human flesh were scattered in every direction. For fully thirty-five minutes our gunners worked at full speed, expending more ammunition than in eighteen months of the Boer War, and at the end of it there were no defences—only blasted earth and mangled bodies.

Our own particular targets included the batteries at Bas Pommereux, Aubers, the Aubers-Fromelles road, and the exits from Aubers; also the Aubers Church, which was a commanding hostile O.P. overlooking our advance. This latter was also a target for the 15-inch, the first round from which missed to the left, but completely demolished a factory; before it could be loaded and fired again, we had hit the target six times with our 6-inch and set the steeple alight. The second round from the giant howitzer detonated on the road beyond the church, demolishing several houses. The zone of its destruction appeared to grow gradually just like the ripples on the surface of a pond when a pebble is dropped into it.

When the preliminary bombardment was over, all guns lengthened their range on to the various targets and the village itself. The houses began to leap into the air, and huge brick and dust clouds rose up to the heavens; trees fell like grass, and the consequent blanket of smoke and debris in front grew denser and denser. Then the whistles blew all along the line and the infantry started their advance.

All day long Gould and myself continued observing from this position, though several stoppages were caused by breaks in our telephone lines to the train when hit by shells. Hostile guns were shelling Laventie, and the church and cross-roads behind us were getting a particularly warm time. As the day progressed news gradually filtered through, keeping us informed of our steady advance. Our troops had practically walked through the demolished German defences, experiencing little opposition from the few half-demented survivors of the awful bombardment; and passing through the remains of the village, established themselves on the eastern outskirts, but the left was experiencing some difficulty from uncut wire. Similarly, the Indians had advanced after some checks, and now were in line with their neighbours on their left. Front of our O.P. the constant stream of fireworks and Verey lights—sent up by our men to indicate their positions, and by the enemy as signals to their own guns to come to their assistance—made a brilliant but confusing display.

Towards noon the firing had appeared to slacken, and we could see several of our batteries moving forward—an encouraging sign. Again, in the afternoon our troops attacked and everywhere advanced, but towards dusk the battle seemed to lessen in intensity of the rattle of rifle and battery fire, and we heard that a check had occurred.

Details arrived in due course. The 7th and 8th Divisions had been held up near the Moulin du Pietre and by the small stream—the Des Layes. The Indians had more than once cleared the Bois du Biez, but each time had to come back to the alignment of those held up on their left. In the neighbourhood of the Des Layes were more strong positions which our guns had not yet touched, and to push an infantry attack would have been needless sacrifice. So as the evening was closing in, we devoted ourselves to strengthening our line on the ground won. Neuve Chapelle was ours; we had straightened out our line and advanced a mile. But we had not broken through, and valuable hours were slipping by.

The plan as arranged for the morning, (Mar. 11th), was that the 4th Corps was to attack the Les Mottes Farm and pass on to Aubers, whilst the Indians were to clear the Bois and wheel to the right upon Halpegarbe. But bad luck continued to follow us, for the morning arrived with a heavy mist over the whole country. Artillery fire was lively on both sides, especially from the enemy farther south. Our own job was to keep up a fire upon Aubers to check reinforcements, and to try and locate and then engage hostile batteries.

The first was simple, but the second almost impossible, for the mist shut out the view. The enemy made an attack from the Bois early in the morning, but were easily driven off by the Indians. Our own advance, however, was impossible on any large scale without the proper artillery support, which the mist prevented. All were very disgusted at this bad luck, for every hour's delay gave the enemy more time in which to bring up reinforcements against us.

The following day, (Mar. 12th), was a little better, though the. fog lay over the country in the morning, but during the afternoon it gradually cleared, and the artillery became very active on both sides, our targets remaining as before.

Throughout the day several messages brought us the news of attacks and counter-attacks, each side fighting hard; the incessant roar of the guns, the rattle of rifles and machine-guns, and the continued display of fireworks indicated this. But we were only able to move forward in places, getting up as far as the Moulin du Pietre. Laventie got its fair share of the shelling, though many were fortunately duds.

A small house alongside our O.P. was occupied by a couple of women and some children, who sat there all day quite fearless, notwithstanding that all the houses on the opposite side of their street and around the church were blown to bits. During the afternoon the field-marshal visited the train.

That evening Estaires was full of German prisoners and our wounded. The casualties on our side had been heavy indeed, but the Germans had lost even more; in fact, in front of our regiments a whole German battalion lay dead—a thousand corpses over a hundred yards' front. The questioning of prisoners was held in the *Hôtel de Ville*, and to relieve the congestion of the streets several hundreds were taken to some barges on the canal, but they could not be persuaded to go on board, for they declared that once there we would sink the barges and drown them all, for they had been told by their officers that we killed our prisoners.

Two young German cadets had just been sent to this front in charge of a draft of reinforcements; they had been awakened in their billets by our opening bombardment, and set out to move forward to join up with their unit in front. Approaching Aubers, they ran into our fire and hid in the woods till dark, when they again moved forward, got lost, and walked straight into our lines, whence they were led to our rear, prisoners, and never having fired a shot in their short career.

We heard that during the preceding night the 6th Division just north of us had created a diversion and had captured L'Epinette.

Saturday morning, (Mar. 13th), was almost as bad as the preceding two days, for the mists were still low and thick. We continued to keep a steady fire on our targets and upon Fromelles. The shelling around us became more violent, and our O.P. looked like being demolished. It had already been hit, so that one side of the house had collapsed and the gardens around were full of holes by now. However, the building continued to bear a charmed life and lived through it. All the news we could obtain was that our offensive movements were stopped for the present, and that the hostile strength was increasing. Next day the whole operation was finally abandoned. The delays caused in the first case by the wretched bad luck of the weather had given the enemy sufficient time to bring up so many reinforcements that attacks now would be at far too costly a price.

Later on, Gould and myself went into Neuve Chapelle itself to visit the scene of the battle. We had some narrow squeaks from snipers who were still hiding in the ruins, for being still dressed in the blue naval uniform we made good targets. Arriving at the remains of the German lines, we found an awful sight of ruin and slaughter. At the time this area was being held by the Rifle Brigade in reserve and a Scottish regiment was clearing up the mess. The German trenches, or rather what was left of them, were full of dead, four and five corpses deep, whilst the shell-holes and dug-outs were littered with hundreds lying and sitting in all manner of positions—almost every face showing signs still of indescribable terror.

Hardly a square yard remained untouched by our bombardment. In our conspicuous rig we made too good an aiming mark to go to the front line, but in and around this ruined village we saw quite enough to last us a lifetime. At the same time the one thing most remarkable was the extraordinary high spirits of the soldiers.

The vigour of our offensive had put new heart into them after the wretched winter. The feeling that at last they were going forward more than repaid their losses, the wounded themselves thinking not of their own afflictions, but spinning wild yarns of the day's incidents.

During the first rush our men crowded into the hostile trenches, all eager to take some part in the fight, and none more so than the Indians, who now could fight in methods more in keeping with their spirit and custom.

Not less marked and noteworthy was the revealing of the conditions under which the enemy had existed during the previous winter. The trenches were narrower than ours and deeper, with quite a foot or more of water in them, but the dug-outs were most comfortable. This contrast might indicate the German officer's custom of looking after his own comfort first and leaving the men to shift for themselves. Furniture and every sort of utensil were to be seen everywhere, probably all having been removed from the village behind.

That evening, I returned to Boulogne to prepare my own train for service, as one was required for some particular work on the Belgian Front.

CHAPTER 6

The Yser, 1915

During the evening of March 18th, I arrived with the train of three 4.7-inch guns, etc., at Dunkerque, and reported on the following day to the British Mission at the Belgian Headquarters, a member of which took me on to the Headquarters of the 3rd Division of the Belgian Army, General Jacques, under whom I was to be placed. The division held the sector in front of Dixmude. It was arranged that I should use a siding at Bray Dunes as a resting place for the train during daylight, for the operations were all to take place at night. I had a Rolls-Royce attached to the train for use in reporting daily at the Headquarters. I was to have the services of three different Belgian observation posts, each of which was to report the lines of direction of our bursting shell; these reports were plotted at a central station and any error reported to me for correction. Such an ideal system of spotting promised to produce good results.

Early in the evening of the 21st we advanced to abreast the Cambron Farm on the Dixmude line and connected up the telephone, getting into touch with the Headquarters and O.P.'s. When everyone was ready the guns moved on to K. 24, laying the connecting telephone line as they advanced. We were so close to the front lines that I kept the guns and the unarmoured sections well separated; my office was in the latter section, in which the reports of the spotting or any revision in targets or orders from the Headquarters were received, and working from my maps there I could telephone the firing orders to the guns in front.

Shortly after 10 p.m. we ranged on to Beerst Village, and then bombarded this area with forty rounds, this firing being the only item of our night's programme.

The following evening, we were out in position by midnight, but our role was merely to be ready to open fire as ordered, in case our

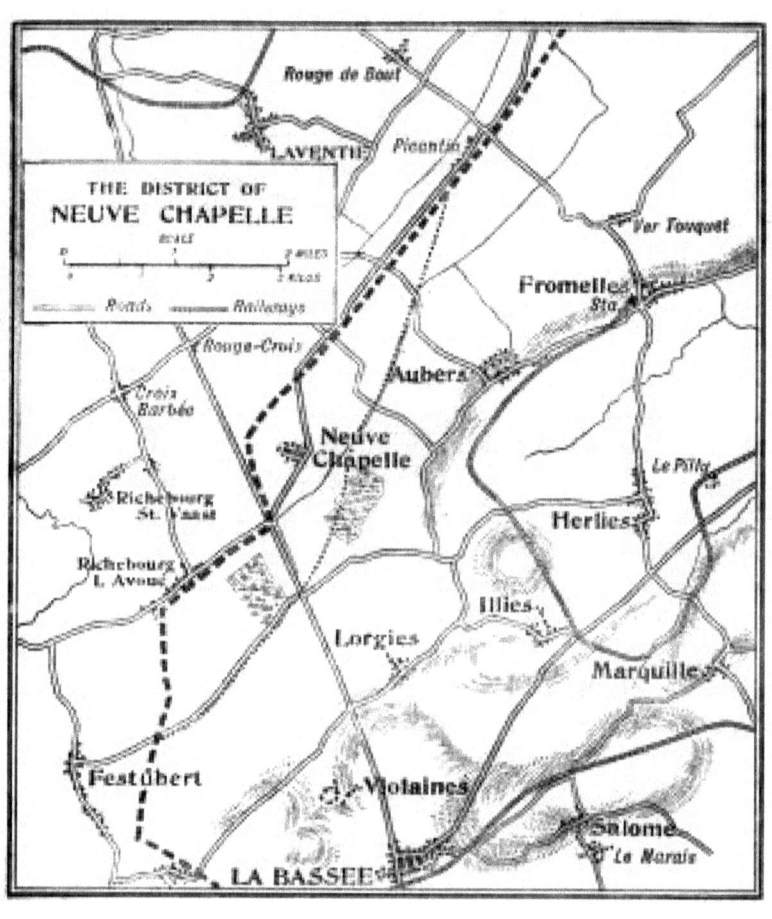

assistance was required in a small operation which was timed to take place at 2 a.m. At this time rifle-firing suddenly broke into the stillness of the night, but all was dead silence again by 2.45 a.m., very little artillery fire having been seen. When dawn began to break, we returned home.

By ten o'clock the same night, (Mar. 23rd), all were ready with the guns at K.24. The nights at this time were most extraordinarily clear and brilliantly illuminated by a full moon, and any tendency to become drowsy during the long silent periods of waiting was checked by the sharp frosts.

Shortly before eleven we opened fire, ranging on Beerst, and, using this index, carried out a ten minutes' bombardment of two battery positions—No. 42, a pair of 8.3-inch howitzers, and No. 27, one of small calibre. The atmosphere was ideal for observation purposes, our bursting shells being very spectacular. The common shell produced a huge brilliant hanging flame which was easily spotted, but the T.N.T. a quick yellow flash which was almost too quick to draw a bead on. Towards the close of our firing a few small shells from some field gun burst around our position, but well clear, and at midnight we went home.

Twenty-four hours later, (Mar. 25th), we went out again, waiting with the guns as far forward as K. 23:4, which was only 1,000 yards in rear of our trenches. At 1 a.m. we ranged upon Vladsloo and Beerst, and then burst into rapid firing upon the former village and No. 42 target. A shower of bullets from the enemy's infantry came over, but being spent, flattened out on the armour. The firing over, the train retired to K. 24:8, and we had to keep quiet till 3 a.m., when, ranging on Keyem, we followed up with a rapid burst on that village and target No. 27.

All these villages were entirely used as rest camps and reserve billets for the Germans, who must have been getting fed up now at having their nights so much disturbed by us. The firing on No. 42 had been particularly good; our first round was spotted 5 yards clear of one emplacement, so probably the unpleasantness of this shoot was the cause of the battery being moved during the following day to another position, as was later observed.

During the day I was introduced to H.R.H., who was much interested in our landship and her mode of working.

Midnight found us ready, the guns being as far forward as possible at K. 23, beyond which the lines were destroyed. At 1.10 a.m. we opened fire on K. 42*a*, getting a hit with the third round; after which we burst into rapid fire for threequarters of an hour, taking in turn No. 27, Hoograad houses and cross-roads, and the route to Roulers. A great commotion was observed in that part of the field, fires breaking out here and there, and lights flitting to and fro showing the panic going on as they tried to get clear. A hostile battery opened fire on the train, but the majority of the shell burst or fell short, though one just missed one gun and fell behind it, and a very few only just short. During this night "Ermyntrude" wandered away on a prowl and only turned up towards dawn. "Jack Johnson" was out in the train with us that evening, and wrote the following yarn, which appeared in a periodical paper under the heading—

Somewhere in France.

It is many months since I first made the acquaintance of Robert E. Lee. Robert E. Lee, I should explain, is a highly respectable, hard-working armoured train of unimpeachable reputation, and so called because the Boches are frequently waiting for him, but (for many reasons) they will most certainly never catch him. And lest the Censor is growing apprehensive, I will hasten to assure him that wild curates will not drag from me the locality where Robert billets and has his being, nor will any information likely to prove of interest to the enemy escape my discreet lips.

There is something about an armoured train that fires the imagination. People like to think that you can sit comfortably in the dining-car eating veal cutlets while bullets and things bounce off the roof and steel window-blinds like hailstones off a tiled outhouse. The idea thrills them to the core. Others, again, are intrigued by the delightful fact that the Government have hired you a special train for your own convenience to do exactly what you like with and no officious guard to hustle you aboard when you would tarry awhile and stretch your legs at a wayside station. Incidentally, it may be noted that heavy pipe-smokers find an armoured train a useful thing to strike matches on. But this by the way.

I well remember the first journey I was permitted to make by the courtesy of Robert's commander. My primary sensation on boarding the train was one of reckless abandon. The whole train was at my disposal. I could sit in (what corresponded to) a first-class carriage with an old third-class return ticket belonging to the Great Eastern

Railway, and there was nobody to make themselves disagreeable about it; I could even place heavy luggage (if I had any) upon the rack for light articles only. The novelty of the thing intoxicated me. I spent my first half-hour in throwing bottles on the line, travelling under the seat, leaning out of the window, leaving and entering the train when in motion, throwing orange-peel at the engine-driver, and pulling the communication cord (£5 or forty days).

The outstanding characteristic of the armoured train is the ability to shake itself about in such a way that it is always in two places at once, and never in the spot where you would have bet a fiver that it would be, and where it might have been if it hadn't hustled out of it five seconds before. In this way, after loosing off your guns at the foe, you have nothing left to do but to stand and shake with laughter while you watch the enemy's shells bursting harmlessly around the spot where you might have been if you hadn't moved off first, and where the foe fondly imagines that you still are. Owing to the darkness he has, of course, only the flash of the guns to give him a clue to his enemy's position.

I should mention in passing that the emotions experienced in the human bosom while the train is performing its celebrated shunting act resemble nothing on this globular planet, and should make a strong appeal to old Indian colonels endowed with a liver of which a Strassburg goose might well be proud; though it is true there come back to mind faded memories of a metropolis of dazzling white in the Shepherd's Bush near where lived a sinister contrivance known as a 'Wiggle Woggle,' which—as the man at the gate earnestly assures bashful youth with a fair escort on their arm—was 'guaranteed to shake the hairpins out of a lady's coiffure within thirty-five seconds. Step up and try your luck.' For this kind of lightning manoeuvre, you need a first-class engine-driver, a man gifted with imagination, a sense of humour, and a quick eye. For this reason, men who in private life embrace the vocation of a juggler or a legerdemain expert are invariably selected for the work in preference to men of more mediocre attainments.

Up to the time of my visit the personnel of Robert E. Lee had barely sustained a single casualty, a remarkable circumstance directly attributable by the men to the presence of 'Ermyntrude,' the train's cat, a sandy-haired feline with a docked tail. 'Ermyntrude' has brought nothing but luck since her advent some seven months back. Before she had been twenty-four hours at the base, out of pure consideration she had passed on to the sentry for the night—a notoriously drowsy

LAVENTIE CHURCH BEFORE THE BATTLE.

LAVENTIE CHURCH AFTER THE BATTLE.

individual—a certain active little stranger which made it quite impossible for the man to drop off to sleep, thus undoubtedly saving him from an ignominious death. 'Ermyntrude' has passed an adventurous life. Of French parentage, she was abandoned upon the entry of the Germans into her native home, and was subsequently found by her present protectors upon the retirement of the enemy from that quarter. Her sympathies are entirely pro-Ally, and if you wish to rouse her from her complacency you have only to exclaim in your throat, '*Himmel! Kreuz! Gott strafe England!*' and she will claw you down the cheek in a moment.

It is the habit of Robert E. Lee to sleep soundly throughout the day and creep out with the falling shadows in the prosecution of his deadly mission. In this way he does not offend the eye of the Huns. On the occasion of my visit, we started out from the base at eleven o'clock. At frequent intervals throughout the earlier part of the night we would drag fretfully to a halt and remain rooted to the spot sometimes for half an hour at a stretch.

And so, the long night would drag slowly to a close, and with the first faint flush of roseate dawn illuminating the heavens the order would be given to 'Up Steam' and 'All aboard for Dixie.'

And just as Robert was about to bound forward in the direction of home and friends somebody discovered that 'Ermyntrude' was missing. To return without 'Ermyntrude' was unthinkable. In a moment big strong men with screwed up lips, headed by the cook, were deploying in every direction, rendering the dawn hideous with what they fondly imagined to be sounds of endearment. The minutes passed, but no sign of the missing feline. Things were getting serious. Every moment it was growing lighter, and it was only a question of minutes before the Germans would discern the lithe, sinuous form of Robert E. Lee in the gathering light. But it was impossible to abandon 'Ermyntrude' to her fate. At this critical juncture the cook, who had returned to his den to begin to get some food ready, suddenly shot his head out of the window and announced in loud and blasphemous terms that that cat was at that moment gorging herself on the men's breakfast. 'Ermyntrude' was safe.

Yours ever,

Jack Johnson.

One of the ultimate results of this successful shoot was that No. 42 had yet again moved to a third emplacement, and No. 27 had also been moved by the following afternoon, information of which points I received from the Headquarters. During the afternoon I went out to the ruins of Pervyse and forward into the Belgian trenches and a couple of machine-gun posts in that sector. The village was quite destroyed, but the trenches were very comfortable. Communication with the advanced posts was very hazardous, for one had to walk along faggot paths and duck-boards built over the flooded country; the waste of water, concealing in its depths the horrors of an avenging death, presents a silent testimony of that act of self-sacrifice which only just stayed the invading hoards.

In the early hours of the morning, (Mar. 27th), we went forward, and by 1.30 were ready at K. 24, just beyond Oostkerke, but not till 3 p.m. did we begin, when, after ranging upon Beerst, we bombarded both batteries for ten minutes; and turned then on to No. 25, a new target at the crossroads west of Beerst. A 5.9-inch battery replied, but all shell fell quite 200 yards short. Many did not burst; all one heard was a squelching thud in the mud, whilst others exploded like squibs. The guns were retired to K. 24.8, and waited till 4 a.m., when we gave Keyem a ten minutes' disturbance.

When we were due to leave, "Ermyntrude" was again missing from the fold, and search high and low brought no favourable results, so as dawn was breaking, we had to leave her behind and get home out of it.

During the afternoon I went out to the Oostkerke O.P.'s, amongst other items looking for the cat in the ruins around, but not a sign of her was to be seen. We were particularly disappointed, for not only had she been a shipmate for so long, but an interesting event was shortly to take place, and I had reckoned upon the Red Cross Funds going yet farther to windward by the proceeds of the sale of such famous animals as kittens born on our train.

We now had thirty-six hours' rest, not going out till 10.30 on the Sunday evening, (Mar. 28th). From K. 27 we opened fire on a new target, Schoorbekke Bridge, which we were to attempt to destroy, but at the second round the communications leading to the O.P.'s were cut by shell-fire.

By midnight we were still out, so began a bombardment of the village of Schoor, (Mar. 29th). However, later on the lines were restored, so we tried again on the bridge, and luckily got a hit in before the lines were again cut, but we continued the firing. This break in the telephone system was still unrepaired when we withdrew at dawn.

The same evening, we were out again by 9 o clock and ranged on a big howitzer position, No. A, from K. 25, at about 11 p.m. Once again, the lines were interrupted and it was midnight before we got them restored again; but this time we got on to the target and bombarded it. The 5.9-inch came over at us again, and though some fell both short and over, none were too near.

At 2 a.m. the guns moved on to K. 23, beyond Oostkerke, and after ranging on Beerst, bombarded the positions of 42*b* and 27*a* and the roads between them. This time the same battery continued to fire at the position we had been in before, but did not hurt the metals.

When we went out in the evening the artillery on both sides was much livelier than usual, and shrapnel was flying around. Shortly before midnight we joined in with the Belgian artillery in a co-operative shelling of the large Howitzer and then went home.

Two days followed without any action, and I lunched with the divisional commander. During luncheon the King of the Belgians visited the Headquarters, a German aeroplane choosing this moment to drop some bombs round the area. An Allied aviator was seen to be in pursuit, so that we were able to watch a fine air fight, which ended in the Hun falling 8,000 feet in flames. Pégoud was the victor.

We were out the same night, and, (April 2nd), shortly after midnight, opened fire upon the cross-roads on the Yser, east of the Vicogne Château. Mists hanging over the river greatly delayed the observers, but between one and two o'clock we were able to get going.

Whilst at Headquarters that afternoon I was told that as things were so much quieter now, it had been decided to keep the train back for a spell. However, I took the opportunity of sending in a report on the excellent conduct of my driver, who had done so well on January 25th, and also my Belgian guard—both of whom were rewarded with the Order of Leopold.

I learnt that I was soon to return to England, and therefore said goodbye to the Headquarters. The general was most kind in his remarks and thanks, as also Commandant Petrie, the Divisional Artillery Officer under whom I had directly worked.

The train was temporarily laid up at Bray-Dunes, and it was here that I said goodbye to my men, and returned in the car to Boulogne. A fortnight later I returned to England on leave, and having received another appointment, my experiences with the armies were brought to a conclusion, having extended over seven of the most interesting months of the campaign.

Appendix 1

Work of the Armoured Train—Enemy Exasperated
(Extract from "*The Times.*")

Flanders, *November 22nd.*—) sent you the other day a brief account of the armoured trains which are operating in Flanders under Naval Command. I spoke of their excellent work in shelling the German batteries within their reach. Their fire has apparently been more effective even than our own gunners supposed. The enemy is exasperated. Five German prisoners who were captured at Furnes a day or two ago declare that the *Kaiser* has offered 20,000 *marks* (£1,000) for the head of the commander of the armoured train.

List of the Personnel of H.M.A.T. "Jellicoe"

Staff:
    Lavers, Chief Petty Officer, Gunner's Mate.
    Roper, Able Seaman, Messenger.
    Clark, Able Seaman, Telephonist.
    Martin, Able Seaman, Telephonist.

4.7-inch Gun "Nelson"
    Dick, Petty Officer, Gunlayer.
    Hood, Leading Seaman.
    Payne, Able Seaman.
    Pakes, Able Seaman.
    Church, Able Seaman.
    Tooke, Able Seaman.

4.7-inch Gun "Drake"
    Blondel, Petty Officer, Gunlayer.
    Lewis, Leading Seaman.
    Read, Able Seaman.
    Sawkins, Able Seaman.

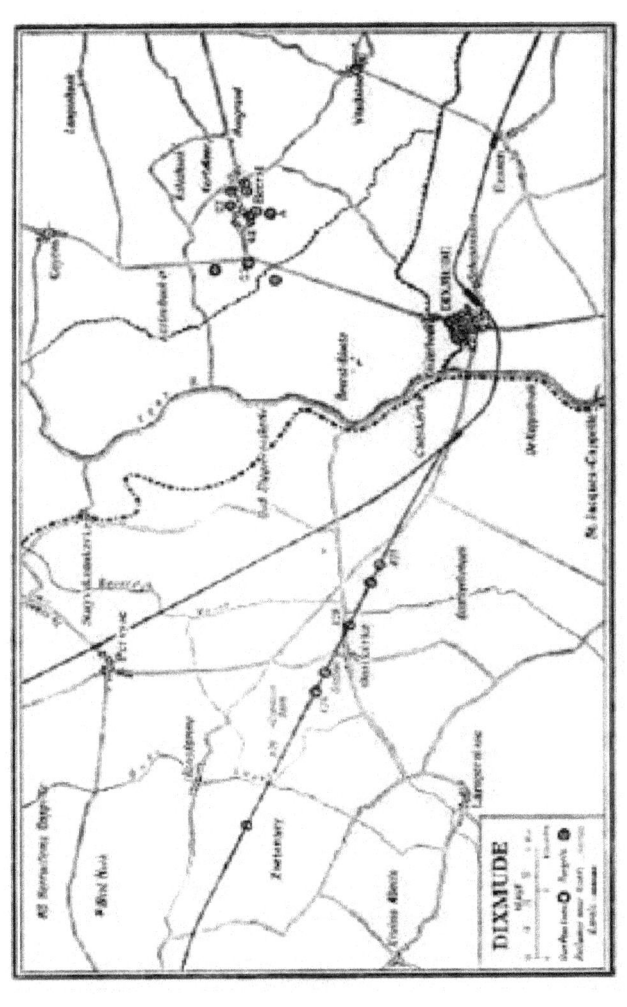

Peet, Able Seaman.
Mockett, Able Seaman.

4.7-inch Gun "Howe"
Collard, Petty Officer, Gunlayer.
Clayton, Leading Seaman.
Gallon, Able Seaman.
Estaugh, Able Seaman.
Blackenridge, Able Seaman.
Fothergill, Able Seaman.

6-inch Gun "Hood"
Etheridge, Petty Officer, Gunlayer.
Pay, Leading Seaman.
Cox, Able Seaman.
Harris, Able Seaman.
Brown, Able Seaman.
Southy, Able Seaman.
Prentice, Able Seaman.

Kaiser's £1,000 Reward—Havoc of the British Armoured Trains

(Extract from the "*Express*.")

Northern France, Sunday, Nov. 22nd.—Almost incredible as it may seem, the Kaiser has offered a reward of £1,000 for the body, dead or alive, of the officer commanding or directing the armoured train which has done so much to hamper the operations of the Germans.

Large as the amount may appear, it is small in comparison with the damage—moral as well as material—done to the German troops by the armoured train, and the *Kaiser* would, doubtless, consider even 20,000 *marks* well spent if it could rid him of such an obstacle to his advance.

Apparently, however, the *Kaiser* has overlooked the possibility that, even if he could catch the commander of the train, plenty of other British officers would be ready to take his place.

The very fact of so large a reward being offered shows to what an extent the good shooting from the train must have affected the German operations; and the apparent impossibility of ever doing any serious harm to so mobile an enemy must be exasperating to the German generals.

So far, the trains themselves and their gunners have escaped almost uninjured, but the damage they have done is known to their cost by the Germans who have come within range of the train's guns.

KAISER'S £1,000 PRIZE—PRICE ON HEAD OF ARMOURED TRAIN
(Extract from the "*Daily Mail*")

North of France, *Sunday*—Five German prisoners captured a few days ago made a statement to the effect that the *Kaiser* had offered a reward of £1,000 to any German soldier who would kill the Commander of the British armoured train that has wrought so much havoc among the ranks of the enemy in Northern France and West Flanders.

I understand that His Imperial Majesty is particularly exasperated at the destruction caused among his crack regiments by this novel and highly original method of warfare. The commander upon whose head such a high price has been fixed may well feel flattered by this genuine if grudging appreciation of his work on the part of the enemy.

AN AUSTRALIAN GUNNER WANTED BY THE *KAISER*
(Extract from the "*Egypt Times.*")

Australia has got some reason to be proud over several important incidents in connection with the war. The sinking of the *Emden* is of course the big feather in her hat. The capture of Germany's Pacific possessions is a matter of no little consequence, but the fact that *Kaiser* William has felt himself called upon to put 1,000 sovereigns on the head of a young Australian officer in charge of an armoured train at Ypres is a good third on our list of peculiar gratifications. Emperor William puts iron on his own heroes in the shape of crosses—he puts gold on our hero in the shape of sovereigns. Lieutenant R—— is wanted by the *Kaiser*. The lieutenant happens to be exceptionally gifted in the handling of guns, and is one of the best, if not the best shot in the British Navy, so he was taken from his ship, where the internment of the German men-of-war had left him small opportunity of showing his ability, and put in charge of an armoured train well within reach of the enemy.

Then the trouble began. It is one of the most persistent worries the enemy had to encounter. Lieutenant R——'s guns were like the Germans' sins—they were always finding them out. The probability is that this one smart Australian is responsible for more damage to the Prussians than any other single man on the job. So irritating has Lieutenant R——'s train been that the *Kaiser* has felt himself called upon to make a big offer for him, dead or alive. Of course, the lieutenant would be cheap at the price mentioned, but he is proud to be made the object of this rare distinction. By the way, Kaiser William has started a new line of warfare—*i.e.*, attack by purchase. How much will it cost him to buy off the British, French, Russians, Belgians, and Serbians at £1,000 per head?

"ERMYNTRUDE," MY CAT.

Appendix 2

Armoured Train Victory—Overwhelming Force Wiped Out
(*A Press Cutting.*)

North-Eastern France, *Saturday*.—News has reached here of the forging of a further link in the chain of successes with which the Allies are slowly but surely ringing the enemy. This week a very considerable force of Germans were completely routed by an armoured train. A skirmish was in progress between a British regiment and about half a division of Germans, a skirmish which was rapidly developing into a struggle of some consequence. The enemy's line had been driven forward, and though neither side was aware of the other's presence, the issue of the fight at this point and at that time was of the first importance.

Greatly, absurdly outnumbered, outnumbered in the proportions which always bring out the finest qualities of our troops, the battle went bravely on for an hour or so. Though the enemy were able, through their numerical superiority, to make three parts of a ring round the handful of British, the single regiment held on doggedly and with that grim determination with which the Germans are now so painfully familiar. By all the laws of warfare our soldiers should have regarded the position as hopeless and have retired before an overwhelming force. Technically considered, the situation probably demanded a retreat. Luckily, technical considerations are generally left out of the reckoning when it comes to the real thing. They held on and did an immense amount of damage to the serried ranks which were steadily hemming them in.

Then came the end—the end of the enemy. Sudden as a thunderclap, deadly as lightning, an armoured train shot up the railway-line which our men were holding. In the pied garb of blue and brown and

OOSTKERKE CHURCH.

yellow, the many-hued coat which makes our land cruisers practically invisible, it was in the middle of the fight before the enemy had an inkling of his danger.

And then came vengeance. Right and left the wicked machine-guns spat out death and destruction, sowing an ever-widening field of swift annihilation. Broadside after broadside was poured into the enemy's inner flanks, wreaking havoc among the closely packed lines. The train moved on to the ceaseless rattle of the machine-guns, mowing down the Germans at every yard, moved on and through. When it came to a standstill at last the thing was done. Most of the ring which had tried to engulf a single regiment was lying in motionless heaps on either side, the rest were flying for their lives. The chameleon-like armoured train had in a score of minutes wiped out some 10,000 Germans and played a big part in wreaking vengeance on land for what the German submarines have done at sea.

Appendix 3

Iron Cavalry—Armoured Trainman's Diary— Bluejackets' Bouts with Bewildered Enemy

(*Extract from the "Daily Chronicle".*)

Northern France, *November 12th.*—A diary showing the peregrinations of a party of bluejackets since the fall of Antwerp has just fallen into my hands.

"It is written a bit rough-like, sir," said the tar apologetically to me, "but it is the truthful log of an armoured train—a train that has scared the German. They call us the 'moving base,' and we don't half laugh at them shelling the spot where we was five minutes ago and where we ought to be always, as they think. We calls ourselves the 'ragtime navy boys.' We are touring artists, and we have put it across those Hewlans and Barbarians something shocking, I can tell you."

The diary gives the movements of one of the armoured trains, and gives a glimpse of the excellent work done by it.

Chatham to Antwerp.

October 1st.—Left R.N. Barracks, Chatham—14 gunlayers, 42 trained men, 14 seamen gunners. Left South Dock for H.M.S. *Engadine*; found her coaling; got aboard safe *en route* for Ostend. During the time, steaming with lights out, we had the misfortune to run mud; but two destroyers skulking about towed us off. But was delayed three hours. But at last arrived about 12 noon Friday.

October 2nd.—The *Engadine's* ship's company gave us a good send-off, and we gave cheer for cheer. We found a train waiting for us, which conveyed us to Antwerp. We passed through Ghent, Bruges (Brugge), St. Nicholas, and Berekem, and arrived Antwerp 7.30 p.m. Belgian officers met us, and we crossed the river in a tug. We passed through the city to our quarters, which was a girl's high school that was converted into barracks. Received orders to be ready by 3 a.m., and went to the station to armoured train, which had on 4.7 guns and one aerial gun. We were told off for guns' crews. We made ourselves acquainted with our surroundings, and was then ready for any emergency. So, being tired, we turned in sail-loft attached to station.

October 3rd (Saturday).—Had breakfast and had a run up and see the position, and finished for the day.

October 4th (Sunday).—Left Antwerp in armoured train at 4 a.m. for Waerlos, where we was shelling all day. We brought down a war balloon at 8,600 yards. . . . We then returned to Antwerp, after being in action nine hours.

October 5th (Monday).—Shelling at Verdron all day. French joined us with centimetre guns. Belgian captain asked for volunteers to rescue three refugees. It was carried out by some of us safe, but little girl shot through thigh.

AT THE BATTLE OF MELLE.

October 6th (Tuesday)—Lay at Antwerp all day resting. Left at 10 p.m. for Vieux-Dieu. The Belgians changing positions, we had orders to leave the guns, and walked to Hoboken, about fifteen miles. We crossed the river and threw our leather gear into it. We slept in brewery for one hour. The colonel gave us a glass of Hollands, and then recrossed ferry for Hoboken Station. We then went right through to St. Nicholas. During the night the 4:7 guns rejoined us. We had expected the Germans had captured them, but they were not touched.

October 7th (Wednesday)—All armoured trains, French included, left for different routes: French guns and our 6-inch guns together, and then arrived Ostend 4.15 p.m.

October 8th.—Had breakfast Hotel Excelsior, and had to wait Ostend waiting orders.

October 9th (Friday).—Stil waiting orders. . . . Highlanders fired volley at German aeroplane, and brought it down.

October 10th (Saturday).—Started to dismount guns for shipment, but gave orders to reassemble gear. Left Ostend for Thourout, arriving 6 a.m. Sunday.

October 11th (Sunday)—Officer christened our guns Drake, Nelson, Jellicoe. Left Thourout for Ghent, arriving 4.30 Left for battle of Melle, the . . . . . in the trenches. We fired 30 rounds of shrapnel and 15 rounds of lyddite, covering the . . . . retreat. We retired to Hansbeke for the night. Lieutenant was highly pleased with the night's work.

October 12th (Monday).—Cleaning out guns and getting for shelling. One 4.7 advanced under our fire and fired two rounds of lyddite. Stayed at Hansbeke til 7.30 p.m. and then returned to Athe. Belgians blew up Ghent Bridge.

"AND KILLED 'EM ALL."

October 13th.—Waiting orders. Lieutenant went rounds; eight hands told off to transport English stores left at Ghent by ... on to our armoured train. Left for Brugge. Civic Guard finished. Belgian Army *en route* for France. Left Brugge 3.15 for Roulers, arrived at 5 p.m. ... Left Roulers for Dixmude, arrived 4 a.m.

October 14th (Wednesday).—Met other part of armoured train, which brought us ammunition from Dunkirk. Our 6-inch guns are at Dunkirk, under Lieutenant ———— Left Dixmude at 5.30 a.m. arrived Lichtervelde 8 a.m. ... Left Lichtervelde, arrived Zonnebeke 12 noon. ... 3 p.m. ... fired on German aeroplane, brought it down, killing two officers.

October 15th.—Waiting orders at Ypres. Stayed all day a mile south of Frezemburgh, covering our artillery till they covered up their guns and got in position. Expecting to have a battle in the morning.

October 16th (Thursday).—Went to Houthem, at 12 noon. Dead horses on line and road, and lot of dead Germans. Captured one *Uhlan* and two infantrymen. ... Went into action; shelled Germans one mile north of Comines.

October 17th.—At Houthem again. Villagers digging holes in gardens burying household things.

October 18th.—Shelled Germans out of farmhouse. They tried to blow up lines, but couldn't.

October 19th (Monday).—At Houthem again. Bombarded church held by Germans and killed 'em all.

October 20th.—Bombarding Germans at Zonnebeke. They had it hot and holy. ... Called Battle of Lille.

October 21st.—Germans retreated five miles from Zonnebeke. We shelled them all the way. It was murdering them, said an officer. Left for Poperinghe. Our brigade hard pressed. Fired 30 rounds of lyddite and cleared Germans off. Our division now advancing back.

October 22nd (Thursday).—Left Ypres for Battle of Lille. Shelling all day. . . . Cavalry. Left for Zillebeke at 5 p.m.; fired 27 shrapnel and 21 lyddite T.N.T. at Germans for a nightcap.

October 23rd (Friday).—Shelled Germans out of Houthem. Fired 4 shrapnel and 28 lyddite T.N.T. Army officer brought fresh orders. A German battery is advanced, so we are off to put it out of action. Did it first round.

October 24th.—General clean-up in train.

October 25th.—Germans retreating from Houthem and Zonnebeke, and Belgian refugees going back home.

October 26th.—Five miles south of Zonnebeke blew up German big gun. Lieutenant said it was "Jack Johnson." Captured 50 prisoners and seven big guns. Prisoners sent to Havre; ages 16 to 19.

October 27th At Bethune for La Bassée. Fired some rounds and drove off German attack.

October 28th (Wednesday).—La Bassée; put another German gun out. French battery on our left put another out. At night went to Ypres; in action 7 p.m. for seven hours. Put 18 guns, three batteries, out of action.

October 29th—Bombarding German batteries all day at La Bassée.

October 30th (Friday).—Shelled German infantry position. Put 'em on the run at La Bassée.

October 31st (Saturday).—At La Bassée; put more German guns out of action. Hundreds of 'em dead all around us! God! it was a sight!

After this the tar had a well-earned rest; but he was overjoyed when I last saw him, because he had just received orders to go to the front again.

"We are goin' in the mornin', sir," he exclaimed, "and by this time tomorrow night we will be chewin 'ell into 'em!"

At Antwerp and the Dardanelles

Contents

Author's Preface,	135
Betteshanger	137
From Dover to Dunkerque	142
Antwerp	148
Vieux-Dieu	152
In the Trenches at Antwerp	156
The Retreat from Antwerp	160
The Retreat from Antwerp—(Continued)	164
Bruges, Ostend, and the Return Home	168
Off to the Dardanelles	173
The Voyage to Lemnos, via Malta	178
Preparing for the Great Landing	184
On the Eve of the Great Landing	190
The Great Landing of British Troops at Cape Helles, April 25 (Sunda), 1915	196
The Story of the Great Landing—(Continued)	202
On The Turkish Shore	213
The Battle of the 6th of May	221
Life in Gallipoli During May, 1915	226
A Chaplain's Work in Gallipoli	231

Events Previous to the Battle of June 4	237
The Battle of the Fourth of June	241
After the Battle	248
The Island of Imbros	254
Farewell to Gallipoli	259
Homeward Bound	266
Conclusion	271

To
Commodore Oliver Backhouse, R.N., C.B.,
And
Old Shipmates of the Upper and Lower
Decks in the Second Royal Naval Brigade,
Whose Courage, Good Humour and Devotion
To Duty in Dark Days Will Always Be
An Inspiration, These Pages Are Dedicated.

Author's Preface

The only excuse I have to offer for adding one more volume to the already vast library of books on the war is that I wish, in a very humble way, to chronicle the immortal deeds of the 2nd Royal Naval Brigade. There are no other books on this subject to my knowledge save the *"Letters and Recollections of Charles Lister,"* so ably edited by his father, Lord Ribblesdale, (also edited and published by Leonaur), and the *"Memoir of Arthur Walderne St. Clair Tisdall, V.C."* To both of these books I owe a deep debt of gratitude.

In these pages my wish has been to chronicle the deeds of the brigade as a whole, and to shew the relations between it and the 29th Division.

May I repeat that the book does not in any sense aspire to be a literary work, and I ask all who read it to forgive its many imperfections,

Henry C. Foster.

The Vicarage, Stocksbridge,
Near Sheffield.

CHAPTER 1

Betteshanger

The First Lord of the Admiralty (the Right Honourable Winston S. Churchill) found that, in the middle of the year 1914, there was a very considerable number of men, belonging to the Royal Naval Reserve and Royal Fleet Reserve, who were not required for immediate service in the Grand Fleet. There was, moreover, another force to be taken into account, and that was the Royal Naval Volunteer Reserve, founded in 1903, and which took the place of the old "Naval Volunteers." The R.N.V.R., as it is popularly known, had thus been working unostentatiously, yet zealously, for eleven years, with a view to assisting afloat, in the defence of our Empire, should the necessity at any time arise.

Great progress had been made at its chief centres on the Thames, the Mersey, the Clyde, and the Tyne, and the same might be said of the R.N.V.R. Divisions in Sussex, Bristol and Wales.

Matters came to a climax when, at the instigation of the First Lord, a conference was called at the Admiralty, at which it was announced that a decision had been arrived at to form the whole of the above units into Two Naval Brigades, to be trained for "land service," and a Third Brigade was to be formed of four Marine Battalions.

The outcome of this was the formation of a large Naval Camp at Deal in August, 1914. The First Naval Brigade Camp was at Walmer, on a cliff overlooking the sea, and that of the Second Naval Brigade was at Betteshanger Park, generously lent for the purpose by Lord Northbourne, At the first, however, both brigades were stationed at Walmer, until it was found that there was not sufficient accommodation for so large a body of men. I propose to deal exclusively with the camp at Betteshanger, because the whole of my time was spent with the Second Brigade.

When I joined up on September 16th Betteshanger was looking

at its best, and no brigade ever had more beautiful surroundings than we had in this spacious park, with its luxuriant foliage. We were a very happy family during our sojourn here, short as it was destined to be, and the smooth working of the camp machinery was, for the most part, due to the capable and energetic staff at the head of affairs. Commodore Oliver Backhouse, R.N., was an ideal brigadier, and exceedingly popular with its officers and men alike; a strict disciplinarian, with unerring judgment and tact, his long service afloat had given him that wonderful knowledge of men and things which we expect to find in the senior officers of His Majesty's Navy. Major Maxwell (Brigade Major) and Captain Saunders (Brigade Captain) were two most capable and energetic officers, and did their difficult, and often disheartening, work with a zeal which was the admiration of all ranks.

The Royal Naval Division, in these early days, had as its officers many men bearing famous names, and in the ranks, one found the real British Bluejacket, the R.F.R. men, stokers, as well as the men belonging to the R.N.V.R.; so that it could hardly be said to be composed of utterly untrained men. They were only untrained as a "land force," and unlearned in regard to military tactics. This must be borne in mind in view of what is to come after.

The name of a famous admiral was given to each battalion; thus, the First Brigade consisted of the Drake, Collingwood, Hawke and Benbow Battalions; and the Second Brigade of the Hood, Howe, Nelson and Anson Battalions. Colonel Quilter, of the Grenadier Guards, was in command of the Hood Battalion, Viscount Curzon in command of the Howe, the Marquis of Graham in command of the Nelson, and Colonel Cornwallis-West, of the Scots Guards, in command of the Anson Battalion.

Betteshanger and the surrounding country was admirably adapted for training purposes, and during the latter days of August, and throughout the month of September, numerous sham fights and night-attacks were arranged. The men acquitted themselves exceedingly well both in the field and at the rifle ranges, which were now in full working order.

I well remember an amusing incident which took place during one of these sham night attacks. The men had been served out with blank ammunition for the first time, and a company of Anson men were placed to guard the main road. Two machine-guns were placed, to support them, on the left flank, and, after a long silence, at about two o'clock in the morning, a vigorous attack was made by the "enemy" on this very position, in order to gain possession of the road.

The machine-gunners, seeing that they could not escape capture, hastily took their guns to pieces, and dashed down a hedge-side into the next field, where I was standing discussing the situation with two marine sergeants. The petty officer in charge of the two guns came solemnly up and said to me: "The enemy are in possession of the road, sir; and we have had to 'run for it.' You, sir, are the only officer we can find; and what are our orders?" I had to tell him gently that a chaplain was a non-executive officer, so could not take upon himself the responsibility of giving an order to two machine-gun crews in the middle of a night-attack.

These night operations had their humorous side, but there can be no doubt whatever that they did prepare both officers and men for the real thing afterwards.

Time passed quickly in camp, and the social side was by no means neglected. Two enormous Y.M.C.A. marquees proved to be a godsend to the men, for here they could read, write letters, or hold an impromptu concert if they felt so inclined. Here, as elsewhere, it is impossible to say too much of the magnificent work done by that great society, now so well-known at home and abroad by the four familiar letters Y.M.C.A.

The Rector of Betteshanger, the late Canon Bliss, and his two nieces did all that lay in their power to help both officers and men during their sojourn in their midst, The rectory bathroom was at the disposal of all officers who were tempted to indulge in the luxury of a hot bath, and in their own grounds the Misses Lindsay worked most zealously night and day at a cosy canteen for the men, under the auspices of the Missions to Seamen.

Lord Northbourne and his friends in the vicinity of the camp always took a kindly interest in the men's welfare, and he was frequently a spectator at the numerous boxing and football contests which were held in the camp. I remember very well a speech that he made at the conclusion of a vigorous boxing match between two rival battalions. He concluded by saying that the men had proved themselves excellent fighters with the gloves, and he had no doubt that when bye-and-bye they were called to take part in "a sterner fight" they would acquit themselves equally as well—a prophecy which, I venture to say, has since been fulfilled.

The religious life of the officers and men was well looked after by the Chaplain of the Fleet, who appointed a chaplain to each brigade, and who himself visited the camps, and saw exactly what was required for the religious needs to be met adequately. Holy Communion was celebrated every Sunday morning in the Parish Church at Betteshanger by the chaplain, and many men availed themselves of the opportunity by coming at 6.30 am, to this picturesque and beautiful little church, so kindly placed at our service by the rector. Parade service was a wonderful sight in these glorious grounds; the place selected was a gradually-sloping piece of ground close to the vicarage, and here, Sunday by Sunday, officers and men made their corporate act of prayer and praise. Lord Northbourne and his friends were present, as a rule, and some of the villagers would group themselves together just outside the railings close by.

One of the bands accompanied the hymns, and to hear the men singing a well-known hymn such as "*Praise, my soul, the King of Heaven*" was indeed an inspiration.

The needs of the Presbyterians were looked after by their veteran chaplain, the Rev. Robert Primrose, a real, sincere "*padré,*" whose friendship, guidance, and. help will never be forgotten by the writer, Other religious bodies were provided for, and some helpful services were held in the Y.M.C.A. tent on Sunday afternoons and evenings.

Another feature of our camp-life, which it is a pleasure to record, is the fact that, taking into consideration the large number of men, their conduct was excellent; there was a certain amount of drunkenness, but practically none of the more serious offences that one might expect where a large body of men is concerned.

Our life in camp was full of surprises and amusing incidents, which the following anecdote will show. I occupied a tent to myself, as brigade chaplain, and one evening I was writing a letter, when the colonel pulled back the flap of the tent, popped his head in and said: "*Padré,* an officer is coming in a few minutes, and he's going to share your tent; his name is Asquith; he's a son of the Prime Minister!" Needless to say, I tidied things up as quickly as I could, and was just finishing my labours when the officer in question arrived. We got on very well together, in spite of the fact that my brother officer said at the end of the second night, "Well, *padré,* I've met a good many "snorers,' but never one that could beat you!" One bright morning I remember finding a motley collection of boots, slippers, books and tins which had been used as missiles by the unfortunate officer aforesaid, who had been trying in vain to get to sleep owing to what he termed my "melodious slumbers!"

It was about this time that Rupert Brooke, whose poems have excited general admiration throughout the world, came to the Anson Battalion as sub-lieutenant. A keen, hard-working officer, he soon endeared himself to the men under his command. His friend, Denis Browne, the well-known writer to *"The Times"* on musical matters, joined up at the same time, and took the same intense interest in his work during this preliminary period of training.

It was my great delight to accompany the Anson Battalion on route marches, and very often do I remember marching along the country lanes with Rupert Brooke as he led his platoon, singing as they went such popular ditties as *"Hello! Who's your lady friend?" "Tipperary"* and *"Sing me a song of Bonnie Scotland."* He seemed to enjoy every minute of it, and greatly admired the rugged nature of the hills surrounding Betteshanger.

There were signs, towards the end of September, 1914, that the staff expected that it would not be very long before we had our first taste of active service. Mysterious orders were issued that all officers must practise the somewhat difficult art of getting all their belongings packed within a given time; sometimes this would mean one hour, sometimes two hours, but suffice it to say that some amusing "packing-up scenes" were witnessed amongst the junior officers, who struggled with valises and camp kit to such an extent that it afforded an excellent morning's entertainment for the senior officers, whose memories carried them back to the time when they were themselves preparing for the South African campaign.

We were all lying in our beds, enjoying the last few hours of slumber before *"Reveille"* on the morning of Sunday, October 4th, when, to our astonishment, we were suddenly awakened at about five o'clock by a bugle call. Had the bugler mistaken the time? We wondered! Woe betide him if it were so! No! There it went again! There was no mistake about it this time; and presently the voice of the brigade major could be heard distinctly shouting, "Officers, get up immediately! We are leaving for France today."

CHAPTER 2

From Dover to Dunkerque

The news that we were to leave immediately for France spread very quickly round the camp, and among the men there was a scene of boundless enthusiasm; loud cheers were raised as they hastily dressed and got their "kit" together. There was no time to lose. Breakfast was at seven a.m., and at eight we were told the transport would be ready to convey our baggage to Dover,

It says a very great deal for the readiness and working capacities of both officers and men when I mention the fact that all baggage and kits were on the road to Dover very shortly after the time arranged.

The Second Brigade started on the march to the pier at about nine a.m., amid scenes of great enthusiasm, two brass bands and a drum and fife band accompanying it. The road from Betteshanger to Dover is one of exceptional interest and beauty, although the hills, which are by no means short, made marching a fairly heavy task. The men had the ordinary seaman's kit, and not the "web equipment," which they took with them to the Dardanelles. A brass band, however, makes marching into a pleasure, and on this occasion, I remember how the men appreciated the strains of well-known music-hall songs, nor did they fail to put plenty of vim into the choruses.

The men select some curious words for their own special "marching songs," and these are, as a rule, set to familiar melodies. It would have astonished, not to say shocked, the Salvation Army, had they heard the following words sung to a hymn tune when passing a public-house:—

There's a man selling beer over there,
There's a man selling beer over there,
Over there, over there, over there, over there,
There's a man selling beer over there.

Another favourite ditty with men on the march is a song with a somewhat unsavoury refrain:—

Wash me in the water
Where you wash your dirty daughter,
And I shall be whiter than the whitewash on the wall,
Whiter than the whitewash on the wall.

This song is sung by all regiments, I believe, and it would be interesting to find out who originally invented it. A song, with more point in it, was a great favourite, "*Going to mow the meadow.*" It commenced:—

One man and his dog went to mow the meadow,

... and the men gradually increased the number of "mowers" until the country lane re-echoed with a chorus which sounded like the following:—

Eleven men went to mow, went to mow the meadow;
Eleven men, ten men, nine men, eight men, seven men, six men, five men, four men, three men, two men, one man and his dog
Went to mow the meadow.

When the number grew to thirty, the reader can imagine the effects of this song upon an officer with a highly sensitive and musical ear! The Scotsmen were, on the whole, the best men for singing on the march, and we could hardly expect them to sing about any topic other than the praises of their native land, and there was one chorus of which they never seemed to tire:—

Hogmanay! Hogmanay!
That's old Scotland's greatest day!
Don't blame us if we all feel happy,
Come along and have a wee, wee drappie,
For it's Hogmanay! Hogmanay!
Let's be blyth and gay,
For we can't foresee
Where we all shall be
On the next Hogmanay.

Singing such ditties as these, we marched to Dover, and as we drew near, the men smartened up. We were accorded a magnificent reception in the streets by crowds of people, who cheered lustily and waved flags and handkerchiefs as we made our way to the pier. We arrived shortly before noon, and the men were given some refreshment. It would be some time, we were told, before our transports would be ready to take us aboard, and so the men had to amuse themselves as best they could.

At about five o'clock our men commenced the somewhat dreary task of getting the baggage on board. We took with us, besides "field kit," our base kit and first-line-of-transport kit. At about 9.30 we were ready to sail, so well had the men worked.

At the very last moment we discovered that no "grub" had been provided for the officers on board, and as they had only been able to secure a hasty breakfast before leaving the camp, and had not had anything but a "snack" at the Lord Warden Hotel since then, we felt that some provision ought to be made. A junior officer and I ran off as quickly as we could to the hotel to see what we could procure in the way of edibles. We knew that there was no time to be lost, as our Transport was ready to sail at any moment, so we did our work as expeditiously as possible. We made our way back to the ship laden with a joint of roast beef, a tongue, bread, butter, three syphons of soda, a bottle of yellow liquid, the praises of which were sung by the Scotsmen, and bottles of lemonade and cyder. We were saved from starvation!

In a short time, we were under weigh and slowly sailing out of Dover Harbour. It was a strange, not to say uncanny, sensation to be leaving one's native land on active service for the first time, The night was dark, but we had not steamed very far before several searchlights were turned upon us. The brilliant light seemed to illuminate every crevice and corner, and gave me an opportunity of making a minute inspection of the ship.

The men lay all over, trying to get some sleep before daybreak, using their great-coats as a covering, but sleep was difficult, because the hilarious spirits insisted on singing music-hall choruses, and for all the night was one of exceptional interest and excitement. Soon the search-lights went off, and it was dark again.

Our escort, consisting of two destroyers, kept close to us during the whole of the night. I lay down on the upper deck, with a great-coat over me to try and get a little sleep, and for a short time succeeded, but in the early hours of the morning I was awakened by what sounded like the clanking of heavy chains—it turned out to be some of the crew getting the boats ready in case of emergency, and seeing that a supply of life-belts was near at hand. The voyage, however, proved to be uneventful, and at about 4 a.m. on Monday, October 5th, we anchored off Dunkerque.

On active service you have to get accustomed to delay; but nobody except those who have experienced it, what it is like to be tossing about at sea for eight hours in a crowded transport, unable to disembark. The feelings of the men on such occasions might be described as those of anticipation, whilst the officers' looks of utter boredom are an index to their true state of mind.

For eight weary hours we lay off Dunkerque, awaiting orders, in a choppy sea. For some of our recruits on board this was the first experience of crossing the Channel, and the effects of the "roll" on them can be easily imagined, and while they "fed the fishes," the majority of the men played "Nap" or watched the French destroyers, as busy as bees, darting hither and thither in their ceaseless vigil.

At last, one of these destroyers came alongside, and a somewhat portly French Naval officer shouted through a megaphone that we were "to proceed into harbour" and moor at the quay. It was just about noon when we entered.

The soldiers stationed at this famous French port, together with the populace, gave us a most cordial welcome, rushing excitedly on to the quays and cheering.

Those were stirring days—the "*Tipperary Days*" we might call them—and the war was but two months old. The cheers from troops and civilians on shore, re-echoed by a thousand throats on our transport, stirred the emotions, and will live in the memories of those who heard them to the end of life. But the most moving incident of all was when our brass band came up on deck and played the "*Marseillaise*"; nothing delighted the French more than this little compliment, and they cheered again and again as the ship moored at the quay.

Our actual destination, so far, had been unknown, but on getting to the quay we were told that we were to entrain for Antwerp immediately to take part in the defence of the city.

The work of unloading the kit, provisions and ammunition from the transport seemed to take a considerable time, and, although in those early days of unpreparedness it was impossible to put the blame upon anyone in particular, it is greatly to be regretted that a great deal of precious time was lost at Dunkerque in disembarking and entraining. We spent the whole of the Monday on the quay, all ranks working like Trojans.

The first train did not leave the quay until 10.45 p.m., with the Nelson and Howe battalions. We had but little food, and that consisted of bully beef and biscuits, with nothing to drink.

Each man received 120 rounds of ammunition before getting into the train, and our *commandant*, Lieut.-Colonel George Cornwallis West, addressed us. He said that there was a possibility of the trains being attacked in the night, that it was uncertain as to whether or not the railway line had been cut by the Germans. "Remember you are British," he said in conclusion, "and I am sure you will give a good account of yourselves." A tremendous cheer greeted this remark, and it echoed and re-echoed through the lofty sheds on the quay.

For hours we had waited for our train, and at last, about 11.30 p.m., it arrived. Our baggage had been sent on in advance by a goods train. The men weary with their labours and the long wait, tumbled into the troop-train with evident joy, in spite of the fact that the journey might be fraught with danger and uncertainty. The anxiety and suspense on this journey were intense—the night was pitch dark, and the train seemed to crawl. Everyone knew that France and Belgium in those early days were full of spies, and we felt that at any moment a bomb might be thrown at the train.

The doctor, Surgeon J. R. Kay-Mouat, R.N., and I had a carriage to ourselves, and he got some bandages ready in case of need. He had come with all the medical stores he could find, but these were by no means complete, as our departure had been hasty and unexpected. Our feet were blistered and sore, because we had been running about more or less for forty-eight hours, without being able to change our socks, and we only had one pair with us, our clean socks having gone on before. So, we took off our boots for a short time, and lay down on the seats to try and get some sleep, which we badly needed. At about 2 a.m. on Tuesday, October 6th, we crossed the Belgian frontier. At all the smaller stations on the line, in spite of the early hour, crowds had turned out to greet us, and there were frequent cheers, with cries of "*Vivent les Anglais*," "England for ever" and "Rule Britannia."

At the more important stations, such as Dixmude and Thielt, large numbers of people brought the men presents of fruit and cakes. Ghent was reached at 5.45 am. It was raining hard, but this did not damp the enthusiasm of the Belgian people. They made coffee for the men, and showered gifts on us of cigars, cigarettes and rolls. Sometimes the train would stop out in the country, where there was no station near, but from a small cottage an old peasant woman would come tripping out with a monstrous jug of hot coffee, with which she regaled the men. All along the line we received the same royal reception; hats and handkerchiefs were waved everywhere, and out of every bedroom window overlooking the railway some face was peeping.

We were feeling very hungry, as our last solid meal had been supper on board the transport on the Sunday evening, and so it was suggested that someone. should get out at the next town or village we stopped at and secure some rolls or chocolate. Lieutenant Asquith suddenly saw his opportunity, and, making a dash for a small confectioner's shop in a town that we had stopped at, returned laden with both commodities. He was instantly acclaimed as a great hero, and I never remember enjoying food as much as I enjoyed those rolls and that chocolate.

We all felt deeply thankful that so far, the journey had been made without danger.

Chapter 3

Antwerp

There were signs about 9 a.m. that we were drawing near to a large and important town. The reader will bear in mind that the date was October 6th, Tuesday, 1914. So far, our journey had been passed amidst peaceful surroundings, and had it not been for the soldiery and the crowds on the station platforms all along the railway, we might haye been travelling to Antwerp under normal conditions.

But now, as we looked out of the carriage windows, we saw quite plainly the first signs that a war was really being waged. Shrapnel could be seen bursting quite distinctly in the vicinity of Antwerp, and two captive balloons were up in the sky directing the German fire. Hundreds, of Belgians were busily engaged, on both sides of the line, in constructing entrenchments, and many fields had been flooded to put a check on the German advance.

Meanwhile, it is necessary to see what had happened before our arrival, in order to understand the exact state of affairs.

After a series of desperate struggles with the gallant little Belgian Army, the Germans, on September 28th, commenced a terrific bombardment of the outer line of forts surrounding Antwerp, with 12-inch, 16-inch, and 17-inch howitzers. This savage attack, which came with startling suddenness, had an electrical effect on the Belgian gunners, with several of whom I had the pleasure of conversing. These forts, stated not long ago to be impregnable, were armed with 4-inch and 6-inch Krupp guns of doubtful quality. It will readily be seen how ridiculously unequal was the contest.

The powerful German projectiles smashed these concrete fortresses into atoms, and the Belgians were forced to fall back across the River Nethe. Meanwhile, the entrenchments, which linked up these forts of the outer ring, were occupied by the Germans, but only after a desperate resistance on the part of King Albert's plucky troops,

The Belgians lost not a moment in their new position; sluices were opened, which caused heavy floods, and these undoubtedly proved to be an awkward obstacle to the main German advance. Beyond the Nethe the Belgians had a fairly strong position, and although the outer ring of forts had fallen, and they formed the main defence of the city, the inner ring of forts was still intact.

The Marine Brigade of the Royal Naval Division, composed almost entirely of regular troops, reached Antwerp on the night of October 3rd (Saturday). Never have war-worn warriors been more delighted to be relieved than were the Belgians when the marines took over the trenches facing Lierre, and enabled them to get a much-needed and well-deserved rest. Armoured trains, with gun-crews formed of British bluejackets, got into action on October 4th, and did excellent work. We of the 1st and 2nd Naval Brigades were due to enter Antwerp on the evening of October 5th, but, as I have shown, an unfortunate delay at Dunkerque meant that we arrived some twelve hours late.

The British 7th Division of Regulars and the 3rd Cavalry Division did not begin to disembark at Ostend until October 6th, and although most important, never-to-be-forgotten work was done by them afterwards, yet they had little or nothing to do with the actual defence of Antwerp.

At this very time Sir John French was quietly and secretly withdrawing his troops from the Aisne and leading them round behind the line, then held by the French, towards St. Omer, so as to concentrate an attack upon Lille, Thus it will be easily seen that if large German forces could be kept at bay in front of Antwerp, even for a few days, it would be of the greatest service for two reasons:—

(1) It would help Sir John French in his designs on Lille.

(2) It would give time to the main Belgian Army to retire behind Ghent and join forces with the main British and French Armies.

We cannot wonder, therefore, that our government felt that it was its bounden duty to answer the cry for help, which came so persistently and piteously from Belgium, and at all costs to endeavour to prevent the fall of Antwerp, if only for some days. October 6th, the very day on which we arrived in Antwerp, was a momentous day in the history of "the second strongest fortress in Europe," and what happened then really brought about the fall of the city earlier than the Belgians expected. The arrival of the Naval Division put new life into the tired Belgians, but things took a turn on October 6th which left no doubt whatever as to what the ultimate issue would be.

During the day, after a fluctuating night engagement, the exhausted Belgians were driven back by the enemy in a furious assault from the direction of Lierre, backed by powerful artillery. The Marine Brigade of the Naval Division, which had continued to hold its position most gallantly and against overwhelming odds, was unable to do anything else but follow suit.

It will be seen, therefore, that the 1st and 2nd Naval Brigades really arrived too late to attempt to save Antwerp, because the Germans had now established themselves on ground from which they were able to bombard the city with powerful howitzers with the greatest ease, to meet which we had only the few naval guns at our disposal and the small guns on the forts in the inner ring. It was not unlike a band of hooligans armed with revolvers being opposed by a crowd of children armed with pea-shooters.

The position was serious and most critical; the most that could be expected now was to hold the Germans at bay for as long a time as possible. While they were busily engaged in getting their heavy guns into position for the final assault, the main Belgian Army withdrew to the left bank of the Scheldt. Such was the position when we arrived in Antwerp shortly before 10 a.m. on Tuesday, October 6th. We were met at a suburban station by the civic guard and several important officials—and then came our march through the streets. It is impossible to say whether or not the people looked upon us as saviours of their city, but we shall never forget the reception they gave us. Huge crowds watched us pass, and at every halt gifts in great profusion were given to the men.

Charming Belgian maidens pinned little flags, made of silk, on to our tunics, and attempted to embrace two of our officers, greatly to their embarrassment and confusion. Large jugs of light beer were brought out of houses, from which the men filled anything that would hold liquid. The scene was one of indescribable enthusiasm. But all the time the distant boom of guns sounded on our ears, and seemed to strike a warning note, telling us that, though it was fine then, the storm might burst at any moment. We marched about four miles to a place on the outskirts of the city, where we had a most welcome rest, The officers were billeted out for meals to various houses.

I found myself in a house where the only occupants appeared to be three old ladies, who could not speak a word of English. I made them understand, however, that I was ravenously hungry, and desired food and drink immediately. The table was quickly set, and I was provided with a delicious omelette and some fried ham, with a bottle of light beer to wash it down.

Whilst I was enjoying this repast the priest from the neighbouring church came and visited me; he spoke a little English, and after his arrival I got on very much better. He was a typical Belgian *padré*, a most genial old gentleman, and started the conversation by firing off a volley of questions. Where had I come from? Was I Roman Catholic or Anglican? Where was I going? How many chaplains were there in my division? How many men were there with us? Needless to say, I was guarded in my answers, for we were taught to be cautious! With difficulty I made him understand that I wanted to buy some new socks, and on giving him some money he ran out to a shop close by and purchased two pairs of black socks, which proved a most valuable asset.

Feeling in need of a sleep, I went upstairs to a bedroom, and was soon in peaceful slumber, in spite of the boom of guns, which every hour seemed to be drawing nearer.

After a glorious sleep of about two hours, I was suddenly awakened by a loud knocking at the door and a voice shouting something in Flemish. The voice sounded rather agitated, and I expected at least that the enemy had broken through, and that a German officer was about to walk upstairs and demand my instant surrender! It transpired, however, that the brigade had fallen in, and was about to move off. I have often felt grateful since to that old woman for her timely warning, because, had I slept on, the difficulties of finding my brigade might have been enormous, and only those who have experienced it know what a half-besieged city is like in war-time.

Rested and refreshed, we marched away, amidst renewed cheering, to further excitement.

CHAPTER 4

Vieux-Dieu

It has already been pointed out that our men were not unlike other British military and naval men in that they sang heartily when on the march, and their love of song did not desert them in a foreign clime. They marched, swinging along in a manner worthy of a brigade of Regulars, singing of "*Tipperary*" and "*Bonnie Scotland*," a fine, straight, manly body of men, with set, determined faces.

A march of some five miles brought us to the village of Vieux-Dieu, a quaint spot, on the confines of the city. Here we found hundreds of Belgian troops resting, after being in the trenches, and on the road through the village there was a scene of bustle and excitement, A continual stream of traffic to and from the Front made it intensely interesting to those of us who had just come from peaceful England. Here we halted, and were told that we were to rest a short time before going up to the firing line, The boom of the enemy's artillery sounded much nearer now, and Vieux-Dieu was surrounded by our own guns, and so the noise can be imagined.

Our officers and men intermingled freely here with the Belgians, a few of whom could speak English. They were very interested in our rifles, ammunition and kit generally.

I saw a horse brought in from near the firing-line; it was literally riddled with bullets. Wounded were continually arriving in Red Cross motor vans, and cartloads of Belgian dead were brought in.

We found an empty house close by, and some of us went and sat down to rest on the window-sill. We had not been sitting there long when someone from the inside gave a loud tap on the window, giving us a great fright. Our nerves had been shaken a little on the journey, and we wondered what the tapping might mean. Suddenly up went the window, and there we saw three or four exhausted Belgian soldiers resting on some straw in this supposed untenanted house. One of them held up a big jug, and, pointing to it, said, "*Café! Café!*" In less time than it takes to tell we held out cups, which were speedily filled with the most delicious cold coffee I have ever tasted; it was almost iced, and freshened us up wonderfully.

A chaplain on active service has to do some strange things at times, and he does a great deal more than merely take services and bury the dead. I found one of the men suffering from violent toothache, and looking very ill, so I gave him a strong dose of brandy and water, which enabled him to "carry on."

Just before arriving at Antwerp, a senior officer came along the corridor to my compartment and said: "I want you to witness my will, *padré*, and then post it for me to my solicitors in London." We found a box just about to be cleared, and luckily the important document reached its destination safely.

After marching into the centre of Vieux-Dieu, we were told that we were to be quartered for the night in an old *château*, standing in its own grounds and surrounded by trees.

There was abundant evidence that its occupants had been wealthy people, and that they had fled away in haste. There was a quantity of valuable furniture, and we found everything just as its owner had left it.

We ascertained, on inquiry, that one of the servants belonging to the house was still at her home in the village, and, after a good deal of persuasion, we succeeded in getting her to come and cook some supper for us, as we were very hungry, and as to the next meal no one knew when or where we should get it.

She cooked us an excellent meal, which consisted of veal, bread and black coffee. Those of us who are still alive will not readily forget the scene in that old room of the *château*. There we sat round the table, a light being supplied by a candle stuck securely in the neck of an empty bottle, eating like the gourmands who haunt Simpson's in the Strand and other famous eating-houses. Plates and forks were scarce, but pocket-knives came in exceedingly handy. The windows had been plastered up with brown paper so as not to let out a single streak of light.

There sat such well-known personages as Lieut.-Colonel George Cornwallis West, Arthur Asquith, Denis Browne and Rupert Brooke, eating pieces of veal with their fingers and drinking coffee out of broken tumblers: and milk-jugs.

It was a most enjoyable meal, in spite of all these petty inconveniences, but all the time there was the feeling of uncertainty, for the distant boom of hostile guns reminded us of the fact that this villa was within range, and that any moment a shell might demolish it and lay it even with the ground.

After bidding farewell to our cook, who was going to flee away from her home with her parents, we retired to rest about nine o'clock.

The men had to bivouac out in the garden as best. they could, and I must say my wish was to do as they did, but the night was bitterly cold, and as I was very uncertain as to what the consequences of spending the night in the open might be, I decided to stay indoors.

At the bottom of the garden, which surrounded this *château*, was one of the Antwerp forts, and so sleep was practically impossible, as the guns were cracking out every few minutes, shaking the house to its very foundations.

Not far off, the six-inch naval guns were also speaking with no uncertain voice, whilst every now and then the whistle of the enemy's shells was distinctly heard, followed by the sound of distant explosions.

I lay down on two armchairs, put together to form a bed, in the hall of the *château*, and tried to sleep. It was an uncanny feeling lying in the darkness, with a. great-coat for bedclothes, and being shaken every few minutes by a loud report from the fort. I was bold enough to take off my tunic and boots in the hope that this would be conducive to sleep, put it was a forlorn hope, for under those conditions sleep was out of the question,

At 2 a.m. next day (Wednesday, October 7th) we were awakened by a Belgian officer, who went up to the commanding officer's room, and talked with him for a few minutes, The result was that we got ready in haste, and were told to fall in at once, and leave for the front trenches.

It was, I believe, only by a merciful Providence that we took this step, because very shortly after, this *château* was smashed by German shells.

It will be remembered by the reader of this account that the main body of the Belgian Army had withdrawn the previous day to the left bank of the River Scheldt. The troops, therefore, which were left to hold the enemy at bay consisted now of the fortress troops, the Second Belgian Division, all very exhausted by incessant fighting, and the three brigades of the Royal Naval Division.

We had a most romantic march in the darkness to Fort No. 7, one of the forts on the inner ring. It was a calm, still night, and the men marched along quietly, having been warned of the serious nature of the task in front of them. We were startled every now and then by a Belgian sentry's challenge, but otherwise the only disturbing element was the distant boom of cannon. We challenged every man we met, and the commanding officer satisfied himself as to his credentials before he was allowed to proceed.

At dawn we reached our destination, and for the first time saw the specially constructed trenches that were to be our home for only two days. These open trenches had been cleverly constructed by the Belgians, but they would have proved utterly useless had they been subjected to a violent bombardment from the enemy's guns. They linked up the forts of the inner ring, which were fifty years old, and mounted with inferior Krupp guns. The real defence of Antwerp was said to lie in the outer forts, designed by General Brialmont in 1879, and finished in 1913. After these had fallen, the only defence remaining was the River Nethe and the infantry behind it.

CHAPTER 5

In the Trenches at Antwerp

Our men were soon in their places, and hoped before long to have their first experience of fighting with the bayonet, a hope which was not realised at Antwerp. It is a strange feeling, going into a front-line trench: for the first time in your life, and knowing that the first men the enemy will have to encounter will be yourselves. At dawn on this particular day (October 7th) all eyes were turned towards the River Nethe, but neither the river nor the enemy could be seen from our trench, occasional shrapnel shell burst overhead and reminded us of his presence,

After a short rest, the men were busily employed in improving the trenches with sand-bags and barbed wire. Meanwhile, the forts were firing away with every available gun.

Our trenches were at the end of a large turnip field, and about 150 yards behind them there was a modern villa, surrounded by a pretty garden. It was empty, and devoid of furniture save one old chair, a stool and a kitchen table. The occupants had evidently made a hasty exit, and had taken all their valuables with them. In this house the doctor and I were installed, and were told to transform it into a hospital.

We procured some straw, and put it all over the floor of one of the rooms, and then took stock of the medical requisites and stores, such as they were. We found that we had not nearly enough stretchers for the Anson Battalion, and so the doctor proceeded to manufacture some. His quick eye had noticed that the blinds of the house would lend themselves for this purpose, and so, without another word, he tore them down. They were then nailed to long pieces of wood, and in the exigency of the moment made stretchers which were quite good enough for all ordinary purposes.

A meal was just about to be prepared in the kitchen of our new home, when the Fleet Surgeon came to tell us to clear out of it immediately, because as a hospital it was quite unsafe, and might be shelled at any moment.

The surgeon frowned severely, but said nothing, and ordered his men in the medical unit to gather up all the straw and his belongings and to follow him.

We did not remove far away, but took up our quarters in an empty farmhouse, very ancient and dilapidated, standing in among thick trees, about fifty yards further back. The trees afforded this house some cover, whereas the former house would have provided a perfect target for gunners,

We made a hospital ward in one of the long, rambling rooms of this farmhouse, with fine old oak beams supporting its ceiling, which was in a very bad state, and looked as if it would descend upon us end cover us the moment a shell burst anywhere in the rear vicinity. We had two cases in already, one man with badly swollen feet, and another with a bayonet wound, received by accident.

On making a tour of inspection in the upper storey, I found a bit of an old mirror in one of the bedrooms, evidently frequented by rats, so I seized the opportunity of having a shave with a safety razor, the first since leaving England. Had the razor been an ordinary one, I am afraid there would have been another hospital case to record, as my hand was a trifle unsteady, and the loud reports of bursting shells, ever increasing as time went on, did not make for improvement!

The colonel, the doctor and myself had the meal, which had been so suddenly postponed in our former abode, in the kitchen of this farmhouse about three o'clock; it consisted of a stew made from tinned beef, biscuits, and coffee.

Dusk was setting in when a Belgian officer and our staff-surgeon came and pronounced this house also unsafe from the enemy's shell-fire. The important question was: Where were we to take our wounded? No place seemed to be safe in face of the heavy siege guns, which were now belching forth their deadly projectiles over our heads into the city.

It was decided that the best and safest course would be to remove to a bomb-proof shelter in the trenches; this would enable the wounded to get immediate attention, and provide the best protection possible from shell-fire.

The surgeon was quiet; twice he had had to move his hospital, and, although he did not say very much, I can guess what he was thinking of.

We took up our abode finally in a bomb-proof shelter or dug-out, some twelve feet long by six feet wide. It was built, of course, underground, the roof being formed. of steel plates an inch thick, laid on strong iron girders, and covered with earth to the depth of six feet. Inside, the ground had been shelved, and so quite a large number of wounded could be accommodated. There was an opening at both ends, through which a stretcher could be carried. In this place the doctor and I lay down to sleep, with the medical unit, consisting for the most part of bandsmen; and it sounded almost ludicrous to hear the doctor saying: "Drum-major, be sure to have all your stretchers ready."

It was a pitch-dark night, and very cold. The hitter wind blew right through our dug-out, and if we felt the cold, the men just outside must have felt it far more severely. They had not had their clothes off for four days, they were loaded up with ammunition, and their shoulders ached. I could not sleep, the shells ever whistling overhead, the guns on the forts close by firing away, and the feeling of insecurity and uncertainty made it a night to be remembered.

Suddenly the alarm was given, and our men opened fire. I went out into the open and watched. There were our men blazing away and peering into the inky blackness of the night. Shells began to burst all round us, I only just had time to run under cover when a shrapnel shell burst over us.

An ex-coastguard stood near me, and I asked him what was happening. He puffed some fumes of raw onions in my face and said: "Enemy seen approaching our barbed wire, sir."

No one can say definitely what happened, except that some Deutschers had evidently crossed the river, and were detected whilst making a reconnaissance. This was by no means unlikely, because one of our scouts in the afternoon got as far as the bank of the River Nethe, and lay on his stomach in among some bushes, and watched the German engineers constructing a bridge. It was a bold, daring act, and they were getting so near, when he left his hiding place, that he could hear them chattering to each other.

There were several other alarms along the line held by the Naval Division during the night, but the fighting never actually got to close quarters,

During the first surprise attack, seven Belgian gunners in the fort close to us were killed. The doctor went out, and said on his return that a big shell had burst on the fort, and the gunners had been blown to bits. We were fortunate in having very few casualties, and they were mainly slight shrapnel wounds, The searchlights on the forts were continually playing on the surrounding country, in the hope of showing up the foe in the act of making a general advance, but all in vain, He had evidently been somewhat astonished at his reception, and had slunk off.

The men had kept remarkably cool during a trying experience, and were only disappointed that no opportunity for using their bayonets had come their way. The brunt of the Antwerp fighting came undoubtedly on the marines, and it is impossible to speak too highly of the courage and bravery they displayed while holding their part of the line against the repeated onslaughts of the enemy. They were called upon to stand and face heavier shelling than either of the two Naval Brigades, and their grit and devotion to duty set us all a noble example.

When all was quiet at last, we lay down and slept.

CHAPTER 6

The Retreat from Antwerp

The night had been restless and devoid of sleep for all of us, and when Thursday, October 8th, dawned, both officers and men looked exhausted and fagged out, and yet there were still to be found some cheery spirits who kept us going.

Stores were getting somewhat low, and for breakfast we had each a tin mug of coffee, one biscuit, a piece of bread and a small bit of cheese. One of the men stated afterwards that Lieut. Asquith had this meal sitting in amongst his platoon and drinking his coffee out of an old tin lid.

It was on this day that we first noticed any marked increase in the enemy's shell-fire. His heavy batteries were very busy, Antwerp being the chief target, and by midday the town was literally deluged by a torrents of big shells, which burst with ear-splitting reports, terrifying both man and beast, The Rev. Robert Primrose (Presbyterian Chaplain) told me that he had taken a walk during the early hours of the day in the centre of the city, and had seen three or four houses blown down, with terrific force, as the wind blows down a house made with playing cards. The loss of life was considerable. Men, women, children, horses, dogs and cats were lying dead in the main streets.

It was evident that the German artillery had advanced considerably nearer during the night. At the invitation of a chief petty officer, I went up into an observation post and saw quite distinctly, with the aid of field glasses, German gunners getting a heavy gun into position. The scream of the shells overhead never ceased, and we got so accustomed to it as not to notice it.

It was almost pathetic to see the gallant little Belgian forts replying to these mammoth guns. When the history of this tragic time comes to be written, it will be told how that they continued to fire to the last shot.

Shortly after midday an extraordinary sight was observed, Dense clouds of black smoke began to ascend into the sky, darkening the sun and the whole horizon for miles, until it began to be more like evening than noonday. Inquiry elicited the fact that these huge columns of smoke came from the petroleum tanks at Hoboken, which had been set ablaze by the Belgians themselves in order the prevent the Germans getting hold of one of the largest stores of petroleum in the world. Hoboken lies on the confines of Antwerp, on the eastern bank of the Scheldt, and its tanks blazed away for two whole days.

Meanwhile the sound of the German guns seemed to have come closer, and shells began to burst unpleasantly near. Every now and then they would give us a taste of shrapnel. We had dinner at about 4.30 p.m. and most of us felt that we needed it, not having tasted food since breakfast in the early morning. It proved to be a most luxurious repast, and consisted of steak which a Belgian soldier had procured for us.

After this the doctor and I started on a tour round the Naval Division trenches, but the German fire was increasing in violence, and Belgian soldiers shouted to us to keep under cover, and, besides, a German aeroplane was overhead, dropping bombs. A violent attack was made on the hostile machine by the Belgian gunners, and French airmen, with great daring and skill, set off in pursuit. The German was flying so high that he was scarcely visible, but we could see the Belgian shrapnel bursting all round him. At last, he made off, and unfortunately succeeded in getting away unharmed.

Some parts of the line held by the Naval Division suffered heavier bombardment than others, but so far, luckily for us, most of the shells were, as the men put it, "Non-stop for Antwerp."

It is, perhaps, somewhat difficult for those who were not there to imagine the utter hopelessness and despair of the men who had been sent with the intention of defending Antwerp. Unknown to us, the fate of Antwerp was decided before we arrived.

The men now fighting, (at time of writing), so bravely on the Western Front know that all their efforts in the field are backed up by powerful artillery; but with us it was different. We had absolutely nothing with which we could reply to the German siege batteries. All that we could do seemed to be to wait calmly for the end, which every hour was bringing nearer,

About five o'clock darkness was setting in. The thunder of the guns increased in fury. Antwerp was seen to be on fire in some quarters. Our baggage party arrived and said that the railway station at Wilryck, in which our baggage had been stored, was in flames. This tragic piece of news made many an officer draw a long face as he proceeded to enumerate the various articles of value, he had tucked away in his valise, which he was never to see again.

The doctor and I had been sitting in our dug-out for a short time, wondering what would happen next, when the drum-major put his head in at one of the openings and exclaimed in a low tone: "We have to clear out immediately, sir, as we are almost cut off on all sides; and they intend using their heavy guns against us tonight." How the latter news reached us I do not know; but it proved to be true,

Our men loathed the idea of a retreat, and some had positively to be dragged from the trenches; but the majority realised that every minute the position was becoming more critical, and that immediate retreat was our only hope of escaping capture.

When the definite order from Headquarters arrived that we were to leave quietly, we hastily gathered together our belongings and passed out of the trenches in good order.

Almost all the Belgians had gone, except those in the forts, and in our covering fort only one Belgian gunner remained. One of our Naval gun-crews gallantly offered to remain and work the guns in order to cover our retreat, which they did up to the very last minute.

When we left the entrenchments, it was dark, and shortly after we had gone, they were pulverised by the German artillery.

Marching across country to a road, which lay to the south of the city, we joined the Howe and Hood Battalions. After a halt of about half-an-hour the Drake Battalion of the First Naval Brigade joined us, and, led by General Paris and Commodore Backhouse, we started our long march of 25 miles to St. Gilles.

In. order to cross the Scheldt we were forced to pass by the blazing petroleum tanks at Hoboken. The road was narrow, but it was the only road left. The fumes were overpowering, and the intense heat proved too much for some of the men. The flames at times blew right across the road, and large German shells were falling in amongst the tanks at the rate of four a minute. Sometimes a shell would burst with a terrific report in the boiling oil, and flames shot up to the height of two hundred feet.

A German captive balloon could be seen up in the sky dropping out coloured fires as signals to their gunners.

As we approached the blazing tanks it was like entering the infernal regions. The burning oil had flooded a field on one side of the road, and dead horses and cattle were frizzling in it.

"Now, boys," shouted an officer, "keep your heads and run through it."

And we did—but I do not know how we did it. I remember at one point I shielded my face with my arms and ran as fast as I could; there was a tremendous explosion, flames leapt up to a terrific height, and when I stopped running, I felt scorched all over for a few minutes. Once we had got past the oil tanks we were in comparative safety for a hundred yards, because the road was sheltered, but then, for some thousand yards, it was exposed again to the enemy's fire.

We were ordered to run at the double over this bit of road, and most of us were fortunate enough to reach the pontoon bridge over the river. There was some doubt as to whether this bridge was still intact, but our doubts were dispelled on arrival, for we found that it was still in position and in good order.

A spy was caught by one of our battalions in the act of trying to blow up this bridge, but his designs were frustrated just in time, and a bayonet ended his career.

Sentries were posted at intervals, while we went across, and shouted "Change your step" every few yards. At last, we were safely on the other side, and breathed again. The relief felt by all ranks on getting across the river can hardly be imagined, and, although even there we were by no means out of danger, yet we knew that a most important step had been taken.

CHAPTER 7

The Retreat from Antwerp—(Continued)

The order to retire had reached all the four battalions of the Second Naval Brigade and the Marine Brigade in the trenches, the Drake Battalion of the 1st Brigade being also informed, with the result that practically all the men in these battalions got safely over the river by the pontoon bridge.

Three other battalions of the 1st Brigade, namely, the Hawke, Collingwood, and Benbow, did not receive the order to retire for some unaccountable reason, and found, some hours later, that they had been left behind. Meanwhile the Belgians realised that the pontoon bridge could not be left for ever, and they determined to wait up to a fixed moment, and if the rest of the Naval Division had not arrived, the bridge was to be destroyed. That moment came, the three lost battalions had not put in an appearance, and the bridge of boats was blown up.

Meanwhile we were marching as quickly as we could through the night to St. Gilles, With us, out of Antwerp, passed an unending procession of refugees; it was the most heart-rending sight that I have ever seen. Nuns and priests, old men and young, old women and girls, mothers with babies in their arms, little children hand in hand, took part in this procession.

The nuns and priests did much to comfort them on their sad journey, but the awful look of utter despair on the faces of old and young as they trudged along, carrying as many of their belongings as they could, will never be forgotten by those who observed it. It resembled a procession of the dead.

Antwerp was burning fiercely now, and the ground shook with the loud reports of bursting shells.

Several times I saw young and old take a last look back at the burning city, thinking, as the tears streamed down their faces, of the homes they were never to see again.

The feelings of anger and disgust against those who were responsible for all this, and the longing to take vengeance on them for all the horrors of this cold, dark night were in the hearts of all our officers and men as they marched on, Belgium will never forget it! Let Great Britain see to it that, when the struggle is over, she also remembers.

Belgian roads are not the best roads for marching on; the cobblestones are very tiring to the feet, and especially to men who are worn out from lack of sleep. Several men collapsed from sheer fatigue, and what happened to them I do not know. I gave them a drink, and then went on with the rest.

We knew that it was a march against time, and that every minute was of the utmost importance, "Come on, boys; there's not a second to lose," was the constant cry of the officers to their men.

On the right side of the road there was an incessant stream of traffic from the burning city. First would come Belgian artillery, then an old London omnibus packed with British Marines, then a small flat cart carrying a Belgian family, with the children asleep on some straw at the back; then some cattle driven by an old man, and darting hither and thither amongst the vehicles—all making their journey with but one end in view, namely, to get away safely before the coming of the ruthless Huns.

The Belgians, for the most part, were silent, as they made the journey, their mental anguish being too acute for words, but every now and then the silence would be broken by a yell from the top of an old omnibus of: "Are we downhearted?" to which a hasty answer of "No!" was returned by men as they tramped along. The answer, perhaps, was hardly a true one, because, as the night wore on, the men began to feel more and more exhausted, and their feet were very sore and blistered. Some of us began to wonder if we could last up to the finish!

I do not know how long I had been marching, as it had become almost mechanical, and my shoulders ached; but I noticed that we were approaching a small town.

At the entrance to this town there was a convent, and none of us will forget the kindness of the nuns, who, at the risk of their own personal safety, remained until the exhausted troops had passed, filled their water-bottles with fresh water, and gave hot coffee to some of the worst cases.

My own water-supply had long since given out, and my throat was parched and dry. I waited in the queue along with the men, and at last I was rewarded with a bottle full of the most delicious cold water I have ever drunk. What happened to the good nuns I have never been able to find out, but their kind thoughtfulness helped many of us to get through who might otherwise have fainted. I have wondered sometimes if there was anything supernatural about that water—who knows?

We were told on entering this small market town that we might lie down and rest for half-an-hour. The news rejoiced our tired hearts, and in a few minutes, we were all fast asleep, lying on the cobble-stones, in the market-place It was a noisy position to choose for a resting-place, as the constant traffic on the road made a considerable din, but we had no other choice, and were so tired that the moment our heads rested on our haversacks we fell asleep.

In the town there was a beautiful church, and one of our officers went to it in hopes of seeing the priest and getting his permission to bring his men in, go that they could lie down on the pews, and have less chance of being disturbed. He entered quietly, and the scene which greeted his eyes will live long in his memory.

The aisles and pews were packed with refugees, who slept soundly, worn out and footsore with their long walk from Antwerp. They were lying right up to the Sanctuary, every bit of space being utilised, and the only indication that the building was a church was the dim light shining from the lamp which still hung in front of the Tabernacle,

Our rest was only to last for three-quarters of an hour, and, when the time was up, we arose feeling more fatigued than before, if that were possible. On and on the road seemed to stretch, and some of the men found at last that the strain of so long a march was beginning to tell on them, I was feeling so tired that I wondered if my feet would carry me for the seven or eight miles that still remained. The march itself, under ordinary conditions, would have seemed as nothing, but it was marching the distance, without having had regular food and sleep for some days, that proved so exhausting.

Suddenly, a voice shouted out my name from an old London 'bus, and there I saw the Rev. C. W. G. Moore, R.N., Chaplain to the Marine Brigade, with several officers, sitting inside. I instantly jumped in, and was never more thankful for a lift. It was only when actually inside one of the vehicles that you got an adequate impression of the great stream of traffic from the city, which never ceased as long as a bridge remained standing over the Scheldt.

All kinds of conveyances went along side by side, sometimes rather too close together. We got a sudden fright, I remember, when there was a terrific crash of glass over our heads; two windows had been smashed in by a lamp projecting from a 'bus driven alongside of us; but luckily none of us was injured.

On the floor of the 'bus I found that some careless soul had left two boxes of sardines, and so, having a weakness for these at all times, I quietly slipped one into my haversack, the other being collared by a Fleet-Surgeon sitting opposite, This ride came to an abrupt termination. The cobble-stones had proved too much for the 'bus, with its heavy load, and our driver, in apologetic tones, said: "One of the wheels will be off her directly," upon which we resumed our tramp. There were some three miles left now; and I will never forget the last "lap."

An officer in front of me appeared to be very exhausted, his determined face being haggard and white. On overtaking him, I found that it was Lieutenant Asquith; he, also, had had a short lift on the journey, but was almost "done up." With him I walked to the railway station at St. Gilles, arriving about 6 a.m. on Friday, October 9th,

Three trains left this place; the first two got safely through, but the third was fired on. The first left just as we arrived, but we got seats in the second, which steamed out of the station at 6.30 am. The compartment in which I found myself was packed almost as tightly as the box of sardines in my pocket! Together with the officers of my own brigade were several marine officers, and we compared notes, and found that they had had even more trying experiences than we had.

Meanwhile, it is interesting to follow the fortunes, or rather misfortunes, of the Hawke, Collingwood and Benbow Battalions. They found out that they had been left behind, as I have already shown, and arrived at the bank of the River Scheldt to find the bridge blown up. Crossing on barges, they marched to St. Gilles, and got into the third train. On arriving at Lokeren, between Antwerp and Ghent, they found that the Germans held the line ahead of them, and so they were faced with the alternative either to surrender, or to cross the Dutch frontier. They decided to choose the latter, and crossed ever into Holland, "in circumstances," as Mr. Winston Churchill says, "on which only those who knew their difficulties are entitled to form a judgment."

Our journey to Bruges was the most tedious I ever remember; it took twelve hours to accomplish, but most of us slept so soundly that we hardly noticed the time. We arrived just after 6.30 p.m., and looked forward to getting a really solid meal, the first since leaving home.

CHAPTER 8

Bruges, Ostend, and the Return Home

The night of Friday, October 9th, was spent in Bruges. It was the first time I had seen the beautiful, picturesque city, with its Town Hall and famous belfry containing the peal of forty-eight bells. My brigade, drawn up in the market-place, had a long wait before: arrangements were completed for billeting and feeding the men. The Belgian officials were kindness itself, and did all they possibly could for us.

Lieutenant Denis Browne, whose contributions to "*The Times*" and musical papers have made his name famous, was suffering very severely from sore feet; they were badly blistered and swollen, and so I stayed with him in the station while the others marched to the Town Hall. Here the men were entertained to a good dinner by the civic authorities, and quartered for the night. The officers were billeted at various hotels, but Lieutenant Browne and myself were invited by one of the Civic Guard to spend the night at his house. This kind and generous gentleman turned out to be Lieutenant Cecele, and he, together with his friend Mr. Lucien Verstuyft, of the Civic Guard of Brussels, entertained us like princes. The latter wrote to my mother, and gave her an account of our arrival, and his broken English makes the letter all the more charming:—

> Madam,—It may be agreeable for you to know that I met the Rev. H. C. Foster, Chaplain 2nd Royal Naval Brigade, about the 8th or 10th of October last, at Bruges.
> My friend and me met him, with a friend, Mr. William D. Browne, Sub-Lieutenant, Royal Naval Division, from London; they had had to walk very far, and their feet were very sore. We took them in a cab, and came with them at the home of my friend at Bruges. We gave them a good foot-bath, and afterwards we had a good time together in the evening. The mor-

row following they were quite well, and they had to go further. I should be very obliged to you if you would give me Rev. H. C. Foster's address that my letter may arrive to him.

We begged to be allowed to contribute something towards the general expenses of the household, but they would not hear of it, and their great kindness to complete strangers will never be forgotten by me. Lieutenant Browne wrote to our host afterwards, and received the following characteristic reply:—

> I ought to add a few words to say that you have not to thank us, for we have done nothing for you at Bruges, and I think that not any Belgians should have done less than we did for English soldiers who come to save our country; that is an opportunity more to be thankful to you all, Good luck and that God save you!

On Friday evening the Market Place was crowded with soldiers, Belgian and English, and we saw some of the Royal Horse Artillery and Northumberland Yeomanry coming in after an engagement.

We had a dramatic interview, I remember, with a Belgian soldier, who told us, sobbing with emotion, how that the Germans had burnt his home and outraged his mother and sister, "A great day of atonement will come soon," he said, wringing his hands, "when the guilty ones shall suffer."

We got a good meal in the evening at the *Hôtel de Panier d'Or,* in the Market Place, and greatly enjoyed it. Meat seemed to be scarce even then, and I remember that liver and bacon formed the staple dish,

After spending a comfortable night under the hospitable roof of our Belgian friend, we had breakfast, and then marched with the men to the station. The station at Bruges is by no means an attractive place to wait in, but we were obliged to wait all day for a train to take us to Ostend.

We had one diversion, however, during this tedious delay. A German spy, dressed in Belgian uniform, was brought in and placed under arrest in a shed in the station. There were some railings close to this shed, and through them there peered a large crowd of people, hissing and crying out for vengeance on the spy, and their excitement knew no bounds when he was marched off to his doom. It was while we were waiting in this station that a train came in packed with the R.F.A. and their guns. They had come from Ostend, and were on their way westward. The men rushed to the train and conversed with their brothers in khaki, and gave them rousing cheers when they left.

Our train arrived at 6.45 p.m. and after an uneventful journey we reached Ostend at 10 o'clock the same night. On marching down to the quay, we were billeted in a transport, and had supper just before midnight. It consisted of a tin of Maconochie stew cold, and two biscuits, which were the nearest approach to dog-biscuits I have ever seen provided for human consumption. Then, tired out, we lay down on the cabin floors and tried to sleep.

In the morning, I had breakfast with two officers at the *Hôtel Majestic*, and then looked round the town. Ostend must have presented a sad picture to those who knew it in its days of sunshine; now a shadow seemed to be creeping over it, and empty houses and deserted shops seemed to tell us of its coming doom.

While I was making my way back to the transport, I met Mr. Garrett, an Old Goole gentleman, from the parish I had been working in, and we shook hands warmly amidst these strange surroundings.

We sailed for England about four o'clock on the afternoon of Sunday, October 11th, and unfortunately a fog came on, which prevented us making the progress we should otherwise have made.

To pass the time away, a mock court-martial was held in the cabin on an officer, the charge being that he had appeared on deck after we had been advised to keep out of sight. The sentence, as far as I remember, was that the officer aforesaid, who was rather portly in build, be thrown out of the cabin through a porthole.

We lay at anchor, off Dunkirk, in a thick fog, until 11.15 a.m. on Monday, October 12th, when the fog lifted and we were able to resume our voyage.

Dover Pier was reached about 7 p.m., and we were glad to be home again, after a short but strenuous time amidst the perils of war. We had not had our clothes off since leaving England, and had been sleeping on the ground with no covering, or on the floor of a ship's cabin. Officers and men had acquitted themselves exceedingly -well under most trying conditions, and it is impossible to say too much in their praise. Many criticisms have been hurled at those in authority in regard to the defence of Antwerp, and the sending of the Royal Naval Division to assist Belgium in her hour of trial, but surely only those who know all the facts are competent to criticise in a matter of such vital importance as this undoubtedly was.

In sending in his report on these operations to the Army Council, Field Marshal Lord French said:—

I have to state that from a comprehensive review of all the circumstances, the force of Marines and Naval Brigades, which assisted in the defence of Antwerp, was handled by General Paris with great skill and boldness.

Although the results did not include the actual saving of the fortress, the action of the force under General Paris certainly delayed the enemy for a considerable time, and assisted the Belgian Army to be withdrawn in a condition to enable it to reorganise and refit, and regain its value as a fighting force. The destruction of war material and ammunition, which, but for the intervention of this force, would have proved of great value to the enemy, was thus able to be carried out.

The assistance which the Belgian Army has rendered throughout the subsequent course of the operations on the Canal and the Yser River has been a valuable asset to the Allied cause, and such help must be regarded as an outcome of the intervention of General Paris's force. I am further of opinion that the moral effect produced on the minds of the Belgian Army by this necessarily desperate attempt to bring them succour before it was too late has been of great value to their use and efficiency as a fighting force.

Some of us, on arriving in England, were allowed to proceed home to our anxious relatives, who, knowing that Antwerp had fallen, were prepared for the worst. The majority of our officers and men, however, returned to Deal, where they were given a hearty welcome by the townsfolk.

I feel that I cannot conclude this chapter without quoting in full the following message, which was sent to the Royal Naval Division on their return by the First Lord of the Admiralty:—

> The First Lord welcomes the Royal Naval Division home on its return from active service. Officers and men of all ranks and ratings have acquitted themselves admirably, and have thoroughly justified the confidence reposed in them. The loss of a portion of the 1st Brigade through a mistake in no way reflects upon the quality or character of the division.
> The Brigade of Royal Marines, throughout the operations, sustained fully, by their firmness, discipline and courage the traditions of the corps. It is not necessary to say more than this. The Naval Brigades bore themselves admirably under the artillery

fire of the enemy; and it is to be regretted that no opportunities of closer contact with his infantry were afforded them.

The dispatch of the Naval Brigades to Antwerp as interrupted for a time the progress of their instruction and training. They were chosen because the need for them was urgent and bitter; because mobile troops could not be spared for fortress duties; because they were the nearest and could be embarked the quickest; and because their training, although incomplete, was as far advanced as that of a large portion, not only of the forces defending Antwerp, but of the enemy forces attacking.

The Naval Division was sent to Antwerp not as an isolated incident, but as part of a large operation for the relief of the city. Other and more powerful considerations prevented this from being carried through. The defence of the inner lines of Antwerp could have been maintained for some days; and the Naval Division only withdrew when ordered to do so in obedience to the general strategic situation, and not on account of any attack or pressure by the enemy. The prolongation of the defence, due to the arrival of the division, enabled the ships in the harbour to be rendered useless, and many steps of importance to be taken. It is too early now to judge what effect the delaying, even for five or six days, of at least 60,000 Germans before Antwerp may have had upon the fortunes of the general battle to the southward. It was certainly powerful and helpful. Apart from the military experiences, which have been invaluable, the Division have been the witnesses of the ruthlessness of the German foe towards a small and innocent State. These facts should inspire all ranks to fit themselves in the shortest possible time for further service in the field, not merely as fortress, but as mobile units.

The Belgian people will never forget that the men of the Royal Navy and Royal Marines were with them in their darkest hour of misery, as, please God, they may also be with them when Belgium is restored to her own by the Armies of the Allies.

CHAPTER 9

Off to the Dardanelles

The experiences at Antwerp did a great deal towards preparing our officers and men for the hard fighting which was to fail to their lot on the Peninsula of Gallipoli; it gave them a foretaste of modern warfare, so that they knew what to expect when they were sent into the field. Before this could take place, however, it was necessary that their training should be complete and thorough. With this end in view, the brigade was sent to various training centres, some battalions going to Sheerness, some to Chatham, and others to Portsmouth.

I myself was quartered for a short time at the Gunnery School at Whale Island, and was privileged in being shown all over that famous training establishment, where so many of those who work the guns of our great ships were trained.

Towards the end of November, 1914, the brigade moved into a camp of huts in Dorsetshire, a healthy, bracing place on the Downs.

I remember how we arrived at the camp towards the end of a dark November day; it had been raining on the previous day, and the whole camp was a sea of mud. The building of this huge camp had necessitated the timber and materials being conveyed for miles over the Downs by means of heavy waggons drawn by traction engines, and it will easily be seen that this did not tend to lessen the amount of mud, which, in places, was two and three feet deep.

Great amusement was caused on the night of our arrival, when it was announced that the waggon containing the officers' baggage had stuck in the mud a mile and a half from the camp. It had commenced to rain heavily, darkness had set in, and I will never forget how we set off with lanterns and searched the Downs for miles before coming to our lost property. We found the waggon at last, deeply embedded in mud, and had to get some of the men to carry the kit to our huts, where they arrived soon after midnight, absolutely drenched through.

An officer, who was one of the wags of the camp, wrote the following parody on a well-known song to commemorate this incident:—

Where our baggage-van has rested,
Bags you'll find upon the grass;
Bags and "ammicks," swords and cases,
You'll find them where the carts can't pass.

Late at night you'll see those heroes
Wandering forth with lighted lamp;
They went forth for love of country—
But they do not love this 'orrid camp.

In spite of the mud and the inconvenience of being so far from shops, we had a very pleasant time of training here. It was ideal country for sham fights and night operations, and some bloodthirsty battles were fought on the hills around. The huts were by no means uncomfortable, and each officer had his own coke-stove. The men's mess-rooms and sleeping quarters were dry and built well off the ground, and their food was plain, but of good quality.

Each battalion had its own flagstaff, and vied with its neighbours in having the best-kept "lines." The whole routine was arranged on the Naval basis, and the watches were rung on a large ship's bell. Men always spoke of "going ashore" when they were going into the town! The camp in itself was a small town of wooden buildings, with its own Cinema and Institute, and here, again, the Y.M.C.A. did an incalculable amount of good by erecting a huge and most palatial hut, where the men could enjoy their favourite recreations and write their letters.

Major-General Sir A. Paris, K.C.B., Royal Marines, was our G.O.C., and lived at a farmhouse a short distance from the camp. I would like to be allowed here to pay, a humble tribute to our G.O.C. Hard-working, keen, thorough in all he undertook, he was a most popular general with all ranks. The late Mr. Gladstone said:

> It is a difficult task to lead the House of Commons, a more difficult one to manage a Cabinet Council; but to lead an army in the field must be the most difficult of all.

And yet General Paris accomplished this difficult task with great success.

In those dangerous days just previous to the evacuation of Gallipoli, I was told by an officer whose word can be relied upon that when heavy shells were bursting round "General Headquarters" no one was more plucky, or kept calmer, than the G.O.C. himself.

The pleasant time we spent at camp came to an end towards the close of February, 1915.

His Majesty the King, accompanied by the First Lord of the Admiralty (the Right Honourable Winston S. Churchill) reviewed the whole Naval Division on February 25th (Thursday), and expressed himself as being highly pleased with the smart appearance of the men, The "Goodbye" given to us all by our king will never be forgotten. It was a gloriously fine day, and the sun shone brightly on swords and bayonets as the whole division marched past the saluting-base in column of companies, the massed bands playing the naval *"March Past."* Then came the final three cheers for His Majesty, and the National Anthem.

For some time, previous to the review, we had had an inkling that we were soon to go abroad again, and that our destination was "Somewhere in the East." We were served out with pith helmets, and the arrangements for our departure were quickly completed.

Meanwhile some changes had taken place in the personnel of the Battalion Commanders of the Second Naval Brigade, Lieutenant-Colonel Collins was now in command of the Howes, and Colonel Moorhouse, D.S.O., C.M.G., in command of the Ansons. The Nelson Battalion, about this time, became part of the 1st Brigade, its place in the 2nd Brigade being taken by the Collingwood Battalion, commanded by Captain Spearman, R.N. The Collingwoods had come direct from the Naval Depot at the Crystal Palace, and remained behind, when we left England, in order to complete their training.

Our last day in camp was February 27th, and in the afternoon of that day a large number of relatives and friends assembled on the Parade Ground to bid us "God-speed." The bands were playing national airs, the most popular being *"For auld lang syne."* How little did we realise then that many fathers and mothers were saying "Goodbye" to their brave young sons for the last time. And yet we tried to "keep smiling," and to look on the bright side, but it was difficult.

It was my privilege, as chaplain, to meet many of the officers' relatives and friends on this occasion, and among others who wished me goodbye was Lady Bonham-Carter, then Miss Violet Asquith.

We left camp at 7.15 p.m., wearing our new "web equipment" and pith helmets, For the first time I had the experience of carrying a pack, and found it very heavy for the first few miles, but soon became accustomed to it. We marched to a small country station named Shillingstone, where we were to entrain. Here there was a long and tedious wait, but our comfort had not been forgotten. Lady Baker, who lived close to Blandford, and who had on many occasions showed a kindly interest in the men's welfare, had arranged for a number of ladies to run a canteen in the vicinity of the station. Here a plentiful supply of hot coffee proved to be a Godsend to us all.

The only excitement was provided by some new mules, who lived up to their reputation for being the most frisky and unmanageable of all animals. I do not think any of us envied the transport officer or his assistants, who experienced the greatest difficulty in getting their charges safely deposited in the special train.

Our train left at 3.30 a.m. on Sunday, February 28th, and we took off our equipment and boots, and had a good sleep in the carriage. It was about eight o'clock when we awoke in the morning, to find ourselves at Avonmouth Docks, Bristol.

Here we boarded a Union Castle Liner, and sailed at about two o'clock in the afternoon; she was a fairly comfortable ship, and was to be our home for some weeks.

There were two battalions on board, the Hoods and the Ansons, and the 2nd Brigade Staff, Commodore Backhouse, R.N., being in command. Two destroyers acted as escort, and kept close alongside until we reached the mouth of the channel, when they bade us farewell.

Next day, March 1st, we entered the Bay of Biscay, and I will here give a few extracts from my diary:—

March 1st, Monday.—"Ship began to roll a lot, and I felt rather sick. Left breakfast half-eaten! Had hearty lunch, however, and remained in my bunk. Dinner also hearty!"

March 2nd, Tuesday.—"Got up and had a delicious salt bath, then ate splendid breakfast. Read in the morning. After lunch sat with Henry (a lieutenant), Asquith and others on the boat deck. Watched dolphins sporting about in the water. Visited the men's quarters. A beautiful night—calm, and nothing but the rippling of the water to break the stillness. Far out we could see the other transport, which had the rest of the brigade on board signalling to us. We replied. Made a discovery today that we are definitely going to the Dardanelles."

March 3rd, Wednesday.—"Beautifully calm day; out of sight of land, and only saw three ships on the horizon. Sang some folk-songs with Denis Browne, F. S. Kelly and Asquith. Uneventful day."

Thus, the time passed for the first few days, and I am sure no one enjoyed a voyage more than we enjoyed this one. We felt that we were earning that title, bestowed upon us in sarcasm by our critics, "Winston's Wandering Wonders."

CHAPTER 10

The Voyage to Lemnos, *via* Malta

Life on a transport, when the voyage is a long one, is busy as a rule, so that the men have not much time to feel weary of it. Our days passed quickly enough in physical drill, boxing, fencing, signalling and various games. In the evening the band played in the officers' mess, whilst on the lower deck a melodeon provided suitable music for various forms of dancing. When we began our voyage, Commodore Backhouse arranged with me to have "Divisions" every morning at 9.30, that is to say "ship's prayers." "I hope you will read the special prayer for the Navy," he said. "I have been accustomed to hear it every morning for the last twenty-five years, and it will be very nice to hear it once more."

It was a magnificent sight to see the men, with bared heads, joining in the prayers, and from what they themselves said I know they were appreciated. Every morning, I said prayers at three different places, so that, all could hear, on the port and starboard sides of the ship, and aft.

We received all the latest news by wireless, and the notice board was scanned eagerly day by day.

On Friday, March 5th, we entered the Straits of Gibraltar about 4 a.m. We did not go up on deck, but from the port-hole I could see the coast of Southern Spain quite plainly. A line of destroyers was stretched across the Straits, and an examination ship came up and asked us who we were before we were allowed to proceed. The following day was beautifully calm, and the view clear, In the distance we could see the African coast, with Algiers nestling in among the hills, with its dazzling buildings of white stone; and, farther away still, the mountains with their snow-clad peaks.

In the evening, when all was still, there was one officer, who was often to be seen pacing the deck alone. No one ever thought of disturbing him, as we knew by instinct that he wished to be alone. It was

Rupert Brooke. He gloried in those quiet nights in the Mediterranean, and remained drinking in their beauty long after the others had turned in. Some of the unthinking ones, perhaps, scarcely understood this love of solitude, but they who knew the poet best could understand. His mother wrote to me:

> It was so like him, however much he liked his companions, he always wanted some time to commune with his own soul.

He had been terribly distressed at what he had seen during the retreat from Antwerp, and his great heart went out in sympathy to the refugees. His mother wrote:

> Of course he hated the idea of fighting, his love of humanity was so great, and his desire to benefit it so deep, but from the first he went off to help his country.

If was only his devotion to beloved England that brought him where he was, and yet he was destined never again to gaze on her quiet valleys, to roam in her woods and fields, or to pluck her wild flowers, of which he was so sweet a singer.

Rupert Brooke had as his companions-in-arms several men of genius; I doubt whether any ship had a more interesting number of officers aboard than the Anson and Hood Battalions together provided on this transport. Sub-Lieutenant Patrick Shaw Stewart, Fellow of All Souls', Oxford; Lieutenant Arthur Asquith, son of the then Prime Minister; Sub-Lieutenant F, S. Kelly, the famous pianist, musician and rowing Blue; and sub-Lieutenant Denis Browne, the musician, were among the poet's most intimate friends; and these, together with Sub-Lieutenant Arthur St. Clair Tisdall, the famous Cambridge: classical scholar; Sub-Lieutenant Waller, son of Mr. Lewis Waller; Sub-Lieutenant Campbell, the playwright, son of Mrs. Patrick Campbell; Lieutenant E. W. Nelson, biologist, of the Scott Antarctic Expedition; and Lieutenant B. C. Freyburg, made up an officers' mess which, for brilliance of conversation and poignancy of wit has scarcely, if ever, been equalled.

It is a great joy and privilege to me to be able to record of these old shipmates of mine that two received the V.C., Lieutenant Freyburg and Sub-Lieutenant Tisdall; five received the D.S.O., one the M.C. and bar, four the D.S.C, and eleven were mentioned in despatches, one officer three times. And it must be remembered that this list does not include the Howe Battalion, which received one D.S.C., while six officers were mentioned for distinguished and gallant services.

The men were just as truly my shipmates as the officers, and I regret that it would take up too much space to record the honours gained by them; but I know of many who gained the M.M., C.G.M, or D.C.M.; and many officers and men lie buried far away in Turkish soil who deserved honours but never received them, and yet we feel that in their eyes it was an honour great enough for them to have died fighting for Britain.

I will not forget my first Sunday in the ship; there was a heavy roll on, and although I felt a trifle unsteady on my legs, I managed to take four services. The commodore attended the first service at 9.30, together with Colonel Quilter and Lieutenant-Colonel Maxwell. The Hood Band accompanied the hymns, but, as Sub-Lieutenant Tisdall remarked, the effect was spoiled by the rolling of the ship, which caused my entire congregation to be jerked, at intervals, from side to side. Tisdall wrote:

> Today being Sunday, we had church on deck in four services for the different parts of the troops; at one service I read the lesson. There was a strong wind and a roll, and occasionally the congregation had a slip to one side.

On Sunday evening we had an excellent lecture on "Bush Fighting" by Colonel Moorhouse, D.S.O., which proved to be most interesting.

We passed the island of Gozo about one o'clock on Monday afternoon, March 8th, obtaining fine view of Rabato, its principal town, and at length arrived at Malta. We saw the harbour at its best, in glorious sunshine, and anchored off the Fish Quay about 3.30, An hour after our arrival a French battlecruiser was sighted coming into the harbour, and a splendid spectacle she made as she steamed in. We stood at the salute, while our band came up on deck and played "*The Marseillaise*"; then her officers and men returned the compliment. Permission to go ashore was granted to officers, but not to the men, greatly to their disgust. Three junior officers went ashore with me in a "*dhycar*" about five o'clock.

We realised that this would be one of the last opportunities for getting supplies in large quantities that would come our way, and so we made use of it. Malta is always picturesque and interesting with its multitude of priests and Jesuits, and its beautiful churches, from the towers of which the bells seem ever to be pealing. We were struck with the weird head-dress of the Maltese women, a relic of the days when they suffered horrible indignities at the hands of the Turks. Five Bedouin Arabs, as black as ebony, with white turbans, looked exceedingly quaint. The shops are well above the average, and it rejoiced our hearts to find a branch of the "Junior Army and Navy Stores."

That evening we dined at the Union Club, which had most hospitably thrown its doors open to all officers of the Naval Division. After a visit to a *café*, we rowed back to the ship and slept on board.

We sailed the following day about 11.30 a.m., and for the next thirty-six hours passed through glorious scenery. Beautiful views of Southern Greece, and those islands with which the Augean Sea is studded made the voyage a very pleasant one. The sun was hot, and the sea that mysterious bluish-green colour which is peculiar to the Mediterranean.

We could see Mount Athos, with its cap of snow, looming in the distance, like an old gentleman in his night-cap. It is hardly to be wondered at that Rupert Brooke said in a letter home:

> If anyone can be said to be lucky in this war, we are.

We reached Lemnos, our destination, about six o'clock in the evening on March 11th (Thursday), and were struck with the spaciousness of this beautiful natural harbour. The entrance is by a narrow strait of water, not more than half-a-mile across, and, at the first approach, you might be led to believe that this was the full extent of the harbour, but soon you would discover your mistake. In Mudros Bay, so called from a village of that name with a modern church, the whole Mediterranean Fleet could lie in comfort, protected alike from storms and submarines. This harbour proved to be a godsend to the Allies during the Dardanelles operations, and within it were accommodated the whole fleet of transports and warships which took part.

As we steamed in, we passed H.M.S. *Queen Elizabeth*, *Agamemnon*, *Lord Nelson*, and other cruisers and destroyers, the crews of which gave us a cordial welcome. We could see numerous small villages in the distance, and an Australian camp of tents.

In the morning, we noticed that the Russian battleship *Askold* had arrived, and was moored alongside the British war-ships. She was instantly nicknamed *The Packet of Woodbines*, because of her five funnels. Mudros Bay was a wonderful sight even thus early, packed with transports and war vessels.

Visits to the island were our great delight in these days, and were full of interest to officers and men alike: Lemnos is a Greek island, and the inhabitants are happy peasants living in small, clean houses, and working here and there on little plots of land, although most of the ground is uncultivated. They speak modern Greek, which is easy to pronounce, and very like ancient Greek. Like most of us, they are fond of talking, and willing to learn anything new. The men look very picturesque in their blue trousers and goat-skin coats.

One day I walked about five miles inland, and visited one of the villages called Leivadi. A heavy shower of rain came on, so I found shelter in the porch of the church, just as the children were coming out of school. They came round me, like flies round a jam-pot, a happy throng of boys and girls, jabbering away, and I was the object of much attention. Presently I got them to understand that I wanted to see inside their Church; a boy then removed a loose stone in the wall, produced a key, which fitted the door, and so we entered,

They all used the Holy Water at the door, even the very little children, some of whom had to stand on tiptoe to insert their fingers in the vase, and then made the sign of the Cross with great solemnity.

It was a disappointment to me not to be able to understand their language; but they showed me all over their church, pointing out its beauties and main features; when I came to the Greek Testament, I read a few verses from it, and they seemed greatly astonished. Suddenly the village policeman and the schoolmaster arrived, and to my great joy I found the former could speak a little English,

We were strictly forbidden, by doctor's orders, to drink any water on the island, because there were some Turks living on it, and spies were a constant source of danger. My own water-supply was at an end, it was very hot, and I was thirsty. So, I took my two friends to the village inn, where I got a bottle of some kind of light beer for two shillings, which I shared with them.

While we were here, the village priest arrived, rather a dirty old man, wearing a hat which resembled a top-hat minus the brim! He seemed interested in me when he heard that I was an English Priest. To my amusement, I found out that he was also the proprietor of the inn. I took his photograph, and on leaving he gave me his name and title: "Papa Athanasios, Ephimerios."

The people travel about on donkeys, and we saw many Biblical scenes being acted over again in real life before our very eyes,

We saw the most glorious sunsets here that we had ever seen, and the hills of Samothrace, lit up with a rich red glow, will never fade entirely from our vision. I can still picture one officer, who would stand motionless, gazing out from the transport to the hills, lit up by the sun's departing rays—it was Rupert Brooke.

Chapter 11
Preparing for the Great Landing

One of my greatest friends in the Anson Battalion was Sub-Lieutenant Arthur Walderne St. Clair Tisdall, who won the Victoria Cross on April 26th, 1915. He was my constant companion during our period of training, and, as we were both keen walkers, frequently went off with me on my tours of exploration. He had a highly successful career at Trinity College, Cambridge, gaining a Major Scholarship, a Bell Scholarship, and many other University prizes. He took his B.A. degree with double first-class honours, and won the highest award of its kind in England, the Chancellor's Gold Medal for Classics, in 1913. I can only look upon it as one of the greatest privileges to have had the friendship and companionship of this highly gifted, yet simple and lovable, man.

We went ashore together on March 16th (Tuesday), and determined to visit, if possible, the three Turkish villages which were said still to be in existence on the island of Lemnos. He had been told off to make maps and observations of the road to Castro, the capital of the island. When his work was finished, we walked four or five miles to a Greek village, and came across the schoolmaster, who seemed to be a most important person. Tisdall's knowledge of Ancient Greek was a valuable asset, and the schoolmaster insisted upon us going into the school, He then made the children sing a patriotic song to us, which was about driving out the Turks and re-establishing Greek and Christian civilisation. Then the girls did a weird sort of scarf dance, keeping excellent time to the music.

Here we also met a boy who could speak English; he took us to his father, who had a small windmill, and earned his living by grinding a kind of flour, consisting of wheat and peas. The old man was a Greek, and had sailed in British ships for twenty-six years; he could speak English well, and was the only Greek I met out there who knew the port of Goole, where I was working as curate,

After bidding "the Ancient Mariner" farewell, we set off into the mountains to find the three Turkish villages; we were rather late in starting, as it was well after three o'clock. On the long, winding road to Castro, which is uphill all the way, we met four journalists riding on donkeys. Two represented French newspapers, one an Italian paper, and the other was a war correspondent from "*The Daily News.*" They asked us many questions, but I am afraid we must have seemed most uninteresting people, and, as it was, Tisdall told me afterwards that he thought I told them too much! We also met a Turk, who could speak no Greek, but he asked for some bread and a penny in Arabic. We gave him the former, but declined the latter request.

Leaving the main road, we walked over the brow of a hill, and reached the first village inhabited by Turks. The second and third were close to it. We found them squalid and dirty, built on either side of a stream; the inhabitants shut their doors in our faces, and evidently looked upon us with great suspicion. However, we managed to have a good look at them. The women wore white trousers, whereas the Greek women wore black, and their veils were not so heavy. The men were dirty, and, unlike the Greeks, had made but poor attempts at cultivating their ground.

"One sees the difference between the Christian and the Turk," Tisdall remarked, "even in their villages and the way they are kept."

We found out the names of two of the villages, Stratia and Lera. Some of the men appeared to be wearing a *fez* with a kind of turban round it, and printed on it were quotations from the *Koran*. While we passed through, they retired into the houses, but came out to take a look at us after we had walked about a hundred yards away.

By the time we had completed our inspection it was getting late, and we set off over the mountains to walk to Smandria, a Greek village not far from the harbour mouth, from which we hoped to get a boat back to our transport. The walk took us longer than we had expected, and dusk was setting in, but at length we arrived, and instantly went in quest of some food. We found the inn, and had a meal of hard-boiled eggs, cheese, and rye-bread, after which the priest came in to converse with us. It was only with the greatest difficulty that we could make him understand us, as he knew neither English nor French.

The greatest difficulty of all, however, was when we tried to make some of the inhabitants understand that we must return to our transport and required a boat. We had forgotten the word commonly used on the island for boat, and it was only after frantic efforts on Sub-Lieutenant Tisdall's part that we got hold of a man eventually, who offered to row us to the ship for five shillings. We walked a long way with this man to the jetty, where he kept his boat, and when we rowed off it was quite dark, We found that the distance was most deceptive, and I will never forget the terrible task we had to find our ship; things seemed to look so different in the darkness, there were but few lights to guide us, and, to make matters worse, the search-lights at the harbour mouth kept playing on to us and blinding us.

Two and a half hours' hard rowing brought us to where the transports lay, but we could not find the right ship. We rowed from one to the other, but all in vain. The boatman at length began brandishing his arms about, and shouting out curses in Greek! He knew neither French nor English, and Tisdall could not understand his Greek. At length, after many adventures, which included a narrow escape from being run down by one of our destroyers, and after asking our way from Greek, French and British ships, we reached the companion ladder of our transport just after eleven o'clock.

The boatman demanded some outrageous sum for his labours, but we managed to get rid of him after a gift of fifteen shillings, and this was only given him to quiet him, as he was beginning to make a disturbance. This we did not want, as we had already disobeyed orders in returning to our ship after eleven o'clock, However, nothing more was said about it; but we found that a search-party, armed with revolvers, had been out to look for us, thinking we had come to some harm. Thus ended an exciting and interesting day.

On Thursday, March 18th, we received orders that we were to sail for Turkish waters at dusk, and, needless to say, great excitement prevailed. Some of us wondered if the landing was to take place immediately, and yet a moment's reflection showed that this could not possibly be so, because the number of troops available was quite inadequate, and the 29th Division had not yet arrived.

We found out later that the idea was merely to make a demonstration, within full view of those on the shores of Gallipoli, while the ships of the Fleet were bombarding up the Narrows. We tumbled out of our bunks at 3 a.m. on March 19th, had breakfast at 4, and at 5 a.m. fell in on deck in full marching kit, The whole fleet of transports then sailed down the coast of Gallipoli, but we saw no signs of the foe, nor was a single shot fired at us. Our warships were busy, however, shelling the forts up the straits, and we could see puffs of smoke from the

Turkish batteries on shore replying to our fire. Passing the mouth of the Dardanelles, we noticed that the lighthouse was still standing. Destroyers, British and French, were cruising about, keeping a ceaseless vigil, and we obtained excellent views of the *Queen Elizabeth, Dublin, Glory, Albion* and *Inflexible*. To our intense disappointment, after we had sailed some distance past the entrance to the Dardanelles, we received a signal to return to Lemnos, which we did in a rough sea.

General Sir Ian Hamilton, on taking command of the Mediterranean Expeditionary Force, found that the first essential, if the landing was to be a success, was a redistribution of troops on the transports, and Egypt was the only country near possessing ports suitable for this purpose. There were no facilities at Mudros, and so we were all ordered to sail to Egypt on March 24th. On the voyage we passed many beautiful islands, including Patmos, Kos, Samos and Rhodes; it was interesting to be so near the places visited by St. Paul, in Passion Week. The sea was calm, and we began to feel the heat of the sun as we drew near to our destination.

Port Said was reached early on the morning of March 27th, and we anchored in the harbour. A shadow was cast over the ship by the death of one of our men, who had been ill for some weeks. We buried him ashore with full Naval honours next day:

All sorts and conditions of Egyptians and Arabs came on board the ship, but the conjurers with their "chicken tricks" caused most amusement. They took a young chicken in their left hand, and with their right appeared to pull off its head, after which the chicken came to life again. One of these sly gentlemen approached a very dignified officer, saying: "Me show you a very good trick for sixpence, Mister Officer."

He turned away, muttering in contempt, "I don't want to see your rotten tricks." As he walked away, the conjurer shouted: "Oh! Mister Officer, give me back my chicken."

The officer looked angrily at the man and said: "I have not got any beastly chicken"; but suddenly, to everybody's amusement, squeals were heard coming from the officer's tunic, and, to his great embarrassment, the chicken stuck its head out of his pocket!

We disembarked on Sunday, March 28th, and encamped just outside the decks, about one hundred yards from the Arab quarter of the town. In writing of this camp, Denis Browne says:—

> The tents were pitched on the sand, and the whole camp might have been in the middle of the desert except for the ships and

the town behind us. If you stood with your back to them there was nothing in sight beyond the camp but desert. The salt lagoons of the Delta and the Canal were there, but they lay below the level we were on, and could hardly be seen. Everything was yellow with sand, and most days we had sand storms, which filled everything with grains.

During our sojourn here, part of the brigade had to go thirty miles up the Canal to occupy some trenches for a few days near El-Kantara. The heat was intense, and luckily the Turks did not appear, so there was no fighting. While bathing near our camp with some officers, I had the misfortune to injure my foot to badly that I was ordered to rest it for a few days, an order that most reluctantly I was forced to obey.

This accident prevented me from taking any services on Good Friday or early services on Easter Day. On Good Friday, April 2nd, parade service was at 7.30 a.m., because of the great heat later on in the day; the Rey. C. W. G. Moore, R.N., Chaplain to the Marine Brigade, officiated for me, and remarked upon the reverence of both officers and men. During the day I was visited by the Roman Catholic Chaplain, Father Green, who was always a good friend and genial companion.

Next day the whole Naval Division was reviewed by the General Officer Commanding in Chief, General Sir Ian Hamilton, on the sand close to the camp. It was a memorable sight at the saluting-base, and the bayonets flashed in the dazzling sunshine.

Easter Day passed most successfully. The chaplains had cards printed for all members of the Church of England in the division, which announced the times at which Holy Communion would be celebrated in the English Church. It was found to be impossible to have any celebration of Holy Communion outside on the sand, as there was a continual sand storm, and the heat was oppressive.

Through the kindness of the English Chaplain, we had our services on Easter morning in the beautiful little Church, which was crowded with earnest and reverent worshippers. So great was the throng that the services timed for 7 and 8 o'clock had to be merged into one, and I will never forget how officers and men knelt side by side to meet the Risen Saviour in loving adoration. For many, alas! it was to be the last Communion; perhaps they had not come for years, but they seemed to realise that they were on the eve of a great fight, and silently they came. I was able to take the parade service at 9.30 a.m., which was attended by officers and men of the Anson, Hood and Howe Battalions. Denis Browne had sat up into the early hours of the morning before leaving the ship, in order that he might copy the music of "*On the Resurrection Morning*" for the band, which was sung with great fervour at this service.

We left Port Said for Alexandria, from whence we were to sail for Lemnos again, on the evening of Easter Monday, April 5th. It was blowing hard, and the sand storm increased in fury, until all our clothes and belongings were covered with it; it got into our food and drink, and it was not without thankfulness that we left Port Said behind.

We had a most interesting journey along the delta of the Nile, and saw some quaint Arabs with their camels, journeying towards the towns, Alexandria was reached next day about 9 a.m., and we marched to a sandy, patch of ground about a mile away to "bivouac" for the night. We lay down at night in holes made in the ground, where our valises had been placed. Had it not been for a considerable number of ants, which made an attack upon me, and a heavy shower of rain, which caused a little streamlet to run down my neck, I might have spent a comfortable night.

CHAPTER 12

On the Eve of the Great Landing

It was pointed out in the previous chapter that a redistribution of troops, guns, ammunition, and stores was found to be necessary, if the landing on the shores of Gallipoli was to be successfully carried out. This entailed an enormous amount of thought and work, but it was an accomplished fact within fourteen days, The Anson Battalion had been specially chosen, out of the Royal Naval Division, to supply working parties, which were to land with various battalions of the 29th Division. Thus, the Ansons were split up into working: parties of one or two platoons each, and told off to go on board different transports.

The ship which I was told to embark in was an old Cunarder, and I went with two platoons of "A" Company, Anson Battalion, under Lieutenant-Commander Peter McKirdy, R.N.V.R. On board this ship was the 1st Battalion, Royal Dublin Fusiliers, Colonel Rooth commanding. The ship was literally packed with troops, and I shared a small cabin with three other officers; but, in spite of the fact that there was no spare accommodation, we were very comfortable, and found her a good sea-going ship. It is pleasant to record that we were a very happy family on board; indeed, I think, on looking back, the happiest times we had were spent in this old ship.

The instant I got on board, a thick-set little man, with a determined face and piercing eyes, came up and introduced himself to me; it was Father Finn, Chaplain to the Dublins. He was a good friend, and a most agreeable companion all the time we were on board. He helped me in every possible way he could, and placed at my disposal a small improvised chapel he had made, under a tarpaulin, in the fore well deck. Here he said Mass daily, and his men attended remarkably well. Strange to relate, all the officers of the Dublins, with two exceptions, were members of the Church of England, whereas in the ranks there were not more than thirty Anglicans.

On our first Sunday on board, Low Sunday, April 11th, Father Finn said Mass at seven o'clock, and then I celebrated Holy Communion at 7-45 in the same place. Ten officers and fourteen men attended, and I found that the Dublins had not had a celebration of Holy Communion on Easter Day, so they gladly availed themselves of the opportunity now. With the Dublins came some of the officers of the 1st West Riding Yorkshire Field Company of the Royal Engineers, who were also on board. After breakfast we had parade service at 10.30 on the Promenade Deck, and about 300 officers and men attended, including Colonel Rooth. We had no band, but the hymns were sung most heartily. We had "*O God, our Help in ages past,*" "*Fight the good fight*" and "*The Church's One Foundation.*"

Father Finn and I became closer friends as the time passed by, and his genial personality, his wonderful broadmindedness, his unselfish nature, and his love for all men made him a favourite with all ranks. We often spoke of the future, and in particular of the landing, and he confessed that he did not expect to live through it; but he was full of fun when talking to the men, so they could never have guessed what his real opinion was. He said one day:

> If you find my body, bury me simply, and say a prayer for my soul, old chap; and if you find any of my boys dying, get them to repeat a short act of contrition.

Then he wrote in my Prayer Book:—

> Oh! my God, I am sorry that I have sinned against Thee, because Thou are so good, and I will not sin again.

In the evening of Saturday, April 10th, we found ourselves lying at anchor once again in Mudros Bay, but we gazed on a very different scene from that which had greeted our eyes one month before. Every available anchorage was used now by the huge fleet of warships and transports, which spread out on all sides to the view. Mr. Ashmead Bartlett asked:

> Will the world ever see such a spectacle again, such a motley collection of types stretching back for well-nigh thirty years or even more?

On Monday evening, April 12th, I went down to the men's quarters, where we had a most hilarious concert. They were no ordinary men, these men; they were among the few remaining men of the British Regular Army. Irishmen are jovial, as a rule; but these Irish Tommies, tanned by the Indian sun, were the merriest souls I have met anywhere. I have often thought of that concert since, and wondered how many of the "bhoys" who were singing that night are alive to tell the tale. For most of them it was their last concert on earth—but how they sang! Anything with a reference in it to shamrock or the Emerald Isle was a certain encore. "*When Irish eyes are smiling*," "*A little bit of Heaven*," "*The dear little Shamrock*," were all sung and re-sung until some of those on board began to wish they had never been written; but it was when they sang "*Tipperary*" at the end that one felt thrilled. I have heard "*Tipperary*" sung by Englishmen, Scots, French, Arabs and others, but I will never again hear it sung as those Dublin Fusiliers sang it on the eve of the great landing. And then came "*God save the King*," every man standing to attention, followed by three Irish cheers!

The sole topic of conversation now became "The landing." It was discussed from every point of view, and all wondered what exactly the date would be, I remember talking it over with two subalterns of the Dublins; they took a somewhat pessimistic view of it, and told me frankly they expected to be "wiped out," to use a soldiers' expression.

Meanwhile, our men were working hard. Moored alongside us was another huge transport which had on board the 1st Battalion Munster Fusiliers, Colonel Tizard in command, and the 1st Battalion Lancashire Fusiliers, commanded by Major Bishop. It was necessary that these troops should keep themselves fit by regular exercise and drill, and so our men were busily employed every day in taking the Dublins, Munsters and Lancashires to and from the shores of Lemnos, The island was admirably adapted for field operations, and the fact that the troops, who made up the 29th Division, had suitable ground for their tactical exercises, went a very long way towards making them ready for the fray which was hourly drawing near.

To be censor of letters on board a transport is a somewhat unenviable task, and yet this fell to my lot as chaplain. In this work the doctors and paymaster gave me valuable assistance in their spare time. It was monotonous but interesting work at times; we noticed that one phrase occurred in every other letter opened, and that was "*We are in the pink.*" This expression is said to have originated with the late Mr. Mark Sheridan, the music-hall comedian. We gained a wonderful insight into the characters of men, and censoring brought one fact to light which has been frequently doubted, that the majority of men have the religious sense very keenly developed.

On the very eve of battle, a shadow was cast over the whole of the Naval Division by the death of Rupert Brooke, whose work has been the admiration of the world. The last occasion on which I visited him was on April 3rd, Easter Eve. I went up to his room in the Casino Palace Hotel at Port Said, and found him complaining of a slight attack of sunstroke and a swelling on his lip; he chatted for about ten minutes, but seemed somewhat dazed. A large mosquito net of white muslin hung over his bed, and when I went into the room, he pulled this to one side. Never had his face looked more beautiful than now; his eyes flashed with a brightness that was unearthly, and as he talked, one read in his countenance that dazzling purity of mind which betrays itself so often in his poems. In his room sat his friend, Patrick Shaw Stewart, who was also unwell, and so, after staying about twelve minutes, I left them, The Hood Battalion, in which both were officers, had been told of to make a "feint" at a landing in the Gulf of Saros, and so they left Port Said in another ship three days after us.

The voyage seemed to have a good effect on Brooke's health, and by the time the ship reached Skyros (Saturday, April 17th) he was to all appearances himself again. For a few days the transport lay at anchor in Trebuki Bay. He landed on this picturesque and beautiful island, and took part in a divisional field day, and this long day, together with the heat, proved too great a strain on his somewhat slender constitution. The next day, Wednesday, April 21st, he stayed in bed, and, although he seemed fatigued, yet was quite cheerful.

Sub-Lieutenant Denis Browne went into his cabin in the evening, and took him a cutting from "*The Times*" about a sermon preached by the Dean of St. Paul's (Dr. Inge), in which the last of his sonnets was quoted. He complained of feeling very unwell, and humorously remarked that he was sorry that the dean did not think him quite as good as Isaiah. Shortly after his lip became swollen again, and he had pains in the chest and back. A consultation was held by the cleverest doctors in the Naval Division, and they took an extremely grave view of the case, with the result that Brooke was moved at once to a French hospital ship, where he was placed in a comfortable cabin on the sun-deck, and here he had every care and loving attention they could give him.

Nothing was left undone that could alleviate his condition or prolong his life. He died at 4.46 p.m. on Friday, April 23rd, his friend Denis Browne being with him. He was unconscious at the end, and the Rev. B, J, Failes, R.N. (Chaplain to the 1st R.N. Brigade), who went to visit him, was only able to pray with him. Denis Browne wrote:

> He died at 4.46, with the sun shining all round his cabin, and the cool sea breeze blowing through the door and the shaded windows, No one could have wished a quieter or calmer end than in that lovely bay, shielded by the mountains and fragrant with sage and thyme.

He was buried the same night on the island of Skyros, and Sub-Lieutenant Denis Browne himself chose his last resting-place. For these particulars I am deeply indebted to Mrs. Brooke, who has most kindly allowed me to make use of Sub-Lieutenant Browne's letter to her, Nothing could be more touching than his account of the poet's burial, and with it I will conclude this chapter:—

> We found a most lovely place about one mile up a valley from the sea, an olive grove above a watercourse, dry now, but torrential in winter. Two mountains flank it on either side, Pephko and Komaro, and Mount Khotrilas is at its head. We chose a place in the most lovely grove I have ever seen or imagined, a little glade of about a dozen trees, carpeted with mauve flowering sage. Over his head droops an olive tree, leaning slightly forward with its upper branches, though its stem is straight; and round it is a little space clear of all undergrowth. .
>
> About a quarter past nine the funeral party arrived, and made their way up the steep, narrow and rocky path that leads to the grave. The way was so rough and uncertain that we had to post men with: lamps every twenty yards to guide the bearers. He was borne by the non-commissioned officers of his own company; and so slowly did they go that it was not till nearly eleven that they reached the grave.
>
> We buried him by cloudy moonlight in the grove. He wore his uniform, and on the coffin were his helmet, belt and pistol. We lined the grave with flowers and olive, and Colonel Quilter laid an olive wreath on the coffin. The chaplain (Mr. Failes), who saw him in the afternoon, read the service very simply; the firing party fired three volleys, and the bugles sounded the '*Last Post.*'
>
> And so we laid him to rest in that lovely valley, his head towards those mountains that he would have loved to know, and his feet

towards the sea, He once said, in chance talk, that he would like to be buried in a Greek island, He could have no lovelier one than Skyros, and no quieter resting place.

On the grave we (his brother officers) heaped great blocks of white marble; the men of his company made a great wooden cross for his head, with his name on it, and his platoon put a smaller one at his feet. On the back of the large cross our Greek interpreter wrote in pencil

> Here lies
> The Servant of God,
> Sub-Lieutenant in the
> English Navy,
> Who died for the
> Deliverance of Constantinople from the Turks.

No one of us knew him without loving him, whether they knew him for ten years, as I did, or for a couple of months, as others. His brother officers and his men mourn him very deeply. But those who knew him chiefly as a poet of the rarest gifts, the brightest genius, know that the loss is not only yours and ours, but the world's. He was just coming into his own; what he had written had reached a zenith of perfection that marked him as belonging to the very finest; and beyond his genius there was that infinitely lovable soul, that stainless heart whose earthly death can only be the beginning of a true immortality.....He has gone to where he came from; but if anyone left the world richer by passing through it, it was he. It was so hard that he should die the day before we opened battle, cut off by disease when he had given himself to die for that England of which his last poem has shown him to be the truest singer.

CHAPTER 13

The Great Landing of British Troops at Cape Helles, April 25 (Sunday), 1915

On April 20th (Tuesday), we ascertained that Sunday, April 25th, was the day that had been chosen for the landing on the shores of Gallipoli. The last days of preparation seemed to pass quickly, and were spent in putting the finishing touches to a scheme the details of which had already been worked out with scrupulous care. They were days of excitement and suspense; transports arrived every hour with fresh troops, receiving & tremendous ovation from those already there. On April 21st, in the evening, we received a message from Major-General Hunter Weston, C.B., D.S.O. It was thus headed:—

> To each man of the 29th Division, on the occasion of their first going into action together.
>
> The Major-General Commanding congratulates the division on being selected for an enterprise the success of which will have a decisive effect on the war.
>
> The eyes of the world are upon us, and your deeds will live in history.
>
> To us now is given an opportunity of avenging our friends and relatives who have fallen in France and Flanders. Our comrades there willingly gave their lives in thousands and tens of thousands for our king and country, and by their glorious courage and dogged tenacity they defeated the invaders and broke the German offensive.
>
> We, also, must be prepared to suffer hardships, privations, thirst and heavy losses by bullets, by shells, by mines, by drowning. But if each man feels, as is true, that on him individually, however small or however great his task, rests the success or failure

of the expedition, and therefore the honour of the Empire and the welfare of his own folk at home, we are certain to win through to a glorious victory. In Nelson's time it was England, now it is the whole British Empire, which expects that each man of us will do his duty.

This was followed soon afterwards by a message from the General Officer Commanding-in-Chief, General Sir Ian Hamilton. It read:—

> Soldiers of France and of the King.
> Before us lies an adventure unprecedented in modern war. Together with our comrades of the fleet we are about to attempt to force a landing upon an open beach, in face of positions which have been vaunted by our enemies as impregnable. The landing will be made good by the help of God and the navy; the positions will be stormed, and the war brought one step nearer to a glorious close. 'Remember,' said Lord Kitchener, when bidding *adieu* to your commander, 'remember, once you set foot upon the Gallipoli Peninsula you must fight the thing through to a finish.'
> The whole world will be watching our progress. Let us prove ourselves worthy of the great feat of arms entrusted to us.
>
> Ian Hamilton, General."

Each man received a copy of these messages, and it was thrilling to hear the British, Australian and French troops cheering as they read them. Every man felt proud to be there, and rejoiced to know that the hour had come in which he was to show his love for his native land. The most explicit orders had been given for the disembarkation of troops on the various transports. The following general instructions were given to the Anson Battalion, R.N. Division:—

> It seems probable that the battalion will disembark in small parties, in some cases consisting of one platoon only, from various ships, and as it may not be possible to issue definite orders for each party, the following general instructions should be carried out as far as circumstances permit by any officer in charge of a party who does not receive any further and more detailed orders.
>
> (1) All details as to time of leaving boats, etc., will be received by officers commanding detachments from the officers commanding troops on board the ships on which the detachments

at present are.

(2) The troops will disembark in full marching order, with 200 rounds S.A.A. and three days' iron rations. Any man who is deficient of his great coat will carry his blanket in his pack.

(3) On landing, the troops will be formed up at some spot on the beach selected by the O.C. Detachment; arms will be piled or grounded, and the packs, haversacks and water-bottles removed. As soon as he is ready, the O.C. Detachment will report himself immediately to the senior naval officer on the beach, and act under his orders. If there is no naval officer in the vicinity, the O.C. Detachment will take what action he considers best to clear his beach, and empty any boats on it; the contents of the boats being temporarily stacked above high-water mark.

N.B.—Water will be scarce. Every man must leave the ship with his water-bottle full, and the men should be warned that this may have to last them for two days. Precautions should be taken by placing the haversack on the top of the pack to ensure the rations not getting wet during disembarkation. If it can be arranged, each man should carry a small quantity of firewood on the outside of his pack.

I have left out some of the technical details in regard to the working-parties, but the above extracts will show how thoroughly the arrangements had been made.

The transports sailed away from Mudros Harbour about 6 p.m. on Friday, April 23rd, escorted by the fleet. The transport in which I was, steamed third in the line, and was escorted by HMS. *Cornwallis*, *Euryalus* and *Dublin*. Each transport, as she steamed out, was vociferously cheered by the troops on the other ships. We dined all together for the last time at seven o'clock that evening, after which I had a long talk to Father Finn and the doctor attached to the 1st Royal Dublins. The men were subdued and quiet, and turned in early in order to get a good night's rest before the excitement and trials of the following night. The doctor gave me some morphia pills in a small bottle, for use in case of need when we landed.

When we awoke on Saturday morning, April 24th, we were lying off the isle of Tenedos, surrounded by battleships, cruisers and destroyers. To our dismay a stiff breeze sprung up, and at one time it looked as if the operations would have to be postponed; at about one o'clock, however, the wind dropped, and it grew wonderfully calm. At 3 p.m. a trawler came alongside to take some of the Dublin Fusiliers to the s.s. *River Clyde.* To quote Sir Ian Hamilton's despatch:—

> The *River Clyde* had been specially prepared for the rapid disembarkation of her complement, and large openings for the exit of troops had been cut in her sides, giving on to a wide gangplank by which the men could pass rapidly into lighters which she had in tow.

Within her holds were also packed the Munster Fusiliers, the West Riding Field Company, Royal Engineers, and the 13th Platoon, "D" Company, Anson Battalion, R.N. Division.

A few hours later, two companies of the Dublins that remained were taken off in a trawler to one of our battleships for the landing. Father Finn went with these latter companies. He shook my hand warmly as he said "Goodbye," and gave me a small medal of "Our Lady of Mount Carmel," such as he had been distributing earlier in the day to his men, he said:

> Take this and wear it, and may it bring you good fortune, and take you safely home.

And, with a wave of the hand, he ran down the gangway on to the trawler.

At about ten o'clock we went on board HM.S. X——, fleet-sweeper. The officers and crew of our transport gave us a hearty send-off, and a gramophone was turned on, on the deck, which played "*Tipperary*" in honour of the remainder of the Dublins who went. with us.

Half-an-hour later all the battleships and cruisers, with the minesweepers and trawlers, weighed anchor, and steamed slowly towards Cape Helles. It was a memorable occasion, and I shall never forget the sight of that huge fleet proceeding silently through the gloom towards their final rendezvous. It must be remembered that a landing was to be made at five chosen positions on the Turkish coast, known by the letters "S.," "V.," "W.", "X" and "Y." Sir Ian Hamilton points out in his first despatch that "V.," "W." and "X." were to be main landings, whereas the landings at "S" and "Y" were mainly to protect the flanks. The s.s. *River Clyde* was to be grounded at "V." beach at the very game moment as the first tow of ships' boats, with three companies of the Dublin Fusiliers, reached the beach.

It was a beautiful, calin night; nothing but the splashing of water broke the stillness. We steamed, of course, without lights, and every man was quiet and subdued, It was the eve of battle, and we knew it; the day for which we had longed and waited, and yet, now that we were on its very threshold, some would willingly have postponed it for a time. We wondered and wondered what would happen—whether we should live to see another sunrise, I lay down on the deck of the fleet-sweeper, and tried to sleep with a coat over me, but it was impossible, the tension was too great; and so I began to smoke a pipe.

Presently I heard a voice saying: "You might try the wardroom, sir; it must be difficult to sleep tonight on deck." I peered through the gloom, and saw that it was a midshipman who thus addressed me. I told him that I was quite comfortable where I was, and that I would go down to the wardroom later. This midshipman was one of the best fellows I have ever met. He came from H.M.S. *Inflexible*, and his present position was only temporary. I saw the other day he had gained a D.S.C., and I know he would deserve it; he was determined, devoid of fear, "white man." After a time, he said quietly: "We are getting very near now, sir; it ought to be a 'topping' sight when, we start; the fleet will give them something to think about."

Soon it grew lighter, and I noticed that we were drifting slowly towards one of our huge warships. At 4.15 a.m. we could just dimly make out the coastline of Gallipoli, but a thin veil of mist obscured from view those hills on which such magnificent heroism was so soon to be displayed. There was no sign of life on shore; nothing stirred. Just before dawn the battleships end cruisers moved proudly forward to their allotted positions, and I believe it was the finest sight I have seen in my life up to the present. As far as the eye could reach, right along the Turkish coast, lay the great ships of the fleet—British, French and Russian. Suddenly a vivid flash of light illuminated the whole scene in the grey dawn, and a terrific report followed.

We knew then what had happened. The bombardment had commenced, and the *Queen Elizabeth* had fired the first shot. Almost immediately every possible gun was brought to bear on the coast. It was a sight unequalled for grandeur to see every one of these gigantic vessels belching forth their deadly projectiles with clouds of fire and smoke, followed by ear-splitting reports. I was quite near the *Queen Elizabeth* when she fired a broadside into the town of Sedd-el-Bahr, and it seemed as if an entire row of houses and the mosque had been blown up into the air at once.

The concussion from the guns was very great, and the naval surgeon came round with cotton-wool, which we stuffed into our ears. The ships we noticed especially active were the *Queen Elizabeth, Lord Nelson, Vengeance, Implacable, Swiftsure, Prince George, Cornwallis* and two French cruisers, with the *Askold* (Russian), but H.M.S. *Albion, Euryalus, Talbot, Minerva* and *Dublin* were also making their voices heard in this amazing display of gunnery.

This terrific bombardment commenced, I believe, with controlled fire for twenty minutes, followed by ten minutes' battle fire, which means that every single gun is firing away as quickly as possible. That final ten minutes was indescribable, "This shows you what the British lion is like when he's roused," remarked a naval officer to me as we stood by in the X watching the never-to-be-forgotten scene. It seemed impossible that anyone could be alive on shore after this heavy fire.

Up to the present, it looked as if the enemy had fled from their entrenchments on the cliff-tops—there was no sign of life; our guns so far were unanswered. About 5.25 a.m., with wonderful regularity and order, the midshipmen could be seen getting their boats filled with the troops who were going to land. Each steam-pinnace towed six or seven ship's boats, and this "crocodile" of boats was called a "tow." At 6.30 precisely, a midshipman brought a tow of boats alongside the X——, and they were quickly filled with the Dublin Fusiliers and men of the Hampshires, who came on board just before we sailed from Tenedos. Wishing them good luck, and raising a cheer, we watched them getting nearer and nearer the hostile shore.

CHAPTER 14

The Story of the Great Landing— (Continued)

To appreciate the difficulties of this memorable morning, it must be borne in mind that the boats, crammed with the men of the 29th Division, were being towed simultaneously to all the five landing places, so that it was very hard to keep the eyes fixed upon any one spot. Our attention, however, was riveted for some time to "V" Beach, towards which we could see the Dublin Fusiliers being towed. At the same time the ss. *River Clyde* (Commander Unwin, R.N.) was heading straight for the shore, The collier and ships' boats drew gradually nearer. So far not a sign of a Turk! But the moment the *River Clyde* was beached, and the first boat touched the shore, a terrible hurricane of lead swept the beach.

The Turks were very much alive, and greeted the Dublins in their open boats with a tornado of fire. Nearly everyone in the boats was killed instantly, amongst the number being Colonel Rooth, the plucky and beloved colonel of the 1st Dublins. The boats and their naval crews were destroyed by the terrible fire from machine-guns and pom-poms, A few managed to escape, and rushed, wounded and exhausted, to the only cover that "V" Beach afforded, end that was a low, sandy escarpment about four feet high. Father Finn was among this number; although badly wounded he shouted through the din to an officer, "I'm going to those fellows," pointing to some of his beloved Dublins who were dying, out on the sand, near the water's edge.

"You'll be a fool if you go," came the answer; "it means death."

"A priest's place is beside the dying soldier," said Father Finn; and ran out and knelt by the side of one of his men, Under heavy fire, and in great pain, he crawled about administering extreme unction, until a shrapnel shell burst over the beach, He was again severely wounded—

in the head this time—and yet, fearless and brave, he continued his work of mercy until he lay down to die from sheer exhaustion and loss of blood. One of the men, said to have been his orderly, ran to him and dragged him under cover. He was in great pain, and just looked up and asked "Are our fellows winning?" and then he passed—amidst the thunder of the guns on land and sea. Thus died the first chaplain to be killed in the present war. His death was a great grief to me, a we had become firm friends on the transport, and a great blow to his men, who well-nigh worshipped him.

He was buried close to the place where he fell, a plain wooden cross marking the grave; Father Harker, Chaplain to the Munster Fusiliers, took the service.

Lieutenant Denholm, R.N.V.R., got ashore with his platoon of Ansons before 6.30 a.m. on this terrible beach. Several of his men were killed in landing, but, on the whole, he and his platoon had wonderful good fortune. The beach was covered with dead bodies, and besprinkled with blood until it resembled a shambles. Meanwhile the galling fire from pom-pom, Maxim and rifle never eased, and every now and then shrapnel would burst over those of our brave men who had managed to land, and who clung tenaciously to the only bit of cover they could find behind the escarpment. All this was seen plainly from the fleet-sweeper through field-glasses.

But let us see now what was happening all this time on the s.s., *River Clyde*. I am greatly indebted to Sub-Lieutenant W. H. Perring, R.N.V.R. (Anson Battalion), then Chief Petty Officer Perring, who was on board the *River Clyde*, for the following most interesting account of his experiences, Perring, who assisted Sub-Lieutenant Tisdall when he won the Victoria Cross for saving the lives of wounded men on "V" Beach, proved himself to be a most efficient chief petty officer, and undaunted when there was dangerous work to do. His C.G.M. was well deserved, and it will go down to his lasting credit that he took part in one of the noblest and brightest episodes in the present war. This is his account, written in his simple, straightforward style:—

> The *River Clyde* was run up on "V" Beach, under the fire of H.M.S, *Albion*. Directly she was beached, the Munster Fusiliers, who were in No, 1 hold, had orders to disembark. In this ship were two doors, cut on either side, for the men to go out on to a platform, along which they ran into a lighter, which was placed in position by the sailors, under Commander Unwin,

Landing the French "75's" on "V Beach.

RN. Directly men showed themselves, the Turks opened a most murderous fire on them, and some poor fellows fell off this platform the moment they placed their feet upon it. So terrible were our losses that in less than half-an-hour the lighter, also a cutter, and the beach itself were covered with dead bodies.

There were nine machine-guns on board the *River Clyde*, and although they opened fire with these guns, very little, if any, damage was done, the enemy keeping himself well out of sight. As soon as ever the ship grounded the Turks opened fire on her from the Asiatic Coast. Three shells hit the ship, and then one of the battleships put the gun out of action, The first shell went in the boiler room without killing or wounding anyone; the second hit. the ship aft, crashed through No, 4 hold, came through the upper deck, then on the main deck, port side, and took off the legs of two soldiers. They died after about twenty minutes, I was only two yards away from these dear men.

The hold was packed with troops as thickly as ever you could stow men together, and the terrible sights and the cries of the wounded will never be forgotten by those who are alive to tell the tale, I often think it was good that one like myself was there, as I did not lose my nerve under fire, and helped to prevent the men from being panic-stricken. I now went down to my men, who were in No, 4 lower hold, and I addressed them, and told them to keep cool, to try and keep their heads as I did. I don't want you to think this is praise of myself, but the 13th Platoon could tell you of my behaviour under fire. I thank God for this courage; He took all fear from me.

While I was talking to the platoon another shell came in and killed three of them., This was the second shell I had seen explode within a few minutes; it was rather bad, especially for young lads like these, but I knew I was there to show them an example and take care of them. I have often wondered since what would have happened had that gun not been put out of action when it was; they had the correct range. After three companies of the Munster Fusiliers had gone out of the ship, with a few of the Dublins, the landing was stopped for a time; the remainder, however, left the ship that night, in the dark, without any difficulty. During the whole of this day (Sunday) I kept my men down below; it was not safe to put your head in sight, as shots were flying everywhere.

During this operation Commander Unwin, R.N., Midshipman Drewry, and many others were getting the wounded in from the beach and the water under an awful fire. Later in the forenoon, Sub-Lieutenant Tisdall also lent a hand, and did good work; then he asked for volunteers of the 13th Platoon to assist with the wounded, Leading Seamen Malia, Curtiss and Parkinson volunteered, and it was now that I lent a hand with them. How we were all not wounded or killed I cannot understand—only by the grace of God. I kept the other men under hatches down below until darkness set in. After we got ashore, we did not do much except outpost duty, attend to the wounded, and do what we could for everyone.

On Sunday, about 1 p.m., they commenced to fire on the *River Clyde* again from Asia; dozens of rounds were fired at the ship and the beach, but I am glad to say no one was touched by any of these shells. The shelling continued on "V Beach every day for over a week. I remember that on Wednesday, April 28th, I and a party of men picked up all the dead on the beach and from the water; we placed in one large grave two hundred and thirteen gallant men who gave their lives for their country. The bombardment of the Dardanelles, the landing, etc., I shall never forget.

By Thursday, April 29th, all the remainder of the Royal Naval Division had landed, and then we formed up afresh and entered into the fighting-line. So, we continued until I was wounded on June 4th, 1915. I am glad to say the Anson Battalion, and the Royal Naval Division as a whole, did all they were called upon to do through that awful struggle.

Thus, ends Sub-Lieutenant Perring's most graphic account. He was promoted on the field from C.P.O. to Sub-Lieutenant for his devotion to duty, and no man ever deserved an honour more. And here I feel that I must give a somewhat fuller account of the incident mentioned in the above narrative of how Sub-Lieutenant Tisdall saved the wounded and won his Victoria Cross.

He was the only officer of the R.N. Division on the ss, *River Clyde*, and was in command of the 13th Platoon, Anson Battalion, which had been told off to form part of the working-party for "V" Beach.

It is said that in the forenoon, Tisdall, hearing the bitter cries for help coming from the wounded lying out on the sand under the burning sun, said: "I can't stand it; I am going over." An eye-witness says that then and there he dived off the gangway into the sea, and attempted to save some of the men, who were lying about the shore in hundreds, suffering untold agonies. Getting exhausted in these gallant efforts, which, it must be borne in mind, were made under the heaviest fire possible in modern warfare, under a perfect hail of lead from rifle, pom-pom, Maxim and shrapnel, he called: for assistance, jumped into the water again, and pushed a boat in front of him to and from the shore, thus saving the lives of several wounded men at the risk of his own.

Tisdall was assisted in his noble work, as we have already seen, by C.P.O. Perring and three leading seamen, Malia, Curtiss and Parkinson. Many thought he had gone mad, others looked on thunderstruck at his cool intrepidity, but Tisdall, I know, would simply look upon it as his duty; and when it was all over it was left to others to tell the immortal story. Tisdall himself never said a word about his glorious deeds. On Tuesday night, April 27th, he volunteered to take up ammunition to the firing line under terribly heavy fire, astonishing everyone by his utter contempt for danger. And on the following days, by his own magnificent example of pluck and grit, he encouraged his men in the hard work of unloading the lighters, which kept arriving at "V" Beach laden with stores, guns and ammunition, amidst continual showers of shrapnel.

This great hero fell in battle on May 6th—the first man in the R.N. Division to gain the Victoria Cross. One of his men, in a letter home, wrote:—

> You would see it in the papers about our dear officer, Mr. Tisdall, 'going down.' He was one of England's bravest men. All his men about cried when he went, because all the boys thought the world of him.

To quote the beautiful words written of him by one of his brother officers:—

> Everyone knew this man was a visionary, an intellectual, a hero. . . . He seemed to be alone in the clouds, but serene—always serene. He could go mad, too—mad with joy and eccentricity. . . . . He could grow sad, too, at times. He proved the genuineness of his ideals, and voluntarily risked his life for others; and one day gave it, doubtless willingly, proud and smiling, I imagine.

The story of how Lieutenant-Colonel Doughty-Wylie and Captain Walford, of the Staff of the 29th Division, pulled the scattered units together on V" Beach, and led the attack on the fort and village of Sedd-el-Bahr is too well-known to necessitate its being re-told here. The whole of "V" Beach was in our hands, including the old castle fand hill, before 2 p.m. on Monday, April 26th.,

The events which I have described were closely watched by us from the deck of H.M.S. *Newmarket*. Three "tows" had already left this ship for the beach, when we found ourselves drifting too far inland. Suddenly four shrapnel shells were fired at us; the first burst about two hundred yards away, the second came much nearer, and the third and fourth only just missed the ship. As it was, a splinter wounded one man. We then put further out to sea, and, at the kind invitation of the officers, went down into the ward room and had an excellent breakfast. The fourth "tow" went away to "V" Beach about 10 a.m., and then, about 11.30 a.m. we were told to get into some boats which had come alongside.

There were seven, and they were towed by a steam pinnace from one of the warships. This was the fifth "tow" to leave for the "Beach." I got into the first boat, with Lieutenant-Commander McKirdy, R.N.V.R., and about twenty men of the Anson Battalion. Just as we were in the very act of starting, a Naval commander came up quickly in a pinnace, and shouted through a megaphone:

Admiral's orders. No more men to be landed on 'V' Beach; you have to go to 'W' Beach.

I have often thought over this incident since, and I am certain that only by a merciful Providence were we spared. Had we landed on "V," as was originally intended, we should have suffered exactly in the same way as the Dublin Fusiliers.

While men were filing into the other boats, I chanced to look down into the bottom of our boat, and what I saw gave me a strange, uncanny feeling. The whole of this little craft was running with blood; there was blood on the oars, blood on the seats, blood all over, and bits of skin here and there. It bore silent testimony to the terrible sufferings which were undergone by the men in the first boats to reach the land. In the bow stood an old salt from one of the battleships, placidly smoking a clay pipe, and helping to get the men settled for their short but precarious journey. The men's packs weighed down these boats considerably, and it will be readily understood that some of us felt no small concern when the old salt said: "She 'as two bullet 'oles in 'er bottom now, sir; but I 'ope she'll last out."

This remark was uttered with a gravity which only served to make it more humorous. And then, huddled together in these blood-besprinkled boats, we made for the beach,

I must confess I held my breath several times as shells burst unpleasantly near, throwing a spout of water up high into the air.

The Beach "W," towards which we were hastening, was taken earlier on in the morning by the gallantry and dogged courage of the 1st Battalion Lancashire Fusiliers. To us, who witnessed the storming of the cliffs and the capture of the whole position by this plucky battalion, it will always be known as "Lancashire Landing." "W" Beach consists of a strip of soft sand, 350 yards long, and from 15 to 40 yards wide, and at its centre a small gully runs down to the sea, opening out a break in the cliffs. On either flank the cliffs are precipitous. The Turks had made the most of their time, and when the first boats, filled with Lancashire Fusiliers, reached the shore, they found that it was covered with barbed wire, which reached to the water's edge, and was even continued under water. Land and sea mines had been laid with great skill.

On the high ground, overlooking the beach, were two redoubts and strong entrenchments, and these, together with a number of cleverly-concealed machine-guns, made this beach almost impregnable. About 6 a.m., "the whole battalion approached the shore together, towed by eight picket boats in line abreast, each picket boat pulling four ship's cutters." Three companies made straight for the sand, but one company made for a ledge of rock on the left. So far not a shot had been fired, but as the first boats touched the bottom a terrible hurricane of bullets swept over the Lancashires. Many men were mown down and remained hanging on the barbed wire; but the others, led in magnificent style by their officers, assisted by those who landed to the left, hacked their way through the network of wire entanglements, and dashed up the hills with a cheer, and drove the enemy from his strong positions.

Nothing could withstand these Lancashire Fusiliers. Although the Turks threw down hand grenades and large stones on them as they stormed the cliffs, they were not to be denied, and, after several truly British charges, the beach was won, The Anzacs farther north did fine work, and so did the Munsters and Dublins on "V" Beach; but the taking of "W" Beach was, in my humble opinion, the finest deed of that great and memorable day. Six Victoria Crosses were awarded the battalion for this glorious deed, which will live in history—but every man deserved a Victoria Cross! As I watched them charge time after time, their bayonets flashing in the sun, I could have yelled with excitement, as men do at football matches, and yet the next moment one would heave a sigh, as men could be seen falling one after another.

Both our commanders-in-chief, on land and sea, were of the same opinion as regards the deeds performed by the Lancashires Let me quote from their despatches. General Sir Ian Hamilton says:—

> It is my firm conviction that no finer feat of arms has ever been achieved by the British soldier—or any other soldier—than the storming of these trenches from open boats on the morning of April 25th. It was to the complete lack of the sense of danger or of fear of this daring battalion that we owed our astonishing success.

Vice-Admiral de Robeck says:—

> It is impossible to exalt too highly the service rendered by the 1st Battalion Lancashire Fusiliers in the storming of the beach; the dash and gallantry displayed were superb.

It was to this beach, then, that we were being towed. We noticed, as we drew near, that the dust and smoke from bursting shells fired by our ships made a screen between us and the beach, and in two minutes we were making our way through it. Bullets were whizzing past in showers, and we dashed out as quickly as we could. The first officer to greet me on shore was. Sub-Lieutenant Bernard Melland, R.N.V.R. (nephew of Mr. Asquith). His arm was in a sling, and I found that. two of his fingers were badly injured by a bullet. And now we found ourselves on the other side of that screen of smoke, and on Turkish ground.

I will never forget what I saw. One hundred corpses lay in rows on the sand, some of them so badly mauled as to be beyond recognition. All over the strip of sand, and on ledges of rock, wherever any cover could be got, men lay about wounded, cut, bleeding and dying. Some of the Lancashires lay dead half-way up the cliffs, still holding their rifles in their cold, clenched hands. Dead and wounded lay about, mixed up together.

Away to the left, among some rocks, stood twenty or thirty Turkish prisoners, with some of my men of the Anson Battalion mounting

Big Turkish Gun on the fort near Sedd-El-Bahr, smashed by the Fleet.

guard.

The whole beach was soaked in human blood, and for fifty yards out the very sea was crimson. But it was no time for looking around; it was the time for action, I went at once to the wounded, and assisted the R.A.M.C. as best I could. To my astonishment, I found that I was the first chaplain ashore, none of the Army chaplains having yet arrived. From man to man I went, ministering to their needs as best I could. The great cry in that hour of anguish was "Water! Water! For God's sake a drink." With many a man I repeated a last prayer to God, and over many said the Last Prayers of the Church, But the full story of those first hours on the beach can never be written; much of it is too sacred to repeat, and it will descend with me to the grave.

CHAPTER 15

On The Turkish Shore

When I had done what I could for the wounded, who were lying all over the beach and cliffs, I turned my attention to the dead. A staff-officer came up and said they should be buried as soon as possible, and so twenty Turkish prisoners were ordered to dig graves, while four sentries kept guard over them. I was told to superintend the arrangements, and under my direction a large pit was dug for the men, and a small grave for four officers.

It was nearly nine o'clock before they had finished, and darkness had closed in upon the strange scene. The bullets kept flying over our heads, the distant noise of battle never ceased. One by one the dead were carried up in waterproof sheets by the men of the R.AM.C,, the only light being a torch. Just as this ghastly work was completed, another chaplain landed, the Rev. H. A. Hall, Chaplain to the 29th Division. Mr. Hall was a true friend to me in those early, difficult days, and I will never forget the example he set of courage and steadfastness in danger.

It was a gruesome picture, this huge pit, five feet deep, containing eighty-four bodies of the fallen brave. Men of the Lancashire Fusiliers, of the Essex and Hampshire Regiments, together with men of the Fleet, lay here sleeping their last sleep. An orderly held up a torch over the grave, and simply I read the beautiful burial service of the Church of England. Never before had I read the words with feelings more intense: "*Blessed are the dead which die in the Lord, yea, saith the Spirit, for they rest from 'their labours.*" In the same way, but in a smaller grave close by, we buried four officers, three of them belonging to the Lancashire Fusiliers. We felt relieved when this sad work was done, knowing that the reinforcements, when they landed on the morrow, would not see the appalling sight which had greeted our eyes when we first reached the shore.

Meanwhile another chaplain had landed on the beach, the Rev. Hankin Hardy, Wesleyan *Padré* to the 29th Division, who proved to be a most devoted companion, and devoid of all sense of danger. Mr. Reid, a Presbyterian chaplain, had also landed on "Y" Beach.

Some of our men bivouacked on this memorable night on one side of the gully near Cape Helle. Many worked from early morning until eleven at night, but their work had been of a very different nature from what they had expected. Instead of acting as working parties on the various beaches, they had the honour of being called to fight side by side with the glorious 29th Division. The Lancashires, hampshires, Dublins and Munsters had lost so heavily that the officers and men of the Anson Battalion, Naval Division, went willingly to their assistance.

Tired out and very sleepy, I lay down to sleep about: 10.30 p.m., but was awakened at midnight to find that the Turks were making a furious counter-attack on the positions already won. A hail of lead was coming over us, when everyone was ordered into the trenches to help to hold the line. The crack of the Turkish rifles sounded nearer every minute, and at one juncture I wondered if they were going to drive us into the sea. I stayed beside the wounded on the beach, and I never remember passing a night of graver anxiety and terror than this. The groans of those in pain, and the din of battle coming closer and closer, made me consider what would be the best course to take in case of emergency.

Every now and then a star shell from the Turks would light up the whole scene, as if by lightning. Worn out by fatigue, I lay down and fell asleep again, but I could not sleep for very long, as the noise was unceasing, and the constant cries of "Ammunition here!" made it practically impossible.

Just before daybreak I noticed a man waist deep in water, helping the beach working party to get the guns ashore, and discovered it was Mr. Hankin Hardy, the Wesleyan Chaplain. Right gallantly he laboured, the bullets falling thick around him. At dawn, the guns of the fleet opened fire again with a terrific roar. This was a welcome sound, because we knew that the Turks could not stand very long in face of a heavy fire from the fleet. In spite of all our fears, our men had stood their ground well, especially the Lancashires, Essexes and Worcesters.

I was proceeding up the gully to get some breakfast, when I was narrowly missed by a sniper, the bullet missing me by inches. Several men saw my escape, and said: "That was a near shave, sir."

During the whole of Monday, April 26th, our men, together with bluejackets from the Fleet, were busily employed in the arduous task of getting the guns, stores and ammunition ashore, This task was cheerfully accomplished, although it was carried out under the burning sun, and under conditions which would have tried the patience of Job had he been in the transport department, So well was this work done that guns of the Royal Field Artillery were in action by midday—a remarkable achievement.

A great deal has been said and written on the landing of the British troops in Gallipoli, but in order to appreciate fully the difficulties and horrors of this great feat of arms, it was essential to have landed on the first day, April 25th. Of those of us who landed then, there are but few remaining who can tell the whole of the immortal story.

I have shown clearly, I hope, that only the Anson Battalion of the Second Naval Brigade landed with the 29th Division in the original landing, and that working parties, formed from this battalion, did excellent work on "W" and "V" Beaches, and earned the praise of all in authority. But let us turn for a minute to see what happened on the beach known as "X."

The troops who landed here were the 1st Royal Fusiliers, and with them was a beach working party formed from "D" Company, Anson Battalion, Lieutenant-Commander Gordon Grant, R.N.V.R., D.S.C., in command. These were all towed ashore under cover of the guns of H.M.S. *Implacable*, and this ship did one of the boldest things that was done on this great day. She stood close in to the beach, firing very rapidly with every gun she had; it looked as if this great floating fortress would ground, but somehow, she just managed to escape. The plan succeeded, the terrified Turks rushing in confusion out of their entrenchments on the top of the cliff. The Royal Fusiliers thus made good their landing with very few casualties; but the Anson men, under Lieutenant-Commander Grant, D.S.C., went up to their assistance in the trenches, when, towards nightfall, the fighting began to grow hot.

Meanwhile, the Hood Battalion was ordered to make a "feint" at a landing further north, up in the Gulf of Saros. This took place about midnight, April 25th-26th, and undoubtedly succeeded, in that many Turks were attracted by the noise made by the Hoods and by the flares which were lit on the shore.

The Hoods were still in the transport in which we had sailed from England, and on this occasion, destroyers accompanied it. Flare lights had to be ignited on the beach, and here Lieutenant-Commander B, C. Freyburg won the D.S.O. in carrying out his self-appointed task. It

The First Officers' grave on "W" Beach.
three of the officers of 1st Battalion Lancashire Fusiliers

had been arranged that a boat containing two or three men should be quietly rowed to the beach, and the flares set alight, but Lieutenant-Commander Freyburg pointed out that this plan would probably fail, as a boat could be heard for a considerable distance, "I'll swim it," he said, "and pull the flares ashore on a kind of raft arrangement." At first, those in authority thought he was joking, but finding he was in earnest, they at length gave way, and agreed that after dusk he should be allowed to make the attempt.

A fine, well-built man, with huge, muscular arms, and a set, determined face, Bernard Freyburg was exceedingly popular both with officers and men, who delighted almost as much as he did in his daredevil escapades. He it was who led the Naval Division in France, at the close of 1916, when they stormed Beaucourt, and for his gallantry and utter contempt of danger on that occasion he was awarded the Victoria Cross,

But to return to our story. Freyburg jumped off the transport in the dark, and, towing a small raft on which the flares were fastened in waterproof, struck out for the Turkish shore. One of the champion swimmers of New Zealand, it was not by any means a difficult thing for this man to swim the distance lying between the transport and the beach, just over a mile; but it was the fact that he was swimming to a hostile coast, where he might be accorded a very warm reception, that made the task precarious in the extreme.

On and on he swam, until at length the shore was reached. Those a mile out to sea on the transport waited with bated breath; presently a jet of light shone out from the coast. Freyburg had succeeded in setting alight the first flare. Quick as lightning he swam off, fired at by the enemy, who expected this was a signal for a heavy attack on his defences. Still undismayed the plucky swimmer swam through the icy-cold waters to point further down the coast and lit another flare, and then his task was done. Flinging himself into the water, he struck out for the transport, and only just in time, as the Turks, suddenly disturbed, came swarming on to the shore from their hiding places.

They fired into the black water, but without avail. Freyburg had been too quick for them, and in the darkness had made good his escape. Freyburg stuck at his task manfully, but to his dismay the current began to carry him out of his course, and it was only after swimming for two hours that he was picked up by the accompanying destroyer and conveyed to the transport, little the worse for his perilous adventure.

Brigadier-General Freyburg, V.C, D.S.O., as he is today, has seen and done many more daring deeds than the one I have just been describing, but the Naval Division will always feel proud to think that it once could claim him as one of its officers,

For the first ten days and nights our men continued to press the enemy—the guns of the fleet were firing almost continuously, and it was magnificent to see how they peppered the peak of Achi Baba, a hill 600 feet in height, which proved to be a veritable fortress, and which held the key to the conquest of Gallipoli.

The whole of the subsequent fighting consisted in attempts to take this hill, with the village of Krithia on its Western slopes,

Here I propose to copy a few pages from my diary as showing how our early days on the Peninsula were spent.

Tuesday, April 27th.—After a somewhat disturbed night, awoke about five o'clock, and went right up to the firing line to talk to the men. They said they had not had a bad time, and were quite cheerful. I saw a wounded Turk. He had been sniping; the doctor ordered his removal to the field dressing station. We were shelled with shrapnel today, but, fortunately, very few of the shells burst. It was rather funny to see people scattering in all directions, whenever they heard them coming. Went up to the trenches with three officers, and sat and talked with a major of the Lancashire Fusiliers. We had one shell right on us, but we ducked, and it passed ever our heads, Had a delightful bathe with the doctor and Lieutenant-Commander Anderson in the sea. The water was 'delicious'—it was no longer coloured red with blood. In the evening watched shells bursting near our trenches, with the doctor.

Wednesday, April 28th—Our men continued to press, and got to the foot of Achi Baba: we got some more prisoners today. Went over to "V" Beach with the doctor in the morning, and passed the forts; whose guns were silenced and put out of action by the fleet on the outbreak of war. They were large Krupp guns, mounted on concrete. I went into one of the gunners' shell-proof shelters, and it was littered with papers of various kinds, I took one of them, and it turned out to be a Turkish military official paper with some notes written in pencil on the back in Turkish.

I am greatly indebted to Dr. W. St. Clair Tisdall, the great Oriental scholar, for reading through this manuscript for me. It was found to contain nothing of very great interest, but probably refers to the firing of the pom-poms, which wrought such havoc amongst our men on "V" Beach. It is headed:—"Instruction concerning 27 millimeter automatic pom-poms." The first clause runs:—"The complement of these guns, along with the marksman, amounts to three men." It then explains what is to be done on certain words of command being given, and there is nothing of real importance.

Wednesday night, April 28th, was very wet; we covered ourselves up as best we could, but it was very damp and cold.

On the following day I took a stroll over the ground on which the recent fighting had taken place, and our Turkish interpreter accompanied me. Some fascinating, though rather gruesome, sights confronted us. Many Turks lay dead on the field, and the very way in which they were lying betokened the haste with which they had fled from their strong positions; the ground was littered with cartridges, spent and unspent, rifles and broken bayonets. It was necessary to keep a sharp look-out for snipers, many of whom remained still secure in their hiding places in the hedges and bushes with which Gallipoli abounds, and at any moment you were liable to be fired at.

It will readily be seen that a brigade chaplain's task is often far from easy. The officers and men to whom he has the privilege of acting as chaplain are frequently scattered about, and so it was on the Peninsula. The Howes and the Hoods did not land until three days after the Ansons, and, as it has been shown, the Ansons were divided up into working parties on the Beaches "W," "V" and "X." Therefore, having visited "W" and "V" Beaches, I determined to set off to wall to "X" Beach to see how Lieutenant-Commander Grant, D.S.C., and his men had fared. I started on the morning of Friday, April 30th, but had the misfortune to get on the sky-line. Shells commenced to whistle all around me, and the Turks probably thought I was an officer leading some reserves up to the front line. At last, it grew too hot to be pleasant, and I decided to postpone my visit for a time.

May 1st opened with glorious sunshine and a terrific bombardment of the Turkish trenches by the ships' guns and the R.F.A. The famous French "75's" had also been landed now, and undoubtedly gave the enemy a warmer time than he had bargained for.

The following message was received now from the General Officer Commanding-in-Chief:—

> General Headquarters,
> Mediterranean Expeditionary Force,
> April 28th, 1915.
>
> I rely on all officers and men to stand firm and steadfast to

resist the attempts of the enemy to drive us back from our present position, which has been so gallantly won. The enemy is evidently trying to obtain a local success before reinforcements can reach us; but the first portion of these will arrive tomorrow, and be followed shortly by a fresh division from Egypt. It behoves us all, French and British, to stand fast, hold what we have gained, wear down the enemy, and thus prepare for a decisive victory.

Our comrades in Flanders have had the same experience of fatigue after hard-won fights. We shall, I know, emulate their steadfastness and achieve a result which will confer added laurels to French and British arms.

Ian Hamilton, General.

We were asleep and in peace in our valises on the night of May 1st, when suddenly the din of battle increased and shells began bursting all over. Major Maxwell (our brigade major) turned up unexpectedly and awakened the officers with the command "Stand to arms."

Chapter 16

The Battle of the 6th of May

At the end of ten days' battling against the Turks, our men had pushed their way forward for some five thousand yards from the landing-places. Both sides had suffered heavy losses. It was evident that a still further advance would have to take place as soon as possible, as a gain of a few hundred yards or so meant a very great deal to us, crowded together as we were on a narrow tongue of land under constant shell fire.

The last chapter closed with an account of how the brigade-major came about midnight on May 1st-2nd. and told us to 'stand to arms." The fact was that some desperate fighting had taken place during the two previous days and nights, the Turks making frantic efforts to break through our line. Many of the troops were tired out and exhausted, especially the French on the extreme right, and it was to strengthen them that our men of the Anson Battalion were ordered up to the line. The battalion moved off to the reserve trenches about 2.30 am. It was a picturesque scene in the moonlight. Colonel Moorhouse marched at the head, and after the officers and men came the ammunition mules, then the doctor and myself, and the stretcher-bearers. Shells came flying across rather too frequently to be pleasant.

Passing over to "V" Beach, where the French Corps *Expéditionnaire* had placed their headquarters, we had to march through the village of Sedd-el-Bahr in order to reach our destination. This was the first opportunity I had of making an inspection of the village which had suffered so severely at the hands of our fleet on April 25th. It was an extraordinary scene of desolation and destruction; a whole row of houses lay in ruins, and on peeping in at the door of one of them, I formed some idea of what it once had looked like. The cooking in that Turkish home had been done at a kind of open range, and at the ruined hearth lay a broken spinning-wheel, a silent reminder of the

The 1st Lancashires having breakfast in the trench. Taken at 6 a.m. on April 28, 1915.

days when there was no war, and the women of all nations did their daily tasks quietly in their homes. Wooden rafters still held up a portion of the ceiling, and the room at one time might have resembled the kitchen of an English farmhouse.

Shells from the Turkish batteries kept shrieking over Sedd-el-Bahr, and bursting with terrific reports near the old castle, while French soldiers were sitting about amidst the shattered walls making their coffee, as unconcerned as if they were at a picnic. Making our way with difficulty along the shell-swept road, we arrived at length at a spot which was christened "Backhouse Post," after Commodore Oliver Backhouse, R.N., our gallant brigadier. There was a small hill close by, and behind it was the field-dressing station for English and French troops. Three men were wounded shortly after I arrived, one in the knee, one on the cheek, and another on-the ankle. The top of the hill behind which we were sheltering was being vigorously shelled, and we had to be careful as to where we placed our wounded. The French medical officers were working hard under difficult and dangerous circumstances, and I noticed that they tended some wounded Turks with as much care as they did their own men. The lighter cases, such as those with leg wounds, were placed on mules to be carried to the clearing station on "W" Beach.

We had no service on this first Sunday in May (May 2nd), as the whole brigade was in action up on the right of the line, and I felt that my place was with the wounded. Finding that I missed many cases by being too near the front line, I went back to the beach, where I was able to see all the wounded as they left the casualty clearing station. On the shore I saw Lieutenant Gamage (of the famous business house of that name) and some wounded men of the Hood and Howe Battalions. Some excitement was caused by a hostile aeroplane which dropped a bomb close to the Red Cross tents; it was said to have been aimed at the ammunition store,

On May 2nd I think I had one of my narrowest escapes. I was with a naval surgeon, who was in uniform, and who had landed at a small bay with some other surgeons (R.N.), in order to assist in the work of getting the wounded away to the hospital ships more expeditiously. We were walking uphill towards the reserve trenches, when a bullet whizzed past us, missing us by inches. Thinking it just a "stray," we went on; but presently another shot came straight for us, followed by another. This third bullet I thought had got me, it was so close. "Let us run for it," said the doctor; "there is a sniper shooting at us somewhere." So, we ran down to the bottom of the hill, and another shot whistled over our heads. However, we escaped safe and sound.

On the night of May 3rd there was some hard fighting, especially on the right, where the French were. The boom of the guns prevented any sleep. On May 4th a portion of the line still held by the French, who had lost heavily, was taken over by the 2nd Naval Brigade. Thus, this brigade, which it was intended to employ as beach working parties, found itself welded together into one whole again, and holding a portion of the front line. Our men had a hard and trying time during the night; fighting was incessant, and I found nine poor fellows of the Anson Battalion lying dead upon the high ground near De Tott's Fort. All were terribly mangled owing to shells, and one man had his head, legs and right arm shot away. We dug a grave near De Tott's Fort, and buried them as decently as we could. May 5th (Wednesday) passed fairly quietly, and everybody was talking of the great advance which was to take place on the morrow. I had a long talk with Arthur Tisdall in his dug-out, and it proved to be the last I was destined to have with my dear friend.

Facing the French Corps *Expéditionnaire* and the 2nd Royal Naval Brigade was a commanding ridge, running from north to south above the Kereves Dere. Sir Ian Hamilton says:

> A foothold upon this ridge was essential, as its capture would ensure a safe pivot on which the 29th Division could swing in making any further advance.

The 29th Division had for its first objective some ground on the south-east edge of the village of Krithia,

The days (May 6th–8th) were perhaps the most terrible that our troops had to pass through. At 11 a.m. on May 6th the bloody fight commenced, the 29th Division leading off. The French, together with my own brigade, followed suit at 11.30 a.m. It was a terrific and awful battle, the rifle and machine-gun fire being very heavy all along the line, while showers of shrapnel were continually pouring down upon our trenches. The officers and men of the 2nd Naval Brigade fought most heroically, and had pushed forward for a considerable distance, but at a great price. Colonel Quilter (Grenadier Guards), of the Hoods, was killed, and many of his men. The Ansons had also lost heavily in the action, Lieutenant Charles Anderson, R.N.V.R., in command of "B" Company, being shot through the heart; Sub-Lieutenant Tisdall also fell in the thick of the fighting.

Sub-Lieutenant Brian Trevor Melland, R.N.V-R., nephew of Mr. Asquith, was also killed. He had advanced with his platoon up to a notable landmark known as the "White House," which was little more than a ruined cottage. Whilst standing in one of its shattered rooms he chanced to drop his field-glasses on the ground, and stooped to pick them up; he never rose again, but fell heavily to the earth. In a moment Lieutenant Waller (son of Mr. Lewis Waller) ran to his side and found that he was dead, a sniper having shot him in the region of the heart. Thus ended a most promising career. If a trifle impetuous, Brian Melland showed indomitable courage in the way he led his men forward, and his fine manliness, his love of fair-play, and his beautiful, unselfish character, endeared him to all his friends.

Never had the doctors a more strenuous time in discharging their duties than now. Wounded were pouring in without ceasing. I went to the field dressing station, and found the brigade surgeons with more cases almost than they could attend to individually, Surgeon Ballance, R.N. (Ansons), Surgeon Schlesinger, R.N. (Howes), and Surgeon Mc-Cracken (Hoods) did magnificent self-denying work, and had been practically without sleep for four nights. They kept cheery, however, amidst their trying work, and the expeditious way in which their duties were performed was beyond all praise.

I went on seeing the wounded until dusk, and then lay down to try and sleep for a few hours. Meanwhile a constant hail of bullets was coming over from the Turkish trenches, and even in the field-dressing station a man was shot who was standing next to me. The battle was not by any means over yet—still harder fighting lay in front of our men.

Chapter 17

Life in Gallipoli During May, 1915

It has been shown already that the month of May opened with a violent assault on the Turkish entrenchments, which was followed by frantic efforts on the enemy's part to retaliate. Such severe fighting meant heavy losses on both sides.

A chaplain, perhaps more than anybody else, sees the seamy side of war, if I may be allowed to use such an expression; one of the saddest tasks that falls to his lot must always be the burial of the dead. On May 7th I read the burial service over the body of Lieut.-Colonel Quilter (Grenadier Guards), who was in command of the Hood Battalion, This brave officer was laid to rest at about eight o'clock in the morning, in the presence of Commodore Backhouse and the staff of the 2nd Naval Brigade, A firing-party from his battalion fired three volleys over the grave as their last token of respect, and the buglers sounded the "*Last Post*," this being the only occasion, as far as I know, on which an officer in Gallipoli was buried with full military honours, Shortly after, I buried Lieutenant Waller, of the Howe Battalion, in the same place. Both funerals took place in a dangerous spot, under a hail of shrapnel, but we managed to get through without a casualty,

Meanwhile, as our men pushed back the Turks, it was necessary that the field-dressing station should be placed in a more advanced position. We moved this time to "The Brown House," an old farm shattered by shell fire, Here I assisted the doctors in getting bandages ready for emergencies.

About 5.30 on the evening of May 8th a vigorous bombardment took place again on the enemy's trenches by every available gun. The din was indescribable, and the whole of Achi Baba was hidden by smoke and dust. A general advance took place after this, and some ground was gained by both British and French. Close to my dug-out there was a battery of Australian guns, and I frequently chatted to the men in the evenings. In the very thick of the fight, I had to bury one of their gunners. It was a touching sight, the men for a few minutes just leaving the gun he had helped so often to fire, in order to pay their last homage.

Mention has been made several times of our popular Brigade-Major, Lieutenant-Colonel Maxwell, and here I must tell of his unfortunate death. He knew no fear, and, in spite of the fact that he wore the red tabs which are always associated with the Headquarters Staff, went about his duties without thinking of his personal safety. Just behind the firing-line he was going his rounds in the early hours of Sunday, May 9th, when he was shot through the heart by a sniper. He was popular with all ranks; we admired him as a soldier, we loved him as man. To many he was known as "the brains" of the brigade, and there is no doubt that it was largely owing to Lieutenant-Colonel Maxwell's knowledge and experience that we met with such astonishing success in the field, His body lay in such a dangerous place that it was impossible to move it, and he was buried quietly at the spot where he fell,

The Officer Commanding the Anson Battalion, Colonel Moorhouse, D.S.O., C.M.G., was chosen to be brigade-major, and Major Roberts, late of the Royal Artillery, was placed in command of the Ansons. War brings many changes, but the saddest, perhaps, are those brought about in the field through death. Major Stuart, D.S.O., now took command of the Hood Battalion, in place of Colonel Quilter.

It has been shown that the officers and men of the Second Naval Brigade had been fighting continuously, practically without a rest, from April 25th, the day of the landing, to May 13th, and it was with great joy they heard on that day that they were to have a well-deserved rest. In the afternoon of that day, we moved to a "Rest Camp" on a small plateau in a pleasant, but rather exposed, position. In spite of shells we all enjoyed a good long sleep.

Next day (Friday, May 14th) we had a great honour conferred upon us. General d'Amade, in command of the French Corps *Expéditionnaire de l'Orient*, came to our Rest Camp and reviewed us. At the close he said he had come there to thank us for the support we had given to the French troops on the right of the line. He was deeply grateful, and thanked us in the name of France. Just as he concluded his speech a shell burst not more than twenty yards from where we were standing, drawn up in line, and a large lump of earth struck me in the back. Needless to say, the visit paid to us by the French general and his staff gave us all great satisfaction and pleasure. The general also told us that he had despatched the following message to the General Officer Commanding-in-Chief (Sir Ian Hamilton):

"In accordance with your orders I am returning the 2nd Naval Brigade to the Composite Division. It is my pleasant duty to place on record how much I have appreciated the brilliant military qualities, the devotion to duty, the courage and intrepidity of the three valiant battalions—Anson, Howe and Hood—of which it is composed. It is a great honour and a great satisfaction to me to have had during the 6th, 7th, 8th and 9th of May the devoted, active and ever-ready collaboration of Commodore Backhouse, an officer who has inspired his troops with those noble qualities to which every French soldier who has seen them at work renders homage."

Our new camp was called a Rest Camp, but we had not been there longer than a few hours when we found that this name was somewhat misleading. Every day we had what the men called "*Our morning and evening 'Hymn of Hate'*" This consisted of a heavy bombardment, which began about 6 a.m. and lasted till 9 or 10 a.m., and then recommenced about 6 p.m., and went on till dusk, Many of the Turkish shells, however, failed to explode; but when they did some distressing scenes were witnessed. Many poor fellows were killed as they lay in their dug-outs enjoying a rest.

I remember one Sunday afternoon three men were having a sleep in one dug-out. A shell came over from the direction of Achi Baba, without warning and burst close by; the fuse fell on to the man who was sleeping in the middle and smashed his skull, killing him instantaneously, while the others on either side of him were untouched. I myself had several very narrow escapes from shells, especially shrapnel.

One evening towards the end of May we gave a dinner party to celebrate the promotion of our colonel to a Staff appointment. We were having a few days' rest, after heavy fighting, and had taken a great deal of trouble to get as sumptuous a repast as circumstances would allow. The menu would astonish housewives, considering it was provided on the inhospitable shore of Gallipoli:—

Vegetable Soup.
Fried Steak, French Beans and Potatoes
(obtained from the French),
Jam Omelette.
Sardines on Toast.
Dessert.

Although it was eaten on tin plates, it was the best meal we had while on active service, and reflected great credit on the colour-sergeant (Royal Marines) who cooked it. Just as we had sat down and were drinking the soup there was a terrific report, followed by a hail of shrapnel bullets of various sizes. We all fell on the ground, and had a miraculous escape; but when the smoke had cleared away, we found that twenty-two men were wounded by this one shell, so for a short time our dinner-party was interrupted. The shell was afterwards found to have been fired by one of the enemy's 5.9in. guns; it was a well-placed shot, and had we not been sitting under a large tree, with thick branches, the casualties amongst officers might also have been serious.

The tables consisted of ration-boxes turned upside down, and on some of them the tin plates were riddled with holes, thus showing how narrow our escape had been. This was not an isolated instance, but in Gallipoli we were continually shelled. A soldier in France has his period in the trenches, and then comes a time of rest in a place where he is comparatively safe, In Gallipoli there was no safety, no getting away from shell-fire, and this fact is overlooked, perhaps, by the general public. One of the amazing things, which it is a pleasure to record, is the fact that amidst all the hardships and dangers in Gallipoli our men kept cheerful and hopeful. The menu I have just given was for a very special occasion, and our fare on ordinary days was the usual bully beef, or tinned stew known as "Maconochie." It became very monotonous, but it was not that we objected to so much as the swarms of flies, which made us almost dread meal-times.

Censoring letters took up a great deal of time, and I sat beneath the burning sun every day engaged on this task for hours on end. Meanwhile the guns were never silent on sea and land, and the question that we asked each other daily was: "Shall we ever get to the top of Achi Baba?"

General D'amade thanking 2nd R.N. Brigade for supporting the French on the right.

CHAPTER 18

A Chaplain's Work in Gallipoli

The short history that I have been trying to give of our experiences in the Near East has dealt so far with the material side of things. In this chapter I propose to deal with the spiritual—with a chaplain's work.

During the earliest days on the Peninsula services were out of the question, because everybody was either fighting or working by day and night. The exigencies of the time called for the undivided attention of every officer and man, otherwise the enemy might have driven us from his coasts into the sea.

There were but few chaplains who landed during the first four or five days, and they found that their work, for the most part, consisted in burying the dead, of whom, unfortunately, there were hundreds, and in ministering to the sick and dying.

In France it frequently falls to the chaplain's lot to have to provide concerts and entertainments for his brigade, but in Gallipoli this was an impossibility, because the whole Peninsula was swept by heavy shell-fire, and any gathering of men would be quickly seen from the enemy's observation posts on Achi Baba and as quickly broken up by his guns. I managed, however, to obtain a supply of illustrated papers and magazines, and the daily newspaper of one sheet, entitled "*The Peninsula Press*," which was printed by the Royal Engineers and sent round to every battalion, proved to be exceedingly popular. I pinned it up in the centre of our Rest Camp on a large tree trunk, where it was eagerly scanned by a large crowd.

The first service I attended was a celebration of Holy Communion for the Nelson Battalion at 7.30 a.m. on Saturday, May 15th. There were about twenty present. The celebrant was the Rev. Bevill Close, who was attached to the Headquarters Staff. While the *Prayer of Consecration* was being said, a shell burst only a few yards off the place where we were kneeling. It was wonderful how the men got accustomed to these strange happenings, and I noticed on this occasion that no one flinched. Mr. Close was ordained deacon in York Minster on the same day as myself, and proved to be a true *padré*, visiting his flock at all hours, and showing his utter contempt for danger. Next day (Sunday, May 16th) was a busy one for me. I celebrated Holy Communion, in a field near the Rest Camp, for the Anson, Hood and Howe Battalions, at 6.30 a.m., when there was an excellent attendance.

Major Stuart, D.S.O., in command of the Hoods, was present with several other officers, and over forty men made their communion. It was a sight never to be forgotten. 'There, in the early morning, amidst the bursting shells, knelt four rows of khaki-clad men in the presence of the Master, solemnly committing both themselves and their loved ones at home into His keeping. The silence, broken every now and then by the thunder of the guns on land and sea was most impressive; indeed, the whole service was a marvellous spiritual experience, such as clergymen may have only once in a lifetime.

It is at these times, more than at any other, that one realises the privilege of being a chaplain, To quote from one of the war-poems in "*The Spectator*":—

In the pale gleam of new-born day,
Apart in some tree-shadowed place,
Your altar but a packing-case.
Rude as the shed where Mary lay;
Your sanctuary the rain-drenched sod,
You bring the kneeling soldier—God.

At 9.30 a.m. came a service for the Howe Battalion, at which all Church of England men were obliged to be present. The men sat in their dug-outs, all round the chaplain, and joined heartily in the hymns. After a short address, I walked over to the Royal Engineers' Camp near the Krithia Road, and asked if I could give them a service. I will never forget the hearty greetings of their colonel, who said: "How delighted I am that we are to have a service. You are the first chaplain I have seen on the Peninsula." Hymn books were quickly distributed, and a nice, bright service followed. Then came a Communion service at noon, with thirty communicants.

In the afternoon I went up to Sub-Lieut. B.T Melland's grave, and read the burial service, as it had not been read before. The rest of the day was spent in censoring the men's letters home, of which there were many on Sundays when they were in the rest camp.

But perhaps a chaplain's most interesting and most useful work lay in individual talks with the officers and men. A man is the same man on active service as he is when living in his parish at home, but fellowship in risk and danger will often cause a man to open his heart to the *padré* in a way such as he never would to an ordinary parish priest. I have had many talks with men on religious matters, but the amount of individual work done depends largely on the chaplain himself and the men to whom he ministers. It was my aim to try and impress the men that I was not an officer to be dreaded, but a friend to be trusted, to whom they could bring all their worries and troubles, knowing that they would find a sympathetic ear.

There is no doubt whatever that the happy relationship existing between the chaplain and his men has done a great deal towards breaking down the fences of "standoffishness" and formality which for so long have stood between the parson and the working man. The war has thus been of service to the Church to an extent which perhaps is not yet realised by the clergy and laity at home, but which, I venture to say, will be realised before the age of the new democracy passes away. In Gallipoli there were chaplains for Anglicans and Roman Catholics, and for the men of other religious bodies, and it is pleasant to record that we lived together in godly union and concord, In the face of major agreements we could afford to forget minor differences.

For once we were content to look at the great things that matter. There was no throwing away of principles, but a keen desire on the part of all chaplains to be friends, however greatly they might differ one from another. It was refreshing to see the Roman Catholic Chaplain, Father le Gros, and his brother chaplain, Dr. Ewing, Presbyterian, walking about arm in arm at the casualty clearing station on "W" Beach,

I myself received many kindnesses at the hands of Roman Catholic and Nonconformist chaplains, When visiting "W" Beach from the front, Mr. Hankin Hardy, the Wesleyan *Padré*, never allowed me to go back without giving me a meal, and when I was seeing the wounded at the Field Ambulance, when a battle was in progress in the early hours of the morning, I was frequently given a meal and told to rest by Father Green (Roman Catholic) or Mr. Hardy (Wesleyan) in their dugouts.

On Whit-Monday we had a conference of all the Church of England chaplains on the Peninsula. This opened with a celebration of

Holy Communion at 8.30 in a tent close to "W" Beach, the officiating priest being Mr. Beardmore, senior chaplain to the Forces. This was followed by the conference itself at 10 a.m., to which every chaplain was invited, I breakfasted that day with Mr. Creighton, son of the late Bishop of London, who was chaplain to the 86th Brigade of the 29th Division.

At our meeting many important matters were discussed, and among them the burial of Turks. Many bodies of Turks lay behind the line, and were being buried daily, and the question at issue was whether or not we should hold a short service over their graves. After quite an animated debate, it was agreed that no Mohammedan should be buried without a short service, in which the Lord's Prayer should form a part.

The happy relationship existing between chaplains representing all Christian bodies was noticed by officers and men, and is still being taken account of in France. Someday the men will return home, and will they see a continuance of this happy friendship when the war is over? It is to be hoped so, because only by this means will the Church of the future be that power, she ought to be among the masses of the people.

A great deal of a chaplain's work lies in ministering to the wounded, and he either accompanies the doctors to the field dressing station, situated as near to the firing-line as safety permits, and even then, the position is often far from secure, or remains at the casualty clearing station, where he may get into closer touch with the members of his flock. His place is not in the firing-line, except when he goes up to visit his men, who appreciate his visits, and say he is "one of the right sort."

On the 18th of May, 1915, I remember the experiences I had during heavy fighting. Our battalions began to advance against the foe, and succeeded in pushing him back some 500 yards. This was at nine o'clock at night, and we had many casualties. A battle at night always seems more horrible and weird than daylight fighting, and so it was on this occasion, Every now and then came flashes from the guns, and in the dressing-stations were the doctors at work, with their small electric-lamps providing the light. Amidst the din of battle came the moaning of those in pain.

The battle had not lasted long before the stretcher-bearers began to arrive with some serious cases. First came a man with a compound fracture of the skull, another with a bullet in his lung, another with a broken thigh. They were wonderful men, both surgeons and patients, and I will never forget the patience, endurance and coolness of all concerned.

Suddenly a man was brought in, shot through the back; he was in fearful pain, the bullet having lodged somewhere in the region of the heart. He had lost a lot of blood, and appeared to be dying. He was very brave, and in all his sufferings made not a single complaint; he looked up at the doctor and said: "Oh! when will I be well enough to go back to my chums in the line!" Such was the spirit of the men who took part in the great landing. I remember the magnificent efforts that were made to save this man's life by Surgeon Schlesinger, R.N., who fought death for two hours. He gave the man hypodermic injections; morphia was tried, strychnine, hot coffee—in fact everything was done in that dug-out for the patient that could have been done in a London hospital, but suddenly the doctor shook his head and said sadly, "Too late!" The man had passed away to that bourne whence no traveller returns.

I have pointed out already the fact that the field dressing station was frequently in a dangerous position, and under fire. We had the misfortune to lose two of our doctors in two days. Surgeon Schlesinger, R.N., was shot through the hand on May 20th, and Surgeon McCracken (Hoods) was wounded in the belly next day. The latter was sitting on a box, upon which I always sat to have my lunch, when he was hit by a sniper and badly wounded. I had accompanied Surgeon Ballance, R.N., on a walk to "W" Beach, and had I been in the doctor's place I should have received the bullet. As it was, we all had narrow escapes from death, and I was nearly hit when on my way to bury one of the Howe battalion just behind the reserve trenches. Bullets were flying all around me, and I had to run and take cover.

It was exceedingly difficult at times to minister to the wounded, the noise being deafening, and, as a Wesleyan chaplain put it to me, "Most of my ministrations so far have taken the form of giving a man a cigarette." And yet even that was no mean service, for a smoke proved to be an inestimable boon under such circumstances,

I have shown that the field dressing station was in a dangerous position, and that two doctors had already been wounded, and it was a matter of regret to me that I was told on future occasions not to go nearer the front line than the field ambulance. A command is a command in the Service, and, therefore, I was obliged to obey, although I did so reluctantly. The exact wording of the order was as follows:—

The commodore is of opinion that during the period that the brigade is occupying the front line trenches it is advisable that you should remain with the field ambulance, to which the wounded men of the brigade are brought as soon as possible.

I sent in a request after this to be allowed to go nearer the front, but without success.

During the time I acted as chaplain I had some unique experiences, and was called upon to do some strange things—to write a letter for an elderly man to his nagging wife, and for a young man to his sweetheart. There is a great deal that is humorous in a chaplain's life, and much that is pathetic. The doctor is with a man up to a certain point, and then hands him over to the chaplain, The *padré* is with the men all through, even when it comes to the end.

I have seen many men die, but I do not think that I ever saw men pass to the other side so peacefully as the men who died amidst the noise and din of the battlefield. With many it was the peace of sins forgiven through the Precious Blood, and the knowledge that they had given themselves for the dear ones at home and that beloved land which they were never to see again. I agree with a great Nonconformist preacher:—

We can leave those who die for England in the hands of Him who died for the world.

It must have been a comfort to many a mother in England to know that her son was not alone when it came to the crossing of the dark river, to know that at the very time when men look for "some last loved hand to hold," the Holy Church was there in the person of her priest, with outstretched hand, and to know that someone tenderly committed his soul into the Father's care.

CHAPTER 19

Events Previous to the Battle of June 4

On May 9th, 1915, General Sir Ian Hamilton wrote from General Headquarters:—

Sir Ian Hamilton wishes the troops of the Mediterranean Expeditionary Force to be informed that in all his past experiences, which include the hard struggles of the Russo-Japanese campaign, he has never seen more devoted gallantry displayed than that which has characterised their efforts during the past three days. He has informed Lord Kitchener by cable of the bravery and endurance displayed by all ranks here, and has asked that the necessary reinforcements be forthwith despatched. Meanwhile the remainder of the East Lancashire Division is disembarking, and will henceforth be able to help us to make good and improve upon the positions we have so hardly won.—

E. M. Woodward, Brigadier-General.

Throughout the month of May, the 2nd Naval Brigade took its place in the front line trenches at regular intervals, and when its officers and men were not in the fighting-line they were busily engaged on fatigue duties. It has been shown that their courage and devotion to duty was recognised by the French general and his staff, and by the general officer commanding-in-chief. Whenever they fought, they succeeded in driving the enemy from his strongholds, and gained the praise and approbation of the regular troops fighting by their side. It is not surprising, therefore, that Colonel Moorhouse, D.S.O., on relinquishing his command of the Anson Battalion in order to become brigade-major, wished to address a few words to the battalion. He made the following speech on May 25th to the officers and men, drawn up in the gully close to the rest camp:—

> Commander Grant, officers and men of the Anson Battalion—The day before we last went into the trenches, I received from the commander-in-chief a copy of a letter which had been addressed to him by General d'Amade, commanding the French troops on the Peninsula, and also a copy of General Ian Hamilton's reply to General d'Amade. General d'Amade, in his letter, pays a very special and glowing tribute to the services rendered by the Anson Battalion to the French troops during the four days we were on the right of the French line. General Ian Hamilton, in reply, thanked General d'Amade, and said he recognised the high compliment that was being paid us by such praise from one of the principal Generals in France. I have taken this, the first opportunity of getting you all together, to give you the contents of these two letters.
>
> I would like to add that you, officers and men, since you landed on the Peninsula, have raised the name of the Anson Battalion to a position equal to that of any other battalion out here; it remains with you to keep its name in the high place to which you have lifted it, and to explain gently but firmly to any recruits that may join you that it is their first duty, too. Since we landed, we have lost many dear and valuable friends; we mourn their loss, but must console ourselves with the fact that their names are written on the Roll of Honour. In conclusion I wish to say that although I only commanded you for a short time, I am very, very proud of having been privileged to do so.

The closing words were interrupted by a really hearty British cheer, which must have re-echoed over the slopes of Achi Baba.

Towards the close of May the shelling became heavier than before, and we all had narrow escapes from death. Lieutenant-Commander Grant, D.S.C., was badly wounded by shrapnel on May 26th, while taking a walk in the evening close to the rest camp, and was removed to a hospital ship.

During the month of May a large number of Turkish prisoners were captured, most of them being dejected and morose. Having with us an Armenian who acted as Turkish interpreter, I learnt from him a few sentences, so that I could address them in their native tongue. The conversation, as a rule, commenced with the question:—"*Ismin Nédir?*" or "What is your name?" On several occasions I visited wounded Turks, but was unable to make much progress with them. There is not a shadow of doubt that the Turk has proved himself to be a much cleaner fighter than the Prussian. I know of several authentic cases where three or four of our wounded have been found in a Turkish trench. The Turks had bound up their wounds and treated them with every consideration.

One day a Turk was carried in to our Clearing Station on "W" Beach, badly wounded. The doctor said: "I am too busy to attend to him immediately."

"Well, sir," said the stretcher-bearers, "he was found crawling about on his belly, with a broken thigh, giving water to our wounded."

An officer of the Lancashire Fusiliers informed me that he found some wounded Turks in a trench, bound up their wounds, put a coat under their heads, and did what he could for them. Before being carried away they kissed his hand in gratitude, A Staff officer (Royal Artillery) told me, in spite of what people said to the contrary, our bombardments had a terrible effect on the Turks. He himself went into a small trench, after the heavy bombardment on June 28th, and saw five Turks lying dead without a scratch on them, all having been killed through concussion. Piles of dead Turks lay about all over, and some of the trenches were filled with corpses up to the parapet. He also said he had to interview, through the interpreter, a Turkish officer, who was trembling in every limb, and looking bewildered and dazed through the effects of the heavy gunfire. He seemed at times almost an idiot, and the sight was pitiable in the extreme.

The same officer gave me an account of two extraordinary escapes from shells he had seen, He saw three mules one day being driven along by an Indian, and a shell came and burst very near, The Indian left his charges and ran away a few yards. Suddenly another shell came and blew the middle mule to bits, all except its head, which was left hanging on the rope in between the other two, which were only slightly hurt. The other incident took place on "W" Beach. A shell burst and knocked a man over; and, on seeing this, another man, who was sitting in his dug-out at the time, ran out to his assistance. While he was attending to the man, another shell fell right in his dug-out and blew it to pieces. A fortunate escape indeed!

Towards the end of May, the flies and other insects began to be almost unbearable. There were literally millions and millions of swarms of these pests, and unfortunately Gallipoli provided an excellent feeding ground for them. At meal times, when your plate of stew was placed in front of you, it was generally half-cold, with the result that it was covered by a huge, crawling, black mass before you had time to sit down. If you tried to beat them off, they returned in greater numbers, I will not enter into too many details, as they are too horrible to write about, but everyone knows that wherever there are flies there will soon be maggots, too; and the effects on the wounded, many of whom had to lie out in the burning sun for, perhaps, a whole day, can be better imagined than described.

And then there was the dust of Gallipoli. There was a stiff breeze blowing, as a rule, from Achi Baba towards the sea, and with it came large quantities of dust, which found its way into our food and clothing, adding considerably to personal discomfort. With the breeze came, also, the smell of dead men. It will go down to the lasting credit of the Government that we were kept well supplied with tobacco and matches, and had, it not been for this, it is my firm opinion there would have been a far more serious outbreak of disease than there was, and life would have been well-nigh intolerable. Cigarettes were scarce at times, but there was a plentiful supply of pipe-tobacco of good quality.

The food supplied to us was wonderfully good considering the immense difficulties of transport and the great heat. In the early days we had hardships to undergo, but they were not as severe as those borne so patiently by the men of the First Expeditionary Force in France in 1914. The staple fare consisted of bacon, bully-beef, biscuits, and Maconochie Rations. Later on, we received good bread from the Australian bakery near "X" Beach, and fruit and vegetables could be procured from Greeks, who brought them from the islands in the Ægean Sea, but only in small quantities.

"Swopping" was a game the men delighted in whenever a Frenchman appeared. They would point to the tin of jam with which they had just been supplied, and shout: "*Confiture! Confiture!*" It ended in the tin of jam being exchanged either for a small bottle of wine or a piece of fresh steak. It is universally known now that out of every dozen tins of army jam ten will be marked "Plum and Apple." To the men's disgust the Frenchman found this out after a time, and would only play "the swopping game" when there was a tin of strawberry or raspberry jam to be bartered.

Throughout the hard fighting of May and June one could not fail to be filled with intense admiration for our wonderful men. They kept cheerful and good-humoured even in Gallipoli, and that is saying a very great deal.

CHAPTER 20

The Battle of the Fourth of June

A brigade consists of four battalions, and it will have been noticed in this history that so far mention has been made only of three battalions in the 2nd R. N. Brigade, namely, the Anson, Hood and Howe. The fourth was the Collingwood, and it was practically a new battalion. The original Collingwood Battalion had the misfortune to be interned, almost to a man, in Holland, during the retreat from Antwerp. Thus, when the other three battalions had completed their training, and were prepared to face the enemy, the Collingwoods were still getting themselves ready at the R.N. Division camp in Dorsetshire. They arrived in Gallipoli in the early hours of May 30 (Sunday), and came to our Rest Camp to sleep.

On that Sunday morning it was impossible for me to have a service, as it was imperative: that the bodily needs of the officers and men should be attended to, The Collingwoods for the moment were without stores, and so we gave them some breakfast, and I remember very well the happy crowd of officers, who sat round the ammunition boxes which formed our table, laughing and joking as they ate their biscuits and bacon.

While the Collingwoods were preparing for their baptism of fire, the other battalions were taking their spell in the trenches. On the morning of June 1st, therefore, I went up to visit them. It was known that a great attack was going to be made within the next three or four days. The line was quiet—perhaps it was the lull before the storm—and in the second line trenches. men were sitting about playing games and reading, with their rifles within easy reach. Next day (June 2nd) they came back to the Rest Camp for a short spell before serious work began. Meanwhile the Collingwoods were having their first taste of real warfare.

During the closing days of May, 1915, our men were occupying their time in trying to work up within rushing distance of the enemy's first line trenches.

On May 25th the Royal Naval Division, together with the 42nd Division, had crept 100 yards nearer to the Turks, and on the night of May 28-29 a still further advance took place along the whole British line. It was welcome news when we heard that same night that the French troops had captured a redoubt on the extreme Turkish left. Every night after this up to June 3-4 the enemy tried his utmost to drive us back and to re-take the redoubt, but without success.

On June 3rd two young officers, who had been wounded early in May, returned to us, and no sooner had they greeted us than there was a loud cry of "Mails!" They arrived at an opportune moment, because many were destined to read their last letters from home. How often have I lived over again those last hours! The feeling of uncertainty and unrest was more marked on this occasion than at any previous time, and every officer and man felt that he was, as it were, standing on the edge of the precipice of fate.

And yet everyone tried to be light-hearted and happy, but somehow it was a happiness that was unreal. That evening, at dinner, the commodore came quite unexpectedly to give Major Roberts, the officer commanding the Ansons, his orders for next day's great battle. Shortly afterwards Captain Spearman, R.N., commanding the Collingwoods, came to find out some information. He was a fine, well-built man, but rather too old for active service. Several officers, I remember, came and gave me their addresses in case they should be killed.

On Friday, June 4th, about 2.30 a.m., the Anson Battalion moved off to battle. In many a reverie since then have I seen the picture and heard the tramp of feet. The light was dim, but I could make out the various officers and men as they waved farewell.

About eight o'clock in the morning our heavy guns began bombarding the Turkish position, and this lasted till 10.30 a.m. At 11 a.m. the bombardment recommenced and lasted till 11.20, when a feint attack was made which caused the enemy to waste needlessly a considerable quantity of ammunition. About 11.45 every gun we had was in action, and two warships assisted. This bombardment, although it was a small affair compared to the gunfire in France we read of nowadays, was the most intense I ever remember. The ground shook with concussion, and the noise was almost indescribable, whilst the shrieking of the shells overhead would have struck terror into anyone unaccustomed to modern warfare.

Precisely at 12 noon the artillery began to increase their range, and our infantry fixed bayonets and advanced along the whole line. It was an extraordinary scene, shells bursting all over the Turkish trenches and on every part of Achi Baba. The fire from the rifles and machine-guns sounded very terrible, and the advance, through clouds of dense smoke, proved to be one of great danger and difficulty. To add to the discomfort of the fighting it was a boiling hot day, and the swarms of flies were almost unbearable.

Everywhere our men dashed forward with the greatest gallantry, with the exception of the extreme left of the French portion of the line, which was unable to gain an inch of ground, and this, unfortunately, proved disastrous, The Turks were in a most formidable position, and their entrenchments were cleverly constructed and very deep, going down in some parts to a depth of fifteen feet. German engineers had doubtless been at work.

This plan will show the exact position of the 2nd Naval Brigade:—

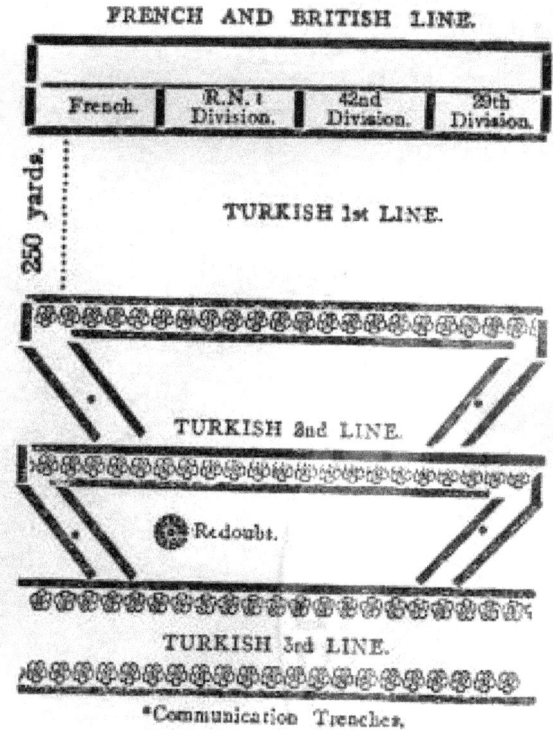

"Lieut.-Commander Spencer-Warwick, R.N.V.R., bringing in 'C' Company, Anson Battalion, after fourteen days incessant fighting on the right of our line." He and most of his men were killed on the 4th.

To quote from Sir Ian Hamilton's despatch:—

> The 2nd Naval Brigade of the Royal Nayai Division rushed forward with great dash; the Anson Battalion captured the southern face of a Turkish redoubt which formed a salient in the enemy's line, the Howe and Hood Battalions captured trenches fronting them, and by 12.15 p.m. the whole Turkish line forming their first objective was in their hands. Their consolidating party went forward at 12.25 p.m.

And now came a terrible blow. The French were forced to fall back, as the Turks were pouring in masses of men down prepared communication trenches, and as they retired the right flank of the Royal Naval Division was uncovered. To quote Sir Ian Hamilton's words:—

> Shortly before 1 p.m., the right of the 2nd Naval. Brigade had to retire with very heavy loss from the redoubt they had captured, thus exposing in their turn the Howe and Hood Battalions to enfilade, so that they, too, had nothing for it but to retreat across the open under exceedingly heavy machine-gun fire and musketry-fire. By 1.30 p.m. the whole of the captured trenches in this section had been lost again, and the brigade was back in its critical position, the Collingwood Battalion, which had gone forward in support, having been practically destroyed.

Thus, the positions, which the brigade had so hardly won, had to be given up through no fault of their own.

During the whole of this day, I was at the Field Ambulance seeing the wounded as they were brought in, and I stayed there until 2.30 next morning. For many reasons this was the most terrible day and night I remember in Gallipoli. In my own battalion seven dear friends lay dead on the battlefield—Major Roberts, our commanding officer; Lieutenant Henry, R.N.V.R., Adjutant; Lieutenant Commander Warwick, R.N.V.R.; Sub-Lieutenant Crow, Lieutenant Richmond, Lieutenant Frazer Brown, and Sub-Lieutenant Flood. In the Hood and Howe Battalions the losses were also terrible, Lieutenant Denis Browne and Lieutenant the Honourable Maurice Nelson Hood being killed. Captain Spearman, R.N., fell dead while leading his battalion into action, and at the close of the battle only two Collingwood officers were alive to tell the tale. The losses among the non-commissioned officers and men were also appalling, and after

June 4th the fighting strength of the 2nd Naval Brigade was reduced to just over one thousand,

My friend, Lieutenant A. P. Herbert, R.N.V.R. (Hawke Battalion), in his capital volume entitled "*Half-hours at Helles*," has described June 4th, this Red Day of Blood, in a striking verse:—

The flies! Oh God! the flies
That soiled the sacred dead.
To see them swarm from dead men's eyes
And share the soldiers' bread!!
Nor think I now forget
The filth and stench of War,
The corpses on the parapet,
The maggots in the floor.

All night long carts full of wounded were being brought along the Krithia road to the Field Ambulance, and with a small electric torch I helped the doctors to examine the cases and to see if any needed operating on immediately. Occasionally a face would light up, and a hand be held out from the cart, and I would recognise someone I knew, and then would follow some remark such as "Thank God, I am out of it." Sometimes stirring tales were told into my ear of how a friend had died, and yet it could be said of all that day they died, as every true British sailor and soldier would wish to die, with their faces towards Britain's foes,

At length, at 2.30 in the morning, the Wesleyan Chaplain, Mr. Halding, whose kindness I will never forget, absolutely insisted upon my lying down to sleep in a dug-out. In spite of the heavy gunfire, which had begun again, I slept, worn out with fatigue and sorrow. The next few days were spent, for the most part, in burying the dead and seeing the wounded. It was evident that, for the present, the brigade's fighting days were done; until fresh drafts arrived from England they would, be useless in the field. Officers and men were worn out, the nerves of some being absolutely shattered; and so they all returned to the Rest Camp on Sunday, June 6th, for one month. Lieutenant-Commander Stuart Jones, R.N.V.R., was temporarily in command of the Anson Battalion, and no one deserved this honour more than he, He had led his men with the utmost gallantry and devotion to duty, showing not the least sign of fear in the thick of the fighting.

The following message was received from the G.O.C., Major-General Paris, C.B.:—

The G.O.C. wishes to express his admiration of the gallant efforts made on June 4th by the 2nd Brigade, and his sympathy and regret for the sad losses incurred. No troops could have shown more devoted courage, and the failure to maintain the ground was in no sense their fault.

CHAPTER 21

After the Battle

On Sunday, June 6th, the 2nd R.N, Brigade return to the Rest Camp war-worn and tired. Most of my time was occupied in the melancholy task of burying the dead, The casualties had been so numerous it was imperative that something should be done towards reinforcing the brigade. For this purpose we had the Benbow Battalion, which was practically a fresh battalion from England, and the remainder of the Collingwood Battalion, consisting of two executive officers and 180 men, These gave up the titles of Benbow and Collingwood and were incorporated into the Anson, Hood and Howe Battalions, Thus Colonel Collins was still in command of the Howes, while Major Myburg was placed in command of the Hoods, and Major Bridges, R.M., in command of the Ansons.

The flies were becoming an intolerable nuisance and settled on the food at every meal, the result being many cases of dysentery. I myself fell ill about the end of June, and under such conditions, and in such a climate, an illness was exceedingly difficult to shake off. So bad were the swarms of flies in the officers' mess that two officers and myself began a little private mess of our own in a dug-out, which was far from ideal, but as good as we could expect in Gallipoli. These officers were the Hon. Kenneth Dundas, Lieutenant R.N.V.R., and Sub-Lieutenant Frewen, R.N.V.R., cousin of Mr. Winston Churchill. Between these officers and myself there sprang up a warm friendship.

On Sunday, June 13th, I celebrated Holy Communion at 6.30 a.m. beneath some shady trees; it was attended by one staff officer, two officers, and two men, in spite of the fact that there was a stiff breeze with large quantities of dust. I discovered that one of the men was a server at S. Barnabas', Pimlico. In the afternoon of this day, we were heavily shelled by a new gun from the Asiatic coast. It was of high velocity, and the shell—which was about a 6in. one—burst with terrific

At The Field Dressing Station, May 1915.

The Hon. Maurice Nelson Hood, Killed June, 4th

force into thousands of fragments,

Towards the end of June a Taube appeared over the Australian trenches and dropped large quantities of bills, on which the following message had been printed in ungrammatical English:—

> Protected by heavy fire of a powerful fleet, you have been able to land on the Gallipoli Peninsula on and since April 25th, 1915. Backed up by these men-of-war, you could establish yourselves at two points on the Peninsula. All your endeavours to advance into the inner part of the Peninsula have come to failure, under your heavy losses, although your ships have done their utmost to assist you by a tremendous cannonade, implying an enormous waste of ammunition. Two fine battleships, the *Triumph* and the *Majestic*, have been sunk before your eyes by submarines, Boats are protected by means against these, but being utterly insufficient. Since these severe losses to the British Navy, your men-of-war had to take refuge, and have abandoned you to your fate.
>
> Your ships cannot be possibly of any help to you in future, since a great number of submarines are prepared to suppress them. Your forces have to rely on sea transport for reinforcements and supply of food, water and every kind of war material. Already submarines did sink several steamers carrying supplies for your consumption; soon all supplies will be cut off from your landed forces. You are exposed to certain perdition by starvation and thirst. More desperate attacks will not avert the fate from you. You could only escape useless sacrifice of life by surrendering. We are assured you have not taken arms against us by hatred, Greedy England made you fight under a contract. You may confide in us for excellent treatment. Our country disposes of ample provisions; there is enough for you to feed you well and make you feel quite at your comfort. Don't further hesitate! Come and surrender! On all other fronts of this war your own people and your allies' situation is as hopeless as on the Peninsula.
>
> All news spread amongst you concerning the German and Austrian Armies are mere lies. There stands neither an Englishman, nor a Frenchman, nor a Russian on German soil. In the contrary, the German troops are keeping a strong hold on the whole of Belgium and a conspicuous part of France. Since many a

month a considerable part of Russian Poland is also in the hands of the Germans, who advance there every day, Early in May strong German and Austrian forces haye broken through the Russian centre in Galicia. Przemysl has fallen back into their hands lately. They are not in the least any handicapped by Italy joining your coalition, but are successfully engaged in driving the Russians in Galicia. These Russian troops, whose co-operation once made you look forward to, are surrendering in hundreds and in thousands. Do as they do! Your honour is safe! Further fighting is stupid bloodshed.

This somewhat craftily-worded document, which bears unmistakable signs of German concoction, caused much amusement among the Australian troopers, and made them more than ever determined to fight to the bitter end.

On Monday, June 21st, there was another terrific bombardment of the Turkish trenches for five or six hours, The French forces, after several vain attempts, succeeded in taking two lines of trenches on the right and a Turkish redoubt, and held what they had so gallantly gained. In this action the enemy suffered heavy losses, which were estimated at 7,000, together with 50 prisoners. The French casualties were 2,500.

After this heavy fighting it was natural that the Turkish authorities asked for a truce to bury their dead, and requested an English officer who could speak German to meet their emissary. Accordingly, Lieutenant the Hon. Kenneth Dundas, of the Anson Battalion, was chosen for this work, and went out under the Red Cross to the barbed wire, and for the first time was able to take a good look round "No Man's Land." He said it resembled a shambles, and was littered with Turkish dead. The stench was almost overpowering.

The Turk held out his hand, and they shook hands, whereupon he formally asked Lieutenant Dundas for an armistice. But it was that officer's mission to point out that previously the Turks had not kept good faith, having used the temporary truce to bring up machine-guns.

"This is terrible," said Lieutenant Dundas, pointing to the heaps of corpses rotting under the burning sun. "Although it is war-time, we are sorry this has to be."

The Turk replied, shrugging his shoulders, "Well, Great Britain started the war."

"Ah!" said the British envoy, "That is where we differ. The blame for that lies with Germany."

The Turk laughed, and said: "Well, as we cannot agree about it, perhaps you will have some Turkish cigarettes."

He handed the lieutenant some cigarettes, struck a match, gave him a light, and then proceeded: "Although I speak German well, I am not a German. I am a Turk. Great Britain has always been our friend in the past." He expressed the hope that he would meet Lieutenant Dundas again and have another interview, and then, shaking hands, they returned to their trenches, when the firing began again as hot as ever.

The chief base for stores and ammunition was at "W" Beach, Lancashire Landing, and a man returning to it after a month's absence would hardly have recognised it as the same shore on which he had disembarked on April 25th. At the end of June, it had been completely transformed into a regular Army base. The Royal Engineers, with prodigious labour, had made excellent roads up from the water's edge, which enabled heavy guns and carts loaded with stores, etc., to be conveyed with comparative ease to their destination. The beach was split up into sections, one section being for the Army Service Corps, where, amidst stacks of boxes of plum and apple jam, ammunition and boxes of water, they toiled like Trojans.

Close to them was the Naval Beachmaster's Office and Post Office, to and from which "snotties" could be seen running at all hours with orders for the steam pinnaces lying at the different piers. The various headquarters were built of sand-bags and planks, which was the only safe mode of building for a beach like this, as it was frequently subjected to heavy bombardment by the enemy. There were numerous jetties built out to sea, and from these stores were landed and the wounded conveyed to hospital ships. Engaged on carrying duties were men of many different nationalities; there were Egyptians, Greeks, Arabs, Russians, Poles, Indians, Senegalese, French, British, Turkish prisoners, Armenians and others. A considerable number of men were employed towards the end of June in manufacturing bombs, made from old jam tins. Until the end of June no bombs were used in Gallipoli by either side.

So far, I have said but little about our glorious navy. It is impossible to express at all adequately one's intense admiration for its marvellous achievement. Sir Ian Hamilton, in closing his first despatch, said:

Throughout the events I have chronicled, the Royal Navy has

been father and mother to the Army. Not one of us but realises how much he owes to Vice-Admiral de Roebeck; to the warships, French and British; to the destroyers, mine-sweepers, picket-boats, and to all their dauntless crews, who took no thought of themselves, but risked everything to give their soldier comrades a fair run in at the enemy.

Throughout the whole of this difficult period, it can be recorded with pride that the Royal Navy, most ably supported by the Mercantile Marine, kept their brethren in the wilderness of Gallipoli regularly supplied with food and ammunition of all kinds, day and night, brought their parcels and letters, and were ready with their powerful guns to come to their assistance at any moment it was needed. Surely the world has no more glorious record than this!

The traditions of the past were worthily upheld by both officers and men, and the discipline was all that could be desired. There was always that respect for their officers on the part of the men, combined with a feeling of comradeship, which comes only of living aboard the same ship day by day. A few days after the landing, I was sitting with a well-known naval officer, who received the D.S.O. for gallant work on April 25th. We were smoking our pipes, and just in front of us on the beach were some blue-jackets from H.M. ships having a rest. Suddenly one of the men came out with some exceedingly strong language, and in an instant the officer called out his name. Cap in hand, he came up and apologised.

"You must be more careful in future," said the lieutenant-commander; "you know I will not allow such language to be used in my presence; there is no need for it."

"Aye, aye! sir," was the reply. "I'm sorry; it's werry 'ot, and I was a-forgettin' meself."

"That will do," came the reply; "remember, we don't allow it in the Service."

CHAPTER 22

The Island of Imbros

When writing or speaking of the operations at the Dardanelles, it must always be borne in mind that that general term also includes a great deal of work done in obscure places on the numerous islands lying close to the peninsula of Gallipoli. One of these islands was Imbros. It was a peaceful, beautiful isle, with lofty mountains, picturesque villages, and cooling streams. Some twenty-five miles from Gallipoli, it was extensively used as an army base, and as a resort to which men, tired out with the long strain of incessant fighting, might go to recuperate. The 2nd Naval Brigade was sent here on June 22nd to rest, after being on Gallipoli's inhospitable shore since the morning of April 25th, 1915. They had taken part in every stern fight that had been fought from the very beginning.

We sailed away from Lancashire Landing about 4 p.m. in trawlers, and arrived without a mishap at 6.30 p.m. Submarines were beginning to be very troublesome about this time in Eastern waters, so that we were glad to be safely anchored at last in the harbour. While awaiting orders to disembark, a boat containing two facetious natives came alongside, and they "did a rearing trade" in postcards, figs and "Turkish Delight," which they vowed was of Greek manufacture! Our men enjoyed "taking a rise" out of these happy salesmen, who made money almost as fast as they could collect it.

We landed about 7.20, and marched to our new quarters, which seemed most luxurious, being a camp of bell-tents. It was a curious sensation to sleep once again with a roof over one's head, although it was merely of canvas; and the knowledge that we were on an island separated from the enemy and his guns by twenty-five miles of water enabled us all to enjoy the first really satisfactory night of sleep we had had for nearly two months. Imbros is some eighteen miles in length, and has an area of 116 square miles. Its highest summit is nearly two thousand feet above sea-level. It is well wooded, and corn, wine and cotton are abundantly grown in the valleys; oil is also produced.

On the afternoon of June 23rd, a delightful surprise was in store for us; the band of H.M.S. *Exmouth* came and gave us an open-air concert. The music had a soothing effect on our tired nerves, and never has a programme given greater satisfaction than the one provided for us on this occasion. In the evening, I went up a beautiful gully with two officers of the Howe Battalion, Lieutenant de la Motte and Lieutenant Browne, R.N.V.R. At the top of this gully was one of the most magnificent views I ever remember of wild mountain scenery. Here, on a kind of a plateau, beneath the shade of a mulberry tree, we found Lieutenant Robertes, the Howe machine-gun officer, encamped with his men. He accompanied us to the top of a rocky peak, from which the views were still more extensive. Gallipoli could be seen very distinctly in the distance, with the famous Achi Baba, on the summit of which shells were still bursting.

After descending, we had one of the most delicious meals I ever partook of in the East. Lieutenant Robertes was evidently a connoisseur when it came to food, and had made friends with some of the natives, The menu consisted of fresh boiled fish, marrows, boiled rice and fresh-stewed mulberries, cheese, lettuce and cucumbers, washed down with lime-juice.

Bathing at Imbros was one of the most delightful of pastimes; nearly every morning I bathed with Major Bridges, O.C. Anson Battalion, or with Brigadier-General Freyburg, V.C.

On June 24th (Thursday) I had the great privilege of a long walk with Commodore Backhouse, R.N. We climbed up wonderful ravines and gullies, and walked for miles over spreading hills, The commodore is a great walker, with a tremendous stride, and few there were in the brigade who could keep pace with him. After going some miles, we sat down by a lovely mountain pool and chatted and smoked. I do not think I ever enjoyed anything more during my experience than this talk with my brigadier. In him one saw the finest type of officer that the navy has produced, and that is saying a very great deal.

We discussed almost everything under the gun, and the mysterious subject of death and afterwards. On the way back to the camp there was a spring of icy-cold water, at which the commodore filled a handsome Grecian jug he was carrying. I was sorry when the time came to part, and I left him, I remember, thinking that as long as such men as he are in command of the ships forming the Grand Fleet Nelson's audacious boast will be more than justified:

The fleets of England are equal to meet the world in arms.

Imbros was the island where General Sir Ian Hamilton had his headquarters, A small marquee and a modest wooden hut were the accommodation which the gallant commander-in-chief kept for his own personal use. Major John Churchill, brother of the Right Hon. Winston S. Churchill, was on the Headquarters Staff, and visited his cousin, Sub-Lieutenant Frewen, at our camp. On June 25th, Sir Ian Hamilton inspected the 2nd Naval Brigade, and, addressing the men, said "the work they had done entitled them to rank with the finest troops in Europe."

Next day I marched over the mountains with "C" Company, Anson Battalion, under the command of Lieutenant the Hon. Kenneth Dundas and Lieutenant Frewen, to Panaghia, the capital of Imbros. It was very hot marching, and the scenery reminded me of our own Lake District on a perfect summer day, except that it was more rugged. Springs of icy-cold water proved a great temptation to us all, and, from what I remember of the after-effects, I am afraid we partook rather too freely. Masses of Persian lilac and oleander grew on either side of the mountain paths.

We found Panaghia a pretty, interesting town, and the inhabitants seemed clean, happy people. The little Greek children were very fascinating, and played about the streets in very much the same way as British children do. The church was a handsome building, its interior gorgeously ornamented with several fine pictures. We talked to two priests, who told us that there was a girl in the town who spoke English. They led us up to a pretty Italian girl, who was knitting, and on asking in French if she could speak English, she replied: "I speak just a very leetle." She told us about the island, and we found she could speak six languages—Italian, Greek, French, English, Spanish and German.

A little *café* provided us with a meal, consisting of omelettes and fruit. There were several interesting relics of the time when the island was under Turkish rule and a Turkish governor resided there. Among them was the ruined mosque, to which the Greeks pointed with glee. On going inside, Lieutenant Dundas gave an imitation of the way in which Turks chant their prayers, greatly to the astonishment of the natives. Near the mosque was the building in which the Turkish governor had lived. It was in a very dilapidated condition, and there was a cupboard strewn with old official papers, which looked as if it had not changed very much since the day its owner had left it in haste.

Soon it was time to wend our way homewards, and none of us were sorry when the camp was reached about 8.30 p.m. It is necessary to say here, because of after events, that I had not felt at all well during this march, and on our return had to go straight to my tent.

Next day, June 27th, was Sunday, and with difficulty I celebrated Holy Communion under some shady trees at 7.30 a.m. I was very much weaker and feverish, but I managed to take parade service at 10 a.m. This proved to be the last service I was to take for the officers and men of my old brigade. General Sir Ian Hamilton had signified his intention of being present, but was prevented at the last minute, owing to the arrival of some other troops from the Peninsula. I remember this service best of all. The commodore was present, with his staff, and the Ansons, Hoods and Howes were lined up in a huge square. We sang:—"*Jesu, Lover of my soul*" and "*O God, our Help in ages past.*" The address was on Hebrews xiii, 8: "*Jesus Christ the same yesterday, and today, and forever.*"

It was a splendid service, but I felt thankful when it was over, as I was in great pain, and the doctor ordered me complete rest. Several men came in and chatted with me during the afternoon. Next day the battalions were ordered back to Gallipoli after a short but delightful holiday. It was evident that I was too ill to go with them, and so very reluctantly I went into the R.A.M.C, Hospital close to the harbour at Imbros. Here I was destined to remain for three weeks, and when the time came for me to leave, I was advised by the doctors that the best thing for me would be to return to England. My complaint had played havoc with my constitution, and I felt very weak. My nerves also were not what they had been.

In the same hospital were several officers who had just come across from Gallipoli. Even the doctors themselves could not escape from the diseases they had come out to cure. Close to me lay Surgeon Taylor, R.N., of the R.N. Division, who was "stroke" of the Cambridge Fight in 1905. I also struck up a warm friendship with Lieut. Killen, of the Egyptian Works Company, Royal Engineers, and we had great amusement over our meals. One of the orderlies announced one day, after we had had a fortnight of "slops," that we were to have some chicken, and the excitement knew no bounds in our tent.

When dinner came to be served, however, we ascertained that the chicken was a curious-looking bird which had emerged from a tin, and, although it tasted somewhat like rabbit, we were rather disappointed. We had "egg flip and brandy," stout and port to help us on the road to recovery, and, on our last night in hospital, a half-bottle of champagne among seven of us. The doctors looked after us most faithfully, and it is impossible to say too much in their praise.

Just before leaving I was visited by the chaplain of H.MS. *Exmouth*, which was the guardship lying in the harbour. I was discharged on the afternoon of July 12th, feeling better, but by no means myself yet. That night I dined with Lieutenant Killen in the Royal Engineers' Mess. Egyptians waited at table, and the cook was of the same nationality. A naval commander and a lieutenant-commander from the *Exmouth* dined with us, and I remember an interesting discussion took place as to the future of the navy and the submarine menace, After dinner Lieutenant Killen was showing me his revolver in his tent, when I happened to remark: "I hope it isn't loaded." Almost as I said the words he pulled the trigger, and there was a loud report. Fortunately, the bullet went into the ground, my foot escaping by about two inches!

Lieutenant Killen wrote to me as late as September 1st, 1915:

> We are faced with the prospect of wintering out in Imbros. We have had a little taste of what the weather can be like when it rains. Two hours' rain last week flooded out the tents and converted the roads into impassable swamps of liquid mud. The operations out here seem to have come to a deadlock; no progress on either side and no prospect of any, unless Bulgaria comes in on our side, which does not seem likely at present, This morning eleven aeroplanes passed over the camp heading for the Peninsula, so I expect there is something in the wind. Possibly they are going to 'spill the Porte' in Constantinople. The Egyptians will soon be leaving here ..... they have done splendid work; still, one can't expect them to stand the cold weather. I have not fired my revolver since the time I nearly punctured your foot!

At 6.30 am, on Tuesday, July 13th, I left in a trawler for Cape Helles, arriving there shortly after 10 a.m., thus beginning my second visit to Gallipoli.

CHAPTER 23

Farewell to Gallipoli

On returning to the Peninsula, I found the position there about the same as when we left for our short rest. The fighting had consisted of several attempts to take Achi Baba, but all efforts were in vain. This hill of 600 feet, as I have tried to point out already in these pages, was a perfect natural fortress, and as long as the enemy had it in his possession, he held the key to the position.

The 52nd Division of Territorials attacked a position of the Turkish line on July 12th. This Division had relieved the Naval Division, which was enjoying a well-deserved rest. The attack succeeded at the beginning, but by the afternoon of the 13th, the 52nd had lost practically all the ground they had gained, and the R.N. Division was ordered to recapture the lost trenches. This task fell mainly to the 1st Naval Brigade and the marines. Five Naval Division battalions took part in this attack, the Nelson Battalion being in the centre. The advance had to be made hastily, and as a result our casualties were severe.

It was a magnificent success, however, and five lines of hostile trenches fell to the Naval Division. During the attack, Sub-Lieutenant F. H. J. Startin (late R.N.), Nelson Battalion, was severely wounded just outside the fire trenches. In spite of loss of blood, and with great gallantry, he continued doing his duty and encouraging his men for thirty-six hours. At first the stretcher-bearers were unable to reach him, but, even when they were able to do so, he would not be carried into safety until other wounded men in front had been brought in, thus setting a noble example to those around him. He died of his wound shortly after on a hospital ship.

While this attack was in progress I arrived back on the Peninsula. On reaching the rest camp I found several of my old friends, who had been wounded early in May, were back at their duties. It was good to see them again, but it brought back the past very vividly with all its memories. I was feeling unwell, and the flies and dust seemed worse than in June. I hated the idea of leaving my old brigade, but on taking further advice, there was no doubt as to what course I should take. A chaplain who is weak with disease, and whose nerves have had a severe shock, is only an encumbrance to a brigade, and cannot be the help to the men he ought to be. Arrangements were made for my passage back to England, and the following are the last three entries made in my diary in Gallipoli:—

Wednesday, July 14th—Had a very bad night last night; not a wink of sleep! Many reports today of surrender of Turks on the right flank. Buried poor Lieutenant Byles, of the Headquarters Staff, today, in the R.N. Division cemetery about 10 a.m. Funeral was attended by Commodore Backhouse, R.N., and his staff. The commodore very kindly sent me some '*Spectators*' with his compliments. I am to get a doctor's certificate today.

Thursday, July 15th.—Got up early—about 5 a.m.—after a fairly poor night. A 'Taube' flew over here this morning and dropped three bombs, which did not appear to do much damage. The French fired off their rifles violently into the sky, but got nowhere near him! Visited Failes (Chaplain to 1st R.N, Brigade) in the evening, who was drinking water with lemonade tablets dissolved in it! Everything for my removal is arranged.

Friday, July 16th.—Said goodbye to three officers and the 'old' men of the Anson Battalion, after having been with them 'through many and great dangers.' My prayer is that they may soon return in triumph, Then I visited the Howes, and shook hands with Colonel Collins and my old friends there. Took leave of the Hoods, and saw Asquith and Charles Lister—they are both magnificent fellows! Went on board the Hospital Ship. Strange to say it was the very same ship we had come out in, the *Union Castle* Liner, but she had been transformed into a hospital ship, I was accorded a splendid welcome by the ship's officers. Nice lunch, after which I sat and talked with Lord Bangor and several other officers. Then went round the wards and visited the sick—some very severe cases. One man died today. I buried him at 8 p.m., the body being covered with the Union Jack and reverently 'committed to the deep.' It was my first burial at sea.

Strictly speaking, I was forbidden to act as chaplain, and had instructions that I had not to do any work whatever. But on getting aboard this ship I found three hundred cases, many of them serious, and no chaplain to visit them. Needless to say, I promised to act as *padré* until the official chaplain should arrive. Fresh cases kept coming in from Cape Helles, and we expected to wait for a time before sailing, as there was accommodation for some six hundred patients. Australia has every reason to be proud of her sailors and soldiers, but she has also cause to be equally proud of her nursing sisters. On board this ship there were six regular Australian Army nursing-sisters and one English nurse (Territorial), The matron was also an Australian.

No women could have been more devoted to their duty than were these gallant souls. Day and night, in calm or rough weather, these Australian girls did their work, without thinking of themselves; and in spite of the many sad tasks that fell to their lot, I never heard a single murmur or complaint. Two sisters slept during the day, and took night duty; and when the number of patients is borne in mind, it will readily be seen how hard was their work. The same might be said of the five surgeons on board, who did all in their power to alleviate suffering and to save life, acting with great skill under difficult circumstances, and with great unselfishness.

The only recreation that these faithful men and women got was an occasional concert in the lounge after dinner. Had we not had something like this to enliven our drooping spirits we should have gone raving mad. And yet, if there was any laughter or gaiety, it had an artificial ring about it, and it was evident that, even in the midst of singing songs from the musical comedies, the sisters often found their thoughts wandering to their cases down below in the wards. Hardly a night passed without one death. Life in a hospital ship is a curious mixture of sadness and mirth.

There are always some slight cases, perhaps of leg wounds, men who will laugh, joke and play cards, whereas only a few yards away a man will be passing on his journey through death to life, and will be whispering to the chaplain a last message home. In fact, one is reminded of those words in "*Sartor Resartus*":—

> The joyful and the sorrowful are there; men are dying there ... men are praying—on the other side of a partition men are cursing; and around them all is the vast void night—while Councillors of State sit plotting and playing their high chess game, whereof the pawns are men. . . . . Two-legged animals without feathers lie around us, in horizontal positions, their heads all in

nightcaps, and full of the foolishest dreams. . . . . . All these heaped and huddled together, with nothing but a little carpentry . . . . between them—crammed in, like salted fish in their barrel.

It is pleasant to be able to record that there was more "praying" than "cursing," and the visits of the chaplain seemed always to be appreciated. Sad to relate, many men died of wounds during the week I acted as chaplain, between July 16th and 22nd, and it was my painful duty to commit twenty bodies to the deep *"to be turned into corruption, looking for the resurrection of the body (when the sea shall give up her dead), and the life of the world to come."*

The men on board came from many different regiments, and I remember visiting dying men from the following:—The 5th Argyll and Sutherland Highlanders, the 1st King's Own Scottish Borderers, the 9th Manchesters, the Royal Horse Artillery, the Royal Marine Light Infantry, the 7th Highland Light Infantry, the Royal Army Medical Corps, the Royal Engineers, the 9th Royal Warwicks, the Royal Welsh Fusiliers, the 7th Royal Scots, the 7th Lancashire Fusiliers, the 6th East Lancashires, and the Royal Navy, Naval Division, and Australian and New Zealand Army Corps.

As I went my rounds the change in accent was remarkable. One minute I would be talking to a "canny Scot," so broad that it was only with difficulty that I could make out what he was saying, and the next minute the voice that talked with me showed unmistakably that its owner lived within sight of the Dome of St. Paul's. In the next bed, perhaps, would lie a typical Yorkshireman, and in the next a man from far-off Australia.

The longer we remained off Cape Helles the more crowded did the ship become. Severe fighting was in progress just at this very time, and so it can be imagined that many critical cases came aboard needing immediate attention.

The Roman Catholic patients had caused me some anxiety, as there was no chaplain for them, but, to my great relief, a Franciscan Father came on board on Monday, July 19th. Father Barry, for such was his name, was one of the most genial of all the *padrés* out in the East. Patriarchal-looking, with a long, flowing beard, he was immensely beloved by his men, He was unable to stay for more than two or three days, because, as a naval chaplain, his duty was to visit all H.M, ships and hospital ships, thus being, as he put it, "a sort of ecclesiastical tramp."

All this time the Turks were exceedingly busy shelling "W" Beach, and, on the night of the 17th July, set fire to the small arms ammunition and some 18-pounder shells. It made a magnificent, but sad, spectacle from our ship. For many reasons we were thankful to be on the water instead of the beach, The blazing boxes, and the cartridges and shells exploding and leaping up into the air, giving a kind of "will-o'-the-wisp" effect, made parts of the shore very dangerous.

This fire was responsible for the arrival on board our ship of a very gallant officer, whose work at Cape Helles, often performed under great difficulty, will always be remembered with gratitude—Lieutenant-Commander Grattan, R.N., D.S.O. He was in charge of the wireless telegraphy station at "W" Beach from May 1st, 1915, to the evacuation, was mentioned in despatches several times, and awarded the D.S.O. in March, 1916. During the fire at the ammunition park, he was severely burnt about the legs and arms, but careful nursing helped him on the way to a complete recovery.

On Thursday, July 22nd, the officially-appointed chaplain came aboard, and so relieved me of my task. About 10 a.m. on this day we were startled by a shell bursting in the water not fifty yards from our ship; this was followed by a second, whereupon the captain thought it advisable to put out to sea another half-mile, There was a good deal of speculation as to why these shots were fired, but the most likely reason is that they were aimed at an ammunition-ship which happened to be passing us at the time. Fragments of shell were picked up on board, and given as keepsakes to the sisters, who kept cool and did their work calmly throughout this somewhat terrifying experience.

I cannot forget one incident that occurred on this day. Early in the morning the sister sent for me to come down to "D" Ward to see a poor fellow who was "passing westward." I talked to him and comforted him to the best of my ability, and then he made a short act of contrition. Just before the end he looked up into my face and said: "May I hold your hand? It will make me feel as if I were at home." And then he passed to that Home where he will be at home for ever.

Next day, July 23rd, the last cases came on board, and we weighed anchor about 10.15 a.m. It was with mixed feelings that I watched Gallipoli growing fainter and fainter in the distance; I was glad to be leaving its inhospitable shore, but could not help a pang of regret at leaving so many good friends behind. Some I left still doing their duty nobly; others, and by far the great majority, had finished the work it was theirs to do, and their bodies lie in the Turkish dust—until the last

Anson Batt. Medical Unit Stretcher Bearers, July 1915

trumpet sounds. And yet their message to us would be:—

> *If I should die, think only this of me*
> *That there's some corner of a foreign field*
> *That is for ever England.*

Chapter 24

Homeward Bound

We sailed direct from Cape Helles to Mudros, arriving in Lemnos Harbour about 3 p.m., on July 23rd. Here we lay at anchor during the night, and started for Alexandria early next morning.

One of the last cases to be brought on board the ship was an officer, whose name has already figured prominently in this short history, Lieutenant-Commander Freyburg, D.S.O. This was the second time he had been wounded, and on this occasion, it was a bad hit in the abdomen. Brigadier-General Freyburg, V.C., D.S.O., as he is known in France today, is a wonderful man! In fact, he seemed to be "made of india-rubber!" Everyone knew him in the Royal Naval Division as a great, tall, happy-go-lucky fellow, who *"didn't seem to know the use of fear,"* as Kipling puts it; and yet, with all his strength and intrepidity, he was a large-hearted man, beloved by all ranks, with a smile and cheery word for all with whom he came in contact.

Just as the ship was about to sail, I was leaning over the side, watching the stretcher-cases being slung aboard, when a voice from the lighter down below shouted: "Hullo! *Padré!* Have you any cigarettes?" It was Freyburg, and before many minutes had passed his wants were supplied. Next day, contrary to orders, he was sitting up in bed, and, long before he was allowed to do so officially, was walking about the deck, saying "there was nothing much the matter with him." The pretty Australian sister shook her head and said: "I guess he's made of india-rubber!"

Professor A. W. Mayo Robson, the famous surgeon, was in our ship during her voyage to Egypt and I was privileged to have several interesting conversations with him.

Just as we were getting near Alexandria, we received a wireless message from H.M.S. *Bacchante*, ordering us to change our course direct to Port Säid. This came as quite an unwelcome surprise; but orders are orders! Port Säid was reached about 9 p.m. on Monday, July 26th, after a delightfully smooth voyage. It took a long time to remove the patients from the ship, but by Tuesday evening every single case had been conveyed ashore. After having spent so long a time in this old ship, both on the voyage out and on the way home, it was with great regret I left her early on the morning of July 29th. Three of the surgeons and several of the sisters were up to say farewell, and gave me a splendid "send-off."

I left Port Säid for Alexandria in the morning, and at the station many Italians had assembled to bid God-speed to some of their compatriots who were going to the war. They came armed with floral offerings and flags, and a brass band led the procession. Tremendous cheers were raised as the train steamed out.

In the opposite corner of the first-class carriage in which I was travelling sat a youngish man, dressed in white duck, and evidently a Government official of some description. We started the usual conversation indulged in by talkative passengers in a railway carriage, and then, somehow, the subject discussed turned to English schools. "I was at the Quaker's School at Ackworth," my fellow-traveller remarked.

"That is rather strange," I replied, "because you were probably there with some cousins of mine named Edmundson."

And so, it was—he knew them every one. It is what the Americans call a "bromidiom" to say "*What a small place the world is!*" but it very often appears to be true!

There were some quaint-looking natives on the platforms of the stations we passed through, and near Ismailia I remember seeing several women smoking *hookahs* outside their dwellings, and chattering to each other as do the village gossips of Great Britain.

We arrived in Alexandria about 3.25. Here I called on Lieutenant F.V. Wilson, R.N.V.R., of the Anson Battalion, who, on account of ill-health, had been left to assist the base-commandant, He made arrangements for my return to England. I left for Port Säid, where I was. to embark, on Monday, August 2nd, and on arrival there met a staff-officer, who asked me if I were returning to England.

On saying "yes," he asked me to accompany him to the Eastern Exchange Hotel, as he was also going home. We dined together, and I found that my companion was Major Lord Montgomerie, 2nd Life Guards, who had been *A.D.C.* to General Hunter-Weston on the Peninsula. The hotel and its inhabitants caused us great amusement; in fact, life in general bore quite a different aspect from what it did previous to the war. We had been in the very thick of the fighting, amidst dangers and great hardships, and now to be back again in civilisation, with properly cooked food and abundant supplies of hot water, caused us to find enjoyment even in the most ordinary things.

For a long time, we had been away from the other sex—in fact so far away that we had not heard a female voice for over four months. One of the queerest sensations that I can remember was arriving on the hospital ship and hearing a woman's voice again. It was only one Australian sister calling out to another: "Right oh! I'll be there in a minute," But how little did she know that a man on deck was standing fascinated by the sound, as though it were a voice from another world, where one had dwelt in the distant past! To the traveller and explorer this may sound absurd, but to one who has hardly travelled at all it was a reality.

About 10.30 am. on August 4th we left for the transport V——, which was to take us to England. There were five officers on board, and two hundred Indian soldiers on their way to see the Motherland for the first time. They were coming as a medical unit to Britain, and had not seen any fighting yet. I found there were eight Christians among them, and with one of these I had a long talk. On telling him that I had been to the Dardanelles and had landed with the 29th Division, so far escaping injury, he looked me up and down and then said: "God has been good to you."

On Sunday morning, August 8th, we had Divine Service on the boat deck. It was a fine, sunny morning, the sea was calm, and we were out of sight of land. My congregation consisted of Colonel Robinson (East Lancashires) Major Lord Montgomerie, the captain, the chief officer, two native Indian Christians, and members of the crew. The hymns were accompanied by a gramophone, which was rather an unusual way of providing sacred music. We sang "*Onward, Christian soldiers,*" "*Eternal Father, strong to save,*" and "*Lead, kindly Light.*" All went well until the second verse of John Henry Newman's beautiful hymn; then something seemed to go wrong with the gramophone's interior, and, to the consternation and dismay of both the chaplain and his congregation, the rest of the hymn was played in "rag-time."

A voyage up the Mediterranean was by no means free from danger even in those days. Submarines were very active and a continual menace to the men of the Mercantile marine. It is impossible to express one's admiration for the gallantry and devotion to duty shown by officers and men. Malta was passed about 9 a.m. on August 9th, and then we had to steam very slowly until 9 p.m., when we entered one of the danger zones. We steamed through at thirteen knots an hour, the captain remaining on the bridge all the night. Fortunately, no hostile submarine made its appearance. Gibraltar was reached on August 13th, and here we lay at anchor for about six hours, while the purser landed to buy some vegetables,

On August 16th we had only five hundred miles to go, but this, from the captain's point of view, was the Most anxious period of the voyage. Four natives were placed as watchers on deck all day until dusk, and were told by the officer in command that they were to report anything they saw that was unusual, even a big fish. One of these men came down and reported that there was a ship on fire. Great excitement prevailed for a minute, but on getting up on deck the captain found that it was merely a small whale throwing up a spout of water!

The natives spent their time in drilling and wrestling, and some lively bouts were witnessed between Mohammedans and Hindoos. The aroma from their kitchens was not of the most attractive kind, and I cannot honestly say that the food looked appetising. Fire-drill was the most sensational amusement; when the syren blew, we had to dash to our respective boats, with life-belts round us. To while away the time two of us began to issue a ship's newspaper entitled "*The Gazette*," which aimed at "ragging" everyone on board, without being too personal. The purser—a handy man with his pencil—drew some wonderful caricature portraits of us all in turns. During the latter part of the voyage the editors, of whom I was the chief, lived in hourly dread of being attacked by the other passengers with a mammoth squirt.

At noon on Tuesday, August 17th, we entered the most dangerous submarine area, and received a wireless message from the Admiralty warning us that two hostile submarines were operating in that area, and that we were to keep a sharp lookout for mines. The captain hardly ever left the bridge, and was evidently anxious. Suddenly, to the westward, we saw what appeared to be a transport with a submarine alongside; even the captain was taken in at first and said: "We are in for it this time." Closer investigation, however, drew from the chief officer the remark: "You're all out of it; it's only a tug."

At dusk the Lizard Light could be seen plainly, and then, after a time, other lights on the British Coast. Although there was still a long way to go, yet these very lights rejoiced our hearts and spoke of home. Nearer and nearer the lights of Plymouth came. "There's no country like it," remarked the captain to me; "and no place like your home." Suddenly three or four searchlights were turned on us, and an examination ship came alongside. We had come safely through all.

That night we lay at anchor in the Sound. In the morning the Indians on board received a great ovation as we steamed up to the landing-place. And then, amid many farewells, we departed on our several ways. It was really too good to be true that we were really in the train for dear old London. We had been through a great deal since we last saw it and paced its streets; but all was forgotten now in the joy of being home again.

On my return the Archbishop of York wrote to me:—

"I am very glad that one of the men whom I have ordained should have been privileged to be the first Anglican Chaplain who landed in that great enterprise, end that you were able, though in the midst of so much danger and distress, to do something to help numbers of wounded and dying men. It is refreshing to hear your account of the way in which, in the presence of danger, men of all kinds turn towards God. I only wish that the nation here at home, face to face with grave realities of another kind, could feel the same stirring of their heart and conscience."

Chapter 25

Conclusion

And everybody praised the Duke,
Who this great fight did win.
'And what good came of it at last?'
Quoth little Peterkin.
'Why, that I cannot tell,' said he,
'But 'twas a famous victory.'

There is one question in Southey's familiar lines on the "*Battle of Blenheim*" which has been asked frequently in regard to the Gallipoli campaign: "What good came of it?"

On the whole, I think it was more useful than people imagine. There are always a certain number of supercilious critics who refuse to hear anything that is good about an enterprise when that enterprise has turned out a failure from the material point of view. This is especially true of war. The Gallipoli Campaign was a failure, but, as Milman said of the Papacy, it was "the most magnificent failure in the world" from the standpoint of the actual fighting. Materially it failed; morally it was a triumph. Politically, the very fact that we gained a footing on the shores of the Peninsula influenced Italy, and most probably it was very largely through this that the gallant little nation launched her attack upon Austria,

Gallipoli did not fail to influence the Balkan States, and Bulgaria would have been in the field against us much earlier in the year 1915 had it not been for our successes at Cape Helles and Anzac Cove. I cannot but think that our presence in the Near East had also an effect upon Egypt.

Dr. Brent, Bishop of the Philippine Islands, writes:

Men are already saying that the two great events of the war are the resistance of Belgium, and Gallipoli, where the immortal will of man willed to dare an undertaking beyond its power, and honoured itself in the failure. Gallipoli was the Charge of the Six Hundred multiplied by a hundred.

But, even from the soldier's point of view, the Gallipoli campaign was not as barren in its fruit-bearing as some would make it appear. We engaged large forces of the Turks' finest troops, and defeated them time after time, and during our stay on the Peninsula we know for a fact that the enemy's losses in killed and wounded were far heavier than our own. It may be shown, someday, that the great successes gained in Mesopotamia were not entirely due to the magnificent bravery and endurance of our troops under Sir Stanley Maude, but that many who rest in the dust of Gallipoli had their share in them too. Suffice it to say that they killed off many who formed "the flower" of the Turkish Army. To have put out of action, or kept from action on some other war-front, nearly 500,000 Turks, is no mean achievement, and yet this was done by the British and French Forces in Gallipoli.

Many adverse criticisms have been hurled at statesmen and generals in regard to this campaign, but it must always be borne in mind that our attempt to seize the Peninsula was not unlike taking a leap in the dark. The actual landing was the treading of an untried way; it was a feat of arms without precedent in military history, unless, perhaps, we look back into the remote past, and read of the campaigns of Xerxes.

It is easy enough to sit in an armchair at home: and to ask:

Why did not the troops land higher up, instead of at Helles, and support the Australians, and make one big push, and get astride the Peninsula?

Every available landing place was used, and used to its utmost capacity, by Sir Ian Hamilton, and yet there are critics who appear to think that the coast resembled the Suffolk coast, with many ideal spots for the landing of men, ammunition and stores. Mistakes were made, undoubtedly; but in my humble judgment it is grossly unfair to attempt to blame anyone in particular when so many of the chief witnesses lie buried in Turkish soil.

It may be true, as has been said, that just at the time of the evacuation of Gallipoli the Turks were feeling the strain of over eight months' incessant fighting and might have surrendered, but we shall have to wait, probably a long time, before anything is known with absolute certainty.

It will always be a matter for pride on the part of the Royal Naval

Division that they were chosen to assist in the defence of Antwerp and in the Gallipoli campaign. "You have been connected," a man once said to me, "with the two mistakes of the war." But that is a statement which needs qualifying. No man, who knows all the facts, could say that the sending of a Naval Force to Antwerp was a "mistake." If anyone knows the truth of the matter it ought to be Sir E. C. Hertslet, who was British ambassador in Antwerp at the time and he has asserted more than once that the coming of a Naval Force to the city in the hour of its need not only saved the Belgian Army, but also the Channel ports.

I have tried to point out in these pages how the 2nd Royal Naval Brigade, to which I was chaplain, was in the beginning almost entirely a Naval Force; but later on, as the needs of the fleet became pressing, the naval element was gradually eliminated, so that, the brigade, as it was constituted at the time of the Gallipoli landing, consisted very largely of Kitchener's Army with six months' training to their credit. Scattered here and there among them one found the old R.N.V.R. hand, and the stoker, R.N., who would make the hair of the new recruits stand up on end as he spun yarns of his old sea-days, puffing at a short clay pipe, as they sat round their dug-out in the evening.

To the 29th Division and the Royal Naval Division fell the hardest work in Gallipoli, That Sir Ian Hamilton recognised this is shown, I think, by the way in which he words the closing sentences of his final despatch:—

> So, I bid them all farewell, with a special God-speed to the campaigners who have served with me right through from the terrible, yet most glorious earlier days—the incomparable 29th Division, the young veterans of the Naval Division.

We have always been proud of being placed second on the list and next to that glorious division which achieved the impossible on the morning of April 25th, 1915. The Australians and New Zealanders fought heroically at Anzac, but we must not forget that:

> The beaches at Helles were as red as those at Anzac, and the Lancashire Landing and the River Clyde are as famous as Hell Spit and Brighton Beach.

The 2nd Naval Brigade, after I left them, had further experience of fighting the Turk in Gallipoli, and were present at the landing at Suvla Bay on August 6th, 1915. The following extract from a letter, dated

August. 27th, is interesting; it is written by one of my old men of the Anson Battalion:—

> I don't know if you have read of the new landing that has been made, but I am glad to tell you it was nothing compared to the one on the 25th of April. But it was "warm" when we had been there a few hours. We had a few losses in the Anson Battalion, killed and wounded, and I am sorry to say that among them was Lieutenant the Honourable Kenneth Dundas and Colour-Sergeant Bedell; but, as you know, Sir, we all have to take our chances and trust to God. We have got the 29th Division with us... We are having some wet weather, and it is not very comfortable.

The rest of their time in Gallipoli up to the evacuation was spent by my old brigade in fatigue work and the usual spells in the trenches. The battalions could not always keep together; for instance, while the Ansons were taking part in the new landing at Suvla Bay, the Hoods were still in the southern part near Cape Helles. They took part in the severe fighting on August 6th, 7th, 25th and 26th.

At the evacuation, January 8th, 1916, there are many who claim to have been the last to leave the Peninsula, but among the last troops to push off in boats from Lancashire Landing were representatives of the Royal Naval Division. It was fitting that those who had been among the very first to arrive should be the last to leave. I was privileged to have a long talk with Lieutenant Alan Campbell, R.N.V.R., who was among these, and he gave a vivid account of the closing hours. The wonderful removal of guns and ammunition, the "silent hour," to which the Turks had grown accustomed, the men going about the trenches with their boots padded with straw, and the heavy bombardments of the last phase by heavy howitzers, made up a memorable picture.

Then he drew a remarkable word picture of the last "silent hour" on January 8th, during which the last men quietly left the trenches. Turkish priests could be heard calling the warriors to prayer; and, almost before those prayers would be ended, the last English and French soldiers would be pushing off from the shore, The great campaign was over.

Lieutenant Campbell also told how an Australian officer spoke of leaving Anzac in December. The men filed down to the boats very quietly, treading lightly as they passed the rows of crosses, where their gallant comrades lay at rest, and one was heard to say to another: "I hope to God, they can't hear us going."

Soon a great explosion shook the whole Peninsula; the time-fuses attached to specially prepared explosives had done their work, and had destroyed abandoned heaps of stores and supplies. This was the end! On April 25th, 1915, the Peninsula was red with blood; on January 8th, 1916, it was red with fire. On the hill at Cape Helles rows of crosses stood out against the fiery background, and onlookers were reminded that the whole campaign had been, as it were, a "Calvary"—one glorious chapter of heroism and self-sacrifice.

As one looks back at past days, it is inspiring to remember that there is still a Royal Naval Division doing valiant service. They are not exactly like the old battalions, who bore the burden and heat of the day, but, as Sir Ian Hamilton said a short time ago:

> A blood akin to that which reddened the waters of Helles runs still in the veins of their successors in France.

The old battalion I used to mess with has changed so completely that I dare say not more than a dozen familiar faces remain; but Commander Stuart-Jones, R.N.V.R., is still with it in France, and only the other day he wrote me a letter, in which occur these splendid words:—

> If any of the men who have gone can look down on the old battalion now, I don't think they'll be ashamed of us; and in my opinion all the good work we have done is almost entirely due to the example they set us in the olden days, up to which we are doing our best to live.

With that spirit running through the officers and men of our Naval and Military Forces, surely, we can face the future with confidence and hope.

★★★★★★★★★★★★★★★★★★★

I feel that I cannot bring this short history to an end without paying a very special tribute of praise to that great depot, which might be termed "The Nursery of the Royal Naval Division," where so many of its officers and men received their early training; I mean the R.N. Depot at the Crystal Palace, It is impossible to praise too highly the untiring efforts made by Commodore Sir R. H. Williams-Bulkeley, Bart., C.B., and Commander T. H. Roberts-Wray, R.N.V.R., to maintain the efficiency and discipline of this great training-centre for the

R.N. Division and the Fleet. It has supplied thousands of men for every branch of the naval service, and the success of the Naval Division abroad, both at the present day, and in the past, is due in no small measure to those responsible for the early training of officers and men at the Crystal Palace Depot. The writer of a poem in one of the best-known periodicals called the Royal Naval Division "*The Crystal Palace Army.*" Perhaps the title was given in satire, but it is by no means a misnomer, for it was the Crystal Palace training staff who turned out men capable of fighting side by side with the 29th Division, men who gained immortal renown at the storming of Beaucourt, and who will give a good account of themselves wherever they serve on sea or land.

★★★★★★★★★★★★★★★★★★★★

But it is time for me to bring these reminiscences to a conclusion; they have been written with but one object in view, and that is to tell the truth about the Royal Naval Division, and to show what its officers and men have gone through for us. This short history has been written, I fear, somewhat disjointedly, and does not aspire to be, in any sense, a work of literary merit. If it has interested any of my readers, or has enabled them to see the truth more clearly than before, it will not have been written in vain, I hope that at no distant date some penman, better qualified than I am, will tell this story over again—the story of the 2nd Royal Naval Brigade—as it is a story which will bear repeating over and over again as long as time shall last.

They tell us that we left behind many thousand wooden crosses in and around Gallipoli. Perhaps, in the future, the Turkish shepherd will pause as he passes, and try to read the names inscribed upon some of them. Will the day come when parents will climb the cliffs at Cape Helles and Anzac, which were stormed so gallantly from open boats on that ever-memorable April morning by their sons? Will they stand one day by the graves of their dear ones and pray that God will grant them perpetual light and eternal rest? Time alone will show. But if, in the future, when fighting days are over, we feel ourselves drifting into the irreligiousness, selfishness and lethargy which were so prevalent in this country before the war, let us think of those wooden crosses; and let them make their silent appeal to us to live the life of the Cross, the life of service for God and men.

ALSO FROM LEONAUR
AVAILABLE IN SOFTCOVER OR HARDCOVER WITH DUST JACKET

ESCAPE FROM THE FRENCH by *Edward Boys*—A Young Royal Navy Midshipman's Adventures During the Napoleonic War.

THE VOYAGE OF H.M.S. PANDORA by *Edward Edwards R. N. & George Hamilton, edited by Basil Thomson*—In Pursuit of the Mutineers of the Bounty in the South Seas—1790-1791.

MEDUSA by *J. B. Henry Savigny and Alexander Correard and Charlotte-Adélaïde Dard*—Narrative of a Voyage to Senegal in 1816 & The Sufferings of the Picard Family After the Shipwreck of the Medusa.

THE SEA WAR OF 1812 VOLUME 1 by *A. T. Mahan*—A History of the Maritime Conflict.

THE SEA WAR OF 1812 VOLUME 2 by *A. T. Mahan*—A History of the Maritime Conflict.

WETHERELL OF H. M. S. HUSSAR by *John Wetherell*—The Recollections of an Ordinary Seaman of the Royal Navy During the Napoleonic Wars.

THE NAVAL BRIGADE IN NATAL by *C. R. N. Burne*—With the Guns of H. M. S. Terrible & H. M. S. Tartar during the Boer War 1899-1900.

THE VOYAGE OF H. M. S. BOUNTY by *William Bligh*—The True Story of an 18th Century Voyage of Exploration and Mutiny.

SHIPWRECK! by *William Gilly*—The Royal Navy's Disasters at Sea 1793-1849.

KING'S CUTTERS AND SMUGGLERS: 1700-1855 by *E. Keble Chatterton*—A unique period of maritime history-from the beginning of the eighteenth to the middle of the nineteenth century when British seamen risked all to smuggle valuable goods from wool to tea and spirits from and to the Continent.

CONFEDERATE BLOCKADE RUNNER by *John Wilkinson*—The Personal Recollections of an Officer of the Confederate Navy.

NAVAL BATTLES OF THE NAPOLEONIC WARS by *W. H. Fitchett*—Cape St. Vincent, the Nile, Cadiz, Copenhagen, Trafalgar & Others.

PRISONERS OF THE RED DESERT by *R. S. Gwatkin-Williams*—The Adventures of the Crew of the Tara During the First World War.

U-BOAT WAR 1914-1918 by *James B. Connolly/Karl von Schenk*—Two Contrasting Accounts from Both Sides of the Conflict at Sea During the Great War.

AVAILABLE ONLINE AT www.leonaur.com
AND FROM ALL GOOD BOOK STORES

ALSO FROM LEONAUR
AVAILABLE IN SOFTCOVER OR HARDCOVER WITH DUST JACKET

FARAWAY CAMPAIGN *by F. James*—Experiences of an Indian Army Cavalry Officer in Persia & Russia During the Great War.

REVOLT IN THE DESERT *by T. E. Lawrence*—An account of the experiences of one remarkable British officer's war from his own perspective.

MACHINE-GUN SQUADRON *by A. M. G.*—The 20th Machine Gunners from British Yeomanry Regiments in the Middle East Campaign of the First World War.

A GUNNER'S CRUSADE *by Antony Bluett*—The Campaign in the Desert, Palestine & Syria as Experienced by the Honourable Artillery Company During the Great War.

DESPATCH RIDER *by W. H. L. Watson*—The Experiences of a British Army Motorcycle Despatch Rider During the Opening Battles of the Great War in Europe.

TIGERS ALONG THE TIGRIS *by E. J. Thompson*—The Leicestershire Regiment in Mesopotamia During the First World War.

HEARTS & DRAGONS *by Charles R. M. F. Crutwell*—The 4th Royal Berkshire Regiment in France and Italy During the Great War, 1914-1918.

INFANTRY BRIGADE: 1914 *by John Ward*—The Diary of a Commander of the 15th Infantry Brigade, 5th Division, British Army, During the Retreat from Mons.

DOING OUR 'BIT' *by Ian Hay*—Two Classic Accounts of the Men of Kitchener's 'New Army' During the Great War including *The First 100,000* & *All In It*.

AN EYE IN THE STORM *by Arthur Ruhl*—An American War Correspondent's Experiences of the First World War from the Western Front to Gallipoli-and Beyond.

STAND & FALL *by Joe Cassells*—With the Middlesex Regiment Against the Bolsheviks 1918-19.

RIFLEMAN MACGILL'S WAR *by Patrick MacGill*—A Soldier of the London Irish During the Great War in Europe including *The Amateur Army*, *The Red Horizon* & *The Great Push*.

WITH THE GUNS *by C. A. Rose & Hugh Dalton*—Two First Hand Accounts of British Gunners at War in Europe During World War 1- Three Years in France with the Guns and With the British Guns in Italy.

THE BUSH WAR DOCTOR *by Robert V. Dolbey*—The Experiences of a British Army Doctor During the East African Campaign of the First World War.

AVAILABLE ONLINE AT **www.leonaur.com**
AND FROM ALL GOOD BOOK STORES

www.ingramcontent.com/pod-product-compliance
Lightning Source LLC
Chambersburg PA
CBHW031622160426
43196CB00006B/240